New Updates in E-Learning

Edited by Eduard Babulak

Published in London, United Kingdom

New Updates in E-Learning
http://dx.doi.org/10.5772/intechopen.97987
Edited by Eduard Babulak

Contributors
Sharon Mistretta, Sibongile Simelane-Mnisi, Ntebogeng Mokgalaka-Fleischmann, Andile Mji, Sibongile R. Ngcapu, Eugenia Kovatcheva, Matjaž Debevc, Peter Čakš, Julija Bele Lapuh, Ines Kožuh, Monika Ferk, Ka Long Chan, Roy Kam, Man Sing Wong, Nilesh Kumar Mitra, Solomon O. Ojedeji, Kehinde O. Kester, Mariel García Leal, María De Jesús Araiza-Vazquez, Pretty Thandiswa Mpiti, Bulelwa Makena

First published in London, United Kingdom, 2022 by IntechOpen
IntechOpen is the global imprint of INTECHOPEN LIMITED, registered in England and Wales, registration number: 11086078, 5 Princes Gate Court, London, SW7 2QJ, United Kingdom

British Library Cataloguing-in-Publication Data
A catalogue record for this book is available from the British Library

Additional hard and PDF copies can be obtained from orders@intechopen.com

New Updates in E-Learning
Edited by Eduard Babulak
p. cm.
Print ISBN 978-1-80355-417-4
Online ISBN 978-1-80355-418-1
eBook (PDF) ISBN 978-1-80355-419-8

Meet the editor

Professor Eduard Babulak is an accomplished international scholar, researcher, consultant, educator, professional engineer, and polyglot with more than thirty years of experience. He has published research that has been cited by scholars worldwide. He has been an invited speaker at the University of Cambridge, England; Massachusetts Institute of Technology (MIT); Purdue University, Indiana; Yokohama National University, Japan; University of Electro-Communications, Japan; Sungkyunkwan University, Korea; Shanghai Jiao Tong University, China; Graz University of Technology, Austria; and other prestigious academic institutions worldwide. He serves as editor in chief, associate editor in chief, co-editor, and guest editor for numerous journals. He communicates in sixteen languages and his biography was cited in the Cambridge Blue Book, Cambridge Index of Biographies, Stanford Who's Who, and several issues of Who's Who in the World and America.

Contents

Preface

Given the current COVID pandemic, E-Learning has become essential to providing quality education to students at all levels all over the world. This book presents state-of-the-art educational technologies and teaching methodologies and discusses future educational philosophies in support of the global academic society.

New Updates in E-Learning is a collection of chapters addressing important issues related to effective utilization of the Internet and Cloud Computing, virtual robotics with best practices, and real-life application of hybrid educational environments to enhance student learning skills regardless of geographical location or other constraints. Over ten chapters, the book discusses the current and future evolution of educational technologies and methodologies and the best academic practices in support of providing high-quality education at all academic levels.

This book is a valuable resource for educators, scholars, and academic administrators who are exploring new educational techniques for use both inside and outside (remote) their academic institutions.

Eduard Babulak
Professor Panelist,
US National Science Foundation,
Alexandria, VA, USA

Section 1

Training and Teaching Evolution

Chapter 1

Technology Integration on Teaching Writing in the Foundation Phase Classrooms in the Eastern Cape Province, South Africa

Pretty Thandiswa Mpiti and Bulelwa Makena

Abstract

Teachers play a significant role in developing writing. They are responsible for teaching the younger generations exposed to technology through various gadgets. This study aims to better integrate technology in teaching writing in the Foundation Phase (FP). The premise for this study is the need to integrate technology in the Foundation Phase in order to attain educational goals. A qualitative case study was conducted that involved semi-structured interviews and the draw and talk/write method to gain in-depth knowledge of integrating technology to develop writing skills. For this study, the cognitive theory of multimedia learning (CTML) and sociocultural theory of learning were used as a theoretical framework. The participants were four Grade 3 teachers and 12 learners from two primary schools. This study indicated the importance of integrating technology in teaching writing, which subsequently led to more positive learning experiences for the FP learners. The study's key finding is that FP teachers are technologically illiterate. As a result, it is suggested that a set of curriculum guidelines based on the interests of this generation of learners be produced to enable teachers and students in successfully integrate teaching and technology in the FP.

Keywords: technology, teaching/learning, writing, foundation phase, township school

1. Introduction

The teaching of writing skills is very important in the Foundation Phase (FP) classroom. It emphasizes developing tactics needed by learners to write effectively in a variety of contexts and disciplines. Learners must master this skill in order to free themselves from the shame and shackles of illiteracy. Since writing skill remains the most common form of communication. It is one of the foundation principles in understanding the content. More significantly, writing allows learners to communicate their thoughts and feelings about a topic as well as demonstrate their understanding of certain content needless to say, this is a difficult task for learners, as seen by their writing, which contains numerous grammatical and spelling errors, as well as a lack of suitable and relevant terminology to communicate their thoughts [1]. Department of Basic Education [2] states that most learners struggle to write. Teachers therefore, provide practical and methodological assistance in engaging learners in clean writing. From the Grade 1 writing class, learners should be confident that their writing is working correctly. Hence, teaching strategies need to be well matched to learners' needs [3]. According to Gadd et al. [4] effective teaching involves understanding and recognizing learners' perspectives and responding to their needs. In the context of this study, the term "need" refers to learners who are technology conscious. As a result, teachers are expected to use a variety of resources, such as films, computers, the classroom, and technology, to enhance writing abilities.

Technology has a remarkable impact on the modern education environment and its positive influences on teaching and learning have been recognized around the globe. Today's technology integration has resulted in inventions that have transformed our societies, affecting people's thinking, working, and living habits [5]. Numerous studies suggest that the use of technology by various user groups is expanding on a daily basis. Gialamas, Kalas et al. [6–8] advocate for the use of technology to aid in the learning and development of young children. Teachers in South Africa (SA) have been asked to incorporate technology into their curriculum. The government has provided technical tools to schools as well as training for teachers on how to use them. The Khanya Project, for example, was launched by the Western Cape Department of Education in 2001 with the goal of "promoting learning and maximizing teachers' capability to employ relevant, accessible, and inexpensive technology throughout curriculum delivery" [9]. In most cases, the Department of Basic Education was also in charge of supplying computers and, more recently, tablets to schools. The primary purpose of delivering tablet computers to schools was to keep learners current with new technology. The focus has changed away from traditional curricula and toward technology-integrated curricula that support learning and teaching experiences [10]. Therefore, technology must be included in the curricula of schools and other educational institutions that are responsible for training learners to live in "information society" [11].

Zevenbergen [12] points out that today's youth are so tech-savvy that even their toys are considered "high-tech," and that they like e-chatting, computer games, high-tech phones, DVDs, pay television, Mp3, and a variety of other technology. As a result of the global technological boom, young children are now born into a "wired" or "connected" environment that includes the Internet, social media (like Facebook and Twitter), instant messaging (like WhatsApp), and always-on digital devices. The latest advancements in modern toys have caused FP teachers to rethink how they teach writing. Prensky et al. [13] highlights this point by arguing that learners have changed as a result of the introduction and quick spread of digital technology in the later eras of the twentieth century, as well as its progression into the twenty first century. The rapid advancement of information and communication technology (ICT) has resulted in significant changes in the twenty first century [14]. Prensky et al. [15] also refers to the present generation of learners as "digital natives," meaning to those born during or after the introduction of digital technology, and "digital immigrants," referring to those born before this period. According to Prensky et al. [13], two-thirds of the world's population owns a cellphone. Teachers are under pressure to adopt and use technology in their schoolrooms as a result of the growing adoption of technology. Therefore, FP schools must be abreast with the need of the community they serve. In other words, technology teaching is a need for the twenty first century generation. Hence, the study is focusing on the integration of technology in teaching writing in the FP classrooms.

Nevertheless, some teachers perhaps fall outside the category of digital populaces. Therefore, they must evaluate and align their teaching methods in order to provide more relevant and effective learning experiences for their learners, referred to as the "digital population." As a result, even when teaching writing in the FP, teachers should keep in mind the role of technology in the classroom. This emphasizes the need for teachers to constantly take steps to advance professional development that allows for a lifelong examination of methods to improve writing teachings in the FP. Beers et al. [16] warns that there is no longer a singular approach for teaching children to write and read. As a result, it's vital to investigate the impact of technology innovations on education, particularly how they affect teaching and learning. The rationale for this study is even more pertinent in light of the move to online and blended provision as a result of the COVID-19 pandemic, as it seeks to emphasize the importance of developing technology-assisted teaching while taking into account the diversity and context of the learners' backgrounds. Hence, this study looked at integrating technology in teaching writing in the FP classroom.

The study was guided by the following research question:

- What are the attitudes and practices of the teachers toward the use of technology in teaching writing in the FP?
- What are learners' experiences toward the use of technology when learning writing in the FP?

1.1 Theoretical framework

The cognitive theory of multimedia learning (CTML) and the sociocultural theory of learning were utilized to assist make sense of the challenges addressed in this study. R.E. Mayer developed the CTML in the late 1990s [17]. It asserts that a person learns and engages more effectively in a learning environment that includes multiple forms of media [17, 18]. It is assumed that when information is provided visually and audibly, the recipient is more likely to respond positively to it [18] and to build a better understanding of it than when only one form of media is employed. It examines how we process information and how our answers are influenced by how we handle that information. To put it another way, cognitive psychology is concerned in what goes on in our heads when input and reaction are linked. It is important because this study has to do with how learning can foster critical thinking that can be applied in real-life situations. Because IsiXhosa learners in the FP lack basic writing abilities, they require direction and support from their teachers in order to complete literacy tasks independently [19]. This theory is relevant to this study because it supports the idea of using a digital platform to create visual graphics, text, and audio recordings to teach FP learners writing skills.

This means that the writing in the FP should include pictures, words, and a textual story when utilizing technology to teach writing. Learners are busy picking and arranging their ideas when they select photos to express their thoughts and create a story about the images' meaning. When learners begin to form links with prior knowledge about a certain topic, such as when studying phonology and phonemes, integration occurs.

In the early 1960s, Lev Vygotsky developed the sociocultural learning theory. It has since been utilized in scholarly discussions about how humans learn from their social environments and the relevance of scaffolding in mental development [20].

The researchers chose this theory because it emphasizes the zone of proximal development (ZPD), information acquisition through social interaction, and scaffolding as a method of learning constructively [21, 22]. The ZPD outlines what learners can achieve with help and what they can do on their own [22]. The researchers propose that similar to how writing is learned through social contact, technology may be used to teach and learn. Scaffolding can be used in conjunction with the ZPD to close the gap between what learners can do with help and what they can do on their own [22]. The researchers believe that most learners are left behind in the ZPD because they have not yet acquired the knowledge and abilities required before moving on to the next level, owing to poor teaching practices.

2. Literature review

Writing has the power to shape the way learners think, reason, and learn. It also has the power to eave an enduring blueprint [23]. According to Taylor et al. [23], learners in the FP should write four times a week, with one extended piece of writing. The following is their requirement for writing per grade: Writing sentences in first grade, paragraphs in second grade, and extended sections in third grade. Teachers must have pedagogical understanding in order to teach writing effectively. Moreso, they need to reconsider the methodology they use in their classrooms that best suit the learners' needs. The learners of the twenty first century are born into a technological culture, and they have access to a wealth of information thanks to the recent technological growth. Technology has enabled young learners to be born into a linked world of the internet, social media, instant messaging, and always-on digital devices [24]. With this in mind, it's become increasingly vital to consider how these changes affect young learners, particularly how technology influences their learning and teaching. Therefore, teachers must learn to teach in a way that is most effective for their students. This does not imply that the meaning of what is significant is changed or that the old curriculum is eliminated. Teachers of the twenty first century, on the other hand, must adapt their materials to the needs of digital learners. The issue is no longer about whether or whether teachers should utilize digital media; rather, it is about how to use new media in a constructive, creative way in FP classrooms to boost learners' writing skills.

2.1 Barriers of technology integration

A lack of technological knowledge and skills, as well as technology-supported pedagogical knowledge and skills and technology-related classroom management knowledge and abilities, has been identified as a key barrier to technology integration. Lack of specific technical knowledge and skills is one of the most common reasons given by teachers for not using technology [25, 26]. For example, a lack of knowledge in the use of databases and spreadsheets was reported as a hindrance by more than 10% of primary school teachers in a study of Scottish schools [26]. Snoeyink et al. [25] discovered that teachers' lack of technology integration was due to a lack of computer expertise or skills in their study of one middle-class school in the United States of America. The teachers in their study did not engage their students in any technology-related activities until they had mastered basic skills such as logging onto a network, opening and closing files and applications, and basic word processing. In addition to their lack of technical competence and skills, some teachers lack familiarity with the pedagogy of using technology. According to Hughes et al. [27], teachers must have a foundation of knowledge and abilities in technology-supported pedagogy that they may draw on when planning to integrate technology into their classrooms. Pedagogy that is supported by technology can be divided into three types, according to how it is used: (a) to replace, (b) to amplify, or (c) to transform [27]. When technology is used as alternative, it is used to attain the same educational aim in a different way.

South Africa's failure to overcome the "digital divide" is due to the challenges faced by schools in the country that do not employ ICT to enhance teaching and learning. The digital divide is the difference between people who profit from digital technology and those who do not [28]. The use of ICT in schools to increase learning could help overcome some of the barriers to boosting the efficiency and productivity of both learning and teaching while also closing the digital divide [29]. The challenge for educators is to stay informed about the various types of information available, the technology used to obtain it, and how this knowledge may affect students. Learners must gain ICT skills in order to perform effectively in society as a whole and to contribute to the long-term use of ICTs.

2.2 Benefits of teaching writing using technology in the FP classroom

Incorporating technology into the teaching of writing in the FP classroom is not a quick fix process. Instead, school management should be prepared to assist teachers as they progress through a technology adoption and acquisition process. Infusing technology in teaching writing is one of the various methods that can be used in the FP. Many studies on technology integration in teaching and learning reach the same conclusion: technology plays a significant role in education at all levels [30]. However, while technology has importance as a learning and teaching tool, its full potential in FP contexts has yet to be realized. Despite this, it is only used in a small number of classrooms since it is considered as going against the grain of play-based pedagogy [31] and developmentally appropriateness [32]. Dietze et al. [33] say, on the other hand, that technology should not be considered as a threat to active play, but rather as a tool that may be utilized to improve it. According to the National Institute for Literacy, "young children need opportunities to develop early technology-handling abilities associated with early digital literacy that is equivalent to book-handling abilities associated with early literacy development." Children, on the other hand, are used to using technology in their homes, but this use is rarely duplicated to its full capacity in the FP context. Shams-Abadi et al. [34] backs up the claims, stating that writing in blended learning produces high-quality writing and answers from students.

3. Methodology

The researchers adopted qualitative methods such as a draw and write/talk technique for learners and semi-structured interviews for teachers as data generation methods. Using qualitative research for this study was suitable because it enabled the researchers and participants to gain a deeper understanding of teaching writing using technology in the FP classrooms. FP learners were able to respond to a researcher's question with a drawing by using the draw and write/talk technique. It also allowed participants to provide written responses to their final drawings. To characterize and clarify the image's content before providing a commentary on which the researchers can base their findings. The participants were taught that the message, not the quality of the drawings, is what matters [35]. Interviews were performed in this study to acquire a better understanding of each teacher's knowledge and experience of teaching writing using technology in the FP class. The data from the interviews were captured and transcribed, and then compared to the data from the draw and write approach. Silverman et al. [36] defined triangulation as the process of comprehending a situation by merging many perspectives.

Data analysis was used to identify and code themes from the raw qualitative data. The data were examined using content analysis. Content analysis is an inductive procedure in which the researcher compares the information gathered [37]. The goal of this form of analysis is to come up with conclusions based on the participants' perceptions, knowledge, attitudes, standards, feelings, and talents [37]. In a member-checking process, themes were circulated to participants for comments. Triangulation of data collection methods, direct quotes from participants' explanations of their drawings, and interview data were used to establish the research's credibility [38]. The data were analyzed by the researchers in terms of how teachers responded to the interview questions.

The sample comprised a total of four Grade 3 classroom teachers drawn from two primary schools in the township in the Eastern Cape Province. Teachers were all females between the ages of 27–58 whose home language is isiXhosa. The sample of learners consisted of 12 Grade 3 learners. Learners were boys and girls between the ages of 9–11. In reporting the data, teachers were labeled as Tc1–Tc4, and learners were labeled as Lr1–Lr12. The schools were purposefully selected because they were typical township primary schools and were accessible.

The appropriate ethical issues were taken into account. The participants were all made aware that their participation was completely optional. The researchers asked the classroom teachers to locate focus-group participants who were willing to speak with the researchers and had their parents' permission to participate in the study. Because the majority of the participants were children, both the children and their parents signed informed consent forms prior to the intervention. Teachers and learners were both informed about the study's contents, research process, and data protection.

In this study, the researchers documented true findings of the teachers teaching writing skills using technology in the FP.

A two-cycle process was used to generate data for the study. These cycles will be explained shortly below.

3.1 Orientation

Twelve Grade 3 learners were purposively chosen from a homogeneous sample and asked to participate in the experiment. The purpose of the first week was to introduce the participants to the drawing/talk technique. Participants in this session exhibited their artworks separately in a classroom. Each participant was required to write a narrative. The teachers were provided with projectors before the lessons had to take place and taken through the process of teaching using technology.

3.2 Cycle 1

The researchers conducted a desktop study of teaching methodologies for FP English First Additional Language (EFAL) sessions that included teaching writing while incorporating technology, as well as how to construct these media tools for FP English First Additional Language (EFAL) courses. Teachers were given an action learning set by the researchers to assist them to reflect on their EFAL insights about teaching writing, as well as the teaching practices they believe contribute to the development of writing skills. Participants' thoughts, as well as transcriptions of the action learning sets, were gathered through draw-and-talk interactions between the participants and the researchers. At this point in the data collection process, both the participants and the researchers kept reflective diaries, which helped them chronicle their experiences as they transpired and categorize critical ideas about what happened.

3.3 Cycle 2

The data from cycle one was utilized to outline how instructors could use technology to teach writing in the classroom during this cycle. These remedial action plans were created collaboratively by teachers and researchers. The remedial action plans were then implemented in their classrooms in the following stage. The participants and the researcher both used laptops and projectors. Teachers were encouraged to keep track of the changes in their learners' attitudes toward writing by taking field notes or filming them. The researchers used field notes, films of the participants, and talks to evaluate the plan they wanted to implement to solve the difficulties noted.

4. Findings

The data analysis for this study was given in a descriptive fashion, owing to the qualitative nature of the research. The themes that arose from the data are addressed with data support and then justified with a theoretical grounding. The findings are explained in terms of the two cycles that drove the study's data collection. Cycle one involved identifying the research problem and planning how to overcome the obstacles, while cycle two involved putting the remedial action plan into action and reflecting on the results of our remedial action plans.

4.1 Teachers' feelings and attitudes on teaching writing using technology in the FP

Three out of every four teachers, according to the teachers interviewed, were reared and schooled in a technologically deficient setting. Only one was given the chance to be exposed to a learning environment in which technology is used to educate and learn. The school systems of the other three participants did not allow for the use of digital learning resources. Teachers were concerned about using technology in the classroom, according to the findings of the interviews. As a result, a teacher's lack of past experience with technology-related supplies is a reliable predictor of their attitudes and beliefs regarding using technology in FP. According to the data, technology was not used in the FP classroom. Despite the benefits and relevance of employing technology in the classroom, some teachers have failed to embrace this innovation. Some teachers still make use of chalkboards and only use the provided laptops for administrative work. This argument is encapsulated in the following verbatim quote.

Tc1 said "*the challenge is the lack of gadgets. Even though I have a laptop which was supplied by the department it is difficult to share the prepared lesson with the whole classroom since we do not have projectors and Wi-Fi in the classroom. When I decide to use the laptop, I divide learners into groups so that they can see what I am teaching on the screen of the laptop"*. Tc2 stated *"It is very critical for us to be provided with the necessary tools of trade more especially for a big class like mine, as interaction with these learners is a challenge because of larger numbers. Yes of course I cannot run for the fact that technology is good, but we cannot only use technology to teach kids, chalk and board is important"*. Tc3 said *"For me, the greatest challenge in using ICT is the lack of knowledge, I struggle a lot to keep up with it. You must know the system very well and be familiar with it to use it effectively. If you do not know the system at all, it's very difficult"*. Tc4: *"The challenges involved are so many, for example, maintaining the facility, safety of infrastructure, lack of proper skills on the part of the teacher. I can go on and on"*. She further said *"I think maybe the people that have been teaching for a very long time do not always incorporate technology, because they are not comfortable. So, for us, newer teachers embrace and incorporate it into lessons like doing a slide show, using DVDs, and the internet"*.

The participants identified several barriers to integrating technology into the FP while teaching writing, including the high cost of procuring equipment, as well as the financial limits associated with educating instructors in technology and maintaining the continuing use of technology. Tc1 expressed her opinion as follows: *"Using computers or the Internet requires planning. It cannot be seen as a distinct plan, but rather as an integral element of the curriculum. Many teachers lack the necessary skills to know how to utilize ICT, which increases the cost load on a school because it is pointless to have the technology if the teachers are unable to use it. As a result, teachers are required to attend training sessions on how to use technology. This, I believe, is one of the primary reasons why schools do not spend money on equipment."* The teachers are one of the main reasons why technology is not being adopted more widely. The success of introducing technology when it is accessible is determined by the teacher's attitude. *"It's about teacher attitude once again,"* Tc2 remarked. *Also, a desire to incorporate technology into the classroom." "You have to have the training, you have to have a laptop, you have to know how to use it,"* Tc3 explained, *"which is a method that the department is trying to support teachers in terms of their workload, planning, and that kind of thing, but it's taking a long time."* Furthermore, the participants noted that pricey electronic equipment in the school is vulnerable due to high crime rates and widespread theft.

Apart from the above participants indicated the influence of planning using a laptop since given by the government. Tc4 said in the current report, *"Yes, having my own laptop influenced me to use technology. It would have been dreadful if I hadn't had it. I gained confidence by using my laptop at home, and the researchers made sure I knew how to do everything."* To this end, three teachers stated that instead of wasting time duplicating notes on a chalkboard, they prepared lessons on their laptops at home and taught using projectors. According to the findings, younger generation instructors who have been qualified in recent years have a more open attitude toward the usage of technology and the necessity to include technology training in their professional development plan. Teaching writing using technology was a challenge to teachers. Although the department of education provided them with computers, data revealed that they were only using it for planning. Only one teacher was using technology due to previous experience.

4.2 Teachers' experience of teaching writing using technology

Their opinions toward the use of technology appear to be tied to their teaching experience. Teachers with more teaching experience were reluctant in the integration of technology in teaching writing in the FP. However, after interventions, all four

DOI: http://dx.doi.org/10.5772/intechopen.103666

teachers agreed to pilot this project. They all agreed that the use of technology helped them to improve teaching writing in the FP. The findings indicated that teachers' perceptions changed. Tc1 indicated *"Kids learn more when they have technology because it is colorful and they can see and is related to their daily lives of technology. Their writing skill has developed".*

The second respondent concurs with the fact that technology integration is a welcome idea; it makes lesson delivery more interesting and enjoyable, especially for learners in the FP classroom. Tc2: *It is very good. The kids like it, they are immediately interested. It is more interesting than books, although it helps, it should not take the place of traditional teaching and teachers must not discard the method of teaching with the textbooks totally.* Tc3 respondent *"apart from making lessons more enjoyable for learners; technology also makes the teacher's work easier, but there is the possibility that it may replace the textbook in the nearest future".* Tc4 further commented, *"instead of preparing notes on a notebook which wasted a lot of time, I prepare my lessons at home with my laptop".* The teachers agreed that technology is good and because learners are familiar with it since they have these facilities at home, they tend to pay more attention in class. Tc4 said *"I think infusing technology provides teachers with different options to present their lessons when teaching the learners*. Furthermore, the majority of teachers thought that the use of technology gave several opportunities for successful teaching, and that aided teaching improves learning.

4.3 Learners' experience of learning writing skills using technology

Data obtained from learners through the write/talk technique also showed that technology in teaching writing enabled the learners to be more active and engaging in the lesson prepared by the teachers.

Hereunder is the evidence of learners writing paragraphs exercise.

Paragraph writing

The **Figures 1–5** below indicate the learners' writing skill development after cycle 2 of writing using technology. The data indicated a huge improvement in learners' writing from the three different classes.

Drawings of learners

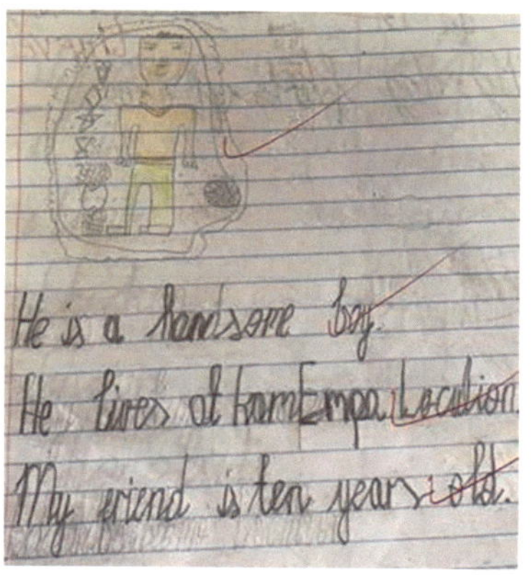

Figure 1.
Drawing by Lr2.

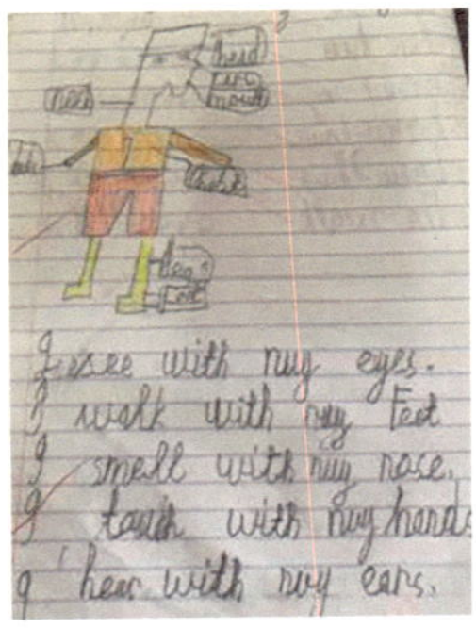

Figure 2.
Drawing by Lr3.

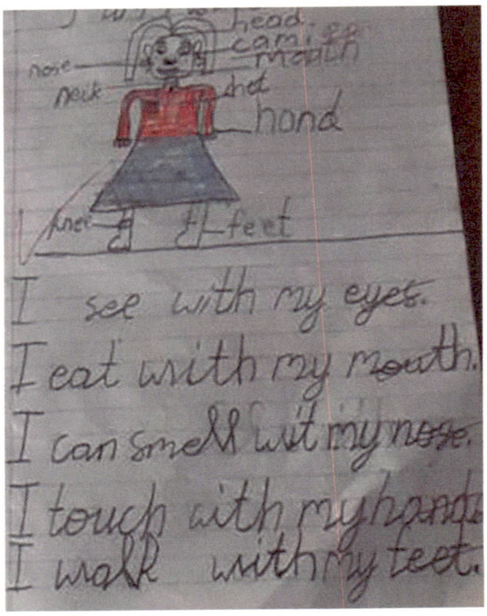

Figure 3.
Drawing by Lr5.

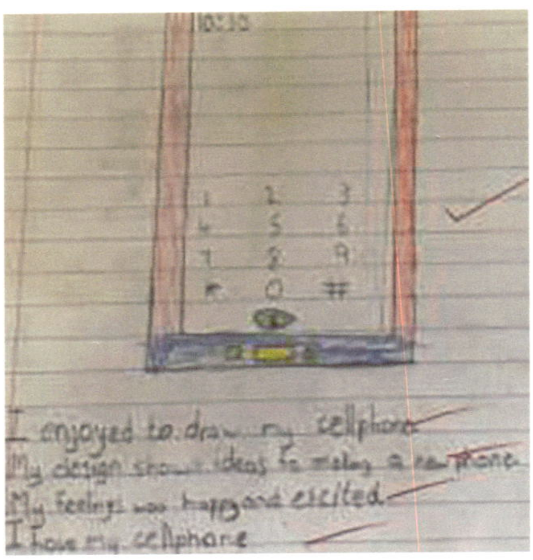

Figure 4.
Drawing by Lr9.

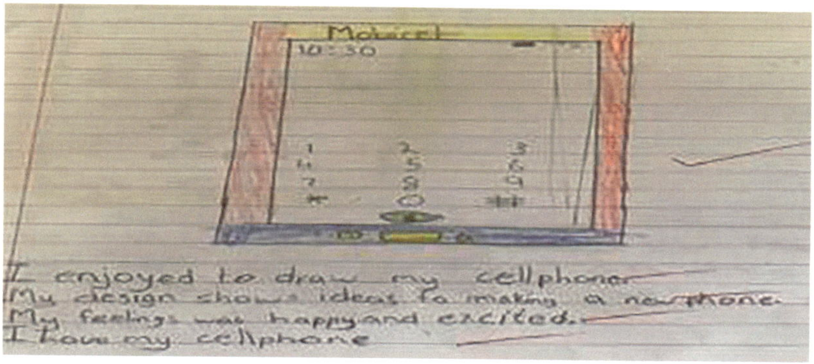

Figure 5.
Drawing by Lr11.

5. Discussion of findings

5.1 Teachers' feelings and attitudes on teaching writing using technology in the FP

Feelings and attitudes about teaching writing with technology are characterized in this study as informal training that affected teachers' willingness to adopt and use technology for teaching writing in the FP. To fulfill the demand of living in the twenty first century, new information and abilities are necessary, and our teachers and students will be asked to learn in creative ways. In view of the foregoing, the Action Plan for 2019 [2] emphasizes the importance of well-designed government initiatives to address the digital gap in South Africa by taking charge of technological advancement. On the other hand, this policy structure does not serve the FP and, worse, does not explain the pedagogical components of employing technology in teaching and learning. Nyambane et al. [14] say that "when technology is used, content and pedagogy, the two core aspects of teaching and learning, must be integrated." As a result, role players must recognize that employing a given technology can change how learners grasp concepts in that content area in order to deliver the required sustenance for choosing the real technology as well as the associated information for the technology. This suggests that teachers need to be taught in using technology to teach writing in the FP.

5.2 Teachers' experience of teaching writing using technology

When applied effectively, the data showed that technology can help pedagogy. When it came to teaching writing while incorporating technology in the FP classroom, participants highlighted several ideas and techniques. It is widely acknowledged that FP learners differ from previous generations, and as a result, the manner they are taught should be different as well. Despite the fact that these learners have a unique learning style that needs a child-centered, play-based curriculum, technology can help in the construction of a plan that is accessible and flexible outside of the classroom. Teachers were unanimous in their assessment of the platform's effectiveness in the FP classroom. Teachers also felt that technology is useful in a variety of ways, particularly in assisting learners in learning to write in an enjoyable, dynamic, and meaningful way. In addition, our findings are consistent with many studies on infusing technology in teaching and learning which agree that technology has a vital role to play in teaching at all levels [30]. Moreover, findings indicated that one area where technology integration has the potential to increase learners learning is in the area of teaching writing. Shams-Abadi et al. [34] back up the claims, stating that writing in blended learning produces good writing and reactions from students.

5.3 Learners' experience of learning writing skills using technology

The findings revealed that learners were enthusiastic about using technology to improve their writing skills. Affectively, the learners expressed a desire to use technology because of its novelty, novelty, and appeal. Learning to write with technology was easy and uncomplicated for the learners, and it encouraged them to write. The overall learner experience of learners was excellent, learners confirmed that technology helped them to learn better about the writing. Much research [30, 33, 34] have come to similar conclusions. In this study, the participants had access to a smartphone and a computer or laptop at home, as well as a positive attitude toward technology use. Prensky et al. [15] highlights this point by arguing that learners have changed as a result of the introduction and quick spread of digital technology in the later eras of the twentieth century, as well as its progression into the twenty first century. This conclusion applies to all language learning situations, both national and international, and allows teachers to better address the requirements of their own learners, especially when learners come from a variety of educational backgrounds and have varying technological skills.

6. Conclusion

This study is significant because it paves the way for a technology-based pedagogical investigation of teaching writing in the FP. Today's learners are socialized in a fundamentally different way than earlier generations because we now all live in a "wired" and connected global information society. The impact of technology at the dawn of the information era was largely focused on information access or transmission, but it should now be extended to encompass how teachers teach (i.e., pedagogy) and how learners learn. It is necessary to integrate technology with knowledge content.

7. Recommendations

This study's recommendations are made from the top-down manner. Starting with the suggestion that the government provides technological assistance to FP teachers. Following that, it is proposed that FP teachers adjust the way they organize their classes in order to respond to the benefits of technology-assisted instruction. Finally, it is advocated that FP learners have access to the most appropriate technology-based information. Therefore, it is advised that schools provide the essential infrastructure for our young learners to take advantage of technology instruments for learning. Because technology allows for the adaptation of classroom procedures as well as the ability to teach and learn in exciting, new ways, its proper deployment still requires assistance. It is, therefore, suggested that a set of recommendations for an emergent curriculum centered on the interests of this generation of learners be produced to aid teachers and learners in successfully integrating teaching and technology in the FP. Teachers' attitudes about technology must be modified, and teachers must have the proper training in how to use technology to teach writing in the FP. Any policy governing the use of technology in the classroom must be simple to understand.

Author details

Pretty Thandiswa Mpiti[1*] and Bulelwa Makena[2]

1 Walter Sisulu University, Queenstown, South Africa

2 Walter Sisulu University, Butterworth, South Africa

*Address all correspondence to: pmpiti@wsu.ac.za

References

[1] Mpiti T, Makena B, Mpahla NE. Applying place-based approach in teaching academic writing in a tertiary english first additional language context in the Eastern Cape. In: Conference Proceedings of International Technology, Education and Development Conference 2021 INTED; 08-09 March 2021. Valencia: INTED; 2021. pp. 10739-10747

[2] Department of Basic Education. Action Plan to 2019 Towards the Realisation of Schooling 2030: Taking forward South Africa's National Development Plan 2030. Pretoria; 2015

[3] Myhill D, Jones S, Lines H. Supporting less proficient writers through linguistically aware teaching. Language and Education. 2018;**32**(4):333-349. DOI: 10.1080/09500782.2018.1438468

[4] Gadd M, Parr JM, Robertson J, Carran L, Ali Z, Gendall L, et al. Portrait of the student as a young writer: Some student survey findings about attitudes to writing and self-efficacy as writers. Literacy. 2019;**53**(4):226-235

[5] KeenGwe J, OnChwari G, OnChwari J. Technology and student learning: Towards a learner-centered teaching model. AACE Review (Formerly AACE Journal). 2009;**17**(1):11-22

[6] Gialamas V, Nikolopoulou K. In-service and pre-service early childhood teachers' views and intentions about ICT use in early childhood settings: A comparative study. Computers & Education. 2010;**55**(1):333-341

[7] Kalas I. Integration of ICT in Early Childhood Education. Torun, Poland: X World Conference On Computer Education; 2013

[8] United States. Department of Education [Internet]. 2016. Available from: http://sites.ed.gov/oese/2016/04/open-discussionon-the-role-of-education-technologies-in-early-childhood-stem-education [Accessed: July 04, 2021]

[9] Du Toit I. The effect of ICT curriculum support on the measured skills levels of learners of two sub-projects of the Khanya project. In: 8th IFIP World Conference on Computers in Education (WCCE 2005). 2005. Retrieved from: www.khanya.co.za/news/events/files/wcceisabel.pdf. Available from: http://www.eranet.co.za/zenex/files/257_Khanya%20Project [Accessed: November 11, 2021]

[10] Hsin CT, Li MC, Tsai CC. The influence of young children's use of technology on their learning: A review. Journal of Educational Technology & Society. 2014;**17**(4):85-99. Available from: http://www.ifets.info/journals/17_4/6.pdf [Accessed: January 11, 2022]

[11] Ghavifekr S, Afshari M, Amla S. Management strategies for E-Learning system as the core component of systemic change: A qualitative analysis. Life Science Journal. 2012;**9**(3):2190-2196

[12] Zevenbergen R. Digital natives come to preschool: Implications for early childhood practice. Contemporary Issues in Early Childhood. 2007;**8**(1):19-29. Available from: http://cie.sagepub.com/content/8/1/19.full.pdf+html [Accessed: May 05, 2021]

[13] Prensky MR. Teaching Digital Natives: Partnering for Real Learning. Corwin Press; 2010. Available from: http://www.marcprensky.com/prensky-teaching_digital_natives-introd [Accessed: August 09, 2021]

[14] Nyambane CO, Nzuki D. Factors influencing ICT integration in teaching—A literature review. International Journal of Education and Research. 2014;**2**(3):1-7

[15] Prensky M. Digital natives, digital immigrants part 2: Do they really think differently? On the Horizon. 2001;**2**:358

[16] Beers CS, Beers JW, Smith JO. A Principal's Guide to Literacy Instruction. Australia: Guilford Press; 2009

[17] Mayer RE, Moreno R. A cognitive theory of multimedia learning: Implications for design principles. Journal of Educational Psychology. 1998;**91**(2):358-368. Available from: https://gustavus.edu/education/courses/edu241/mmtheory.pdf [Accessed: January 15, 2022]

[18] Sorden SD. A cognitive approach to instructional design for multimedia learning. Informing Science. 2005;**8**:263

[19] Fani T, Ghaemi F. Implications of Vygotsky's zone of proximal development (ZPD) in teacher education: ZPTD and self-scaffolding. Procedia-Social and Behavioral Sciences. 1 Jan 2011;**29**:1549-1554

[20] Newman F, Holzman L. Lev Vygotsky (classic edition): Revolutionary Scientist. Australia: Psychology Press; 24 Jul 2013

[21] Mcdevitt TM, Ormrod JE. Cognitive development 2: Cognitive process. In: Child Development Education and Working with Children and Adolescents. 2nd ed. Oxford: Pearson; 2004. pp. 91-98

[22] Brewer JA. Introduction to Early Childhood Education: Preschool through Primary Grades. Boston: Allyn and Bacon; 2001

[23] Taylor N, Draper K, Muller J, Sithole S. The state of literacy teaching and learning in the foundation phase. X World Conference On Computer Education

[24] Codrington G. Mind The Gap: Own Your Past, Know Your Generation, Choose Your Future. Oxford: Penguin Random House South Africa; 2012

[25] Snoeyink R, Ertmer PA. Thrust into technology: How veteran teachers respond. Journal of Educational Technology Systems. 2001;**30**(1):85-111

[26] Williams D, Coles L, Wilson K, Richardson A, Tuson J. Teachers and ICT: Current use and future needs. British Journal of Educational Technology. 2000;**31**(4):307-320

[27] Hughes J. The role of teacher knowledge and learning experiences in forming technology-integrated pedagogy. Journal of Technology and Teacher Education. 2005;**13**(2): 277-302

[28] Best ML, Maclay CM. Community Internet access in rural areas: Solving the economic sustainability puzzle

[29] Chitamu PJ, Van Olst R, Vannucci DE. How can the cost of telecommunications access in Africa be driven downwards. In: Southern African Telecommunications and Applications Conference (SATNAC), Proceedings (CDROM). New York: Psychology Press; 2013. ISBN 0-620-30949-0

[30] Padayachee K, Kritzinger E. Teaching safe and secure usage of ICTs in South African schools [Online]. Available from: http://www.uir.unisa.ac.za/handle/10500/3986 [Accessed: August 13, 2021]

[31] Murcia K, Campbell C, Aranda G. Trends in early childhood education practice and professional learning

with digital technologies. Pedagogika. 2018;**68**(3):233. DOI: 10.14712/23362189.2018.858

[32] Langub LW, Lokey-Vega A. Rethinking instructional technology to improve pedagogy for digital literacy: A design case in a graduate early childhood education course. TechTrends. 2017;**61**(4):322-330. DOI: 10.1007/s11528-017-0185-1

[33] Dietze B, Kashin D. Shifting views: Exploring the potential for technology integration in early childhood education programs/Changement d'opinion: Exploration du potentiel d'intégration de la technologie dans les programmes d'éducation de la petite enfance. Canadian Journal of Learning and Technology/La revue canadienne de l'apprentissage et de la technologie. 2013;**39**(4):233. DOI: 10.21432/T25P4Z

[34] Shams-Abadi BB, Ahmadi SD, Mehrdad AG. The effect of Edmodo on EFL learners' writing performance. International Journal of Educational Investigations. 2015;**2**(2):88-97

[35] Theron L, Stuart J, Mitchell C. A positive, African ethical approach to collecting and interpreting drawings. In: Picturing Research. SensePublishers; 2011. pp. 49-61

[36] Silverman D. Doing Qualitative Research: A Practical Handbook. Athens: Sage; 2013

[37] Nieuwenhuis J. Introducing qualitative research. First Steps in Research. 2007;**5**:224-254

[38] Creswell JW. Mapping the field of mixed methods research. Journal of Mixed Methods Research. 2009;**3**(2):95-108

Chapter 2

New Updates in Online Learning

Nilesh Kumar Mitra

Abstract

During the COVID-19 pandemic, a rapid transformation happened overnight in the teaching-learning strategy in primary, secondary and tertiary education. All educators started using web-conferencing tools as principal element of online learning. However, in spite of health concerns among the pandemic situation, strong student preferences towards returning back to face-to-face or hybrid mode brought challenges to the effectiveness of online learning. Students cite many reasons for dropping out of online courses. Increased workload and poor organization of remote learning have been found to be the principal reason for the students' dissatisfaction. The orientation of online learning needs alignment towards the principle of course design along with the flexibility to attain the instructional goals, objectives, and outcomes. Sophisticated technology often makes online and even hybrid course design to change track from well-designed pedagogy leading to loss of functional relevance for the students. Instructors should be flexible and employ multiple strategies to improve online learning experiences in both asynchronous and synchronous learning environment. Studies have proved that using the best practice of the alignment of learning outcome, online learning activities and repeated online knowledge-checks foster student motivation towards the completion of online courses.

Keywords: online education, instructional design, engagement in online learning, asynchronous online learning, synchronous online learning

1. Introduction

Online education has been growing continuously for the last two decades. With the reduction of budgets and shrinking spaces, many Universities continue to use online education as a long-term strategy to handle increasing student enrolment. Compared to 3.2 million students enrolled in at least one fully online course during fall semester 2005, in fall 2019, 7.3 million students enrolled in at least one distance education course in the USA. Since the days of 1840, when Sir Isaac Pitman introduced teaching shorthand through the post, distance learning became available through television in 1965 with the first Open University in England broadcasting the lectures through BBC. However, today crossing the borders of postal services and television broadcasting, the advent of newer technology and web-based connectivity has turned remote learning into agile and flexible virtual classrooms [1, 2].

Analysis of the status of online learning in different parts of the world indicates a strong presence of country-level factors. A close look at the globalization of online education explains its dependence on bridging the digital divide, accommodation of various languages, standardized curriculum across different countries and use of universal technology platforms. A shift from the agricultural or industrial economy to the digital economy, automation of jobs requiring lower grades of skills and impending need of lowering infrastructure costs have led the government administration and higher education institutions to make major structural changes [3].

After an initial peak in the enrolment of the students in the online courses, US Universities have been experiencing the burden of increased faculty training costs, lack of appropriateness of teaching of all subjects in the online mode and increased cost of technological updates. Some students are concerned about the reduced quality of instruction and increased cognitive load of mastering new technology. Among the developing countries, Indian Universities have established themselves as major drivers of online or blended education with people using online education reaching 9.6 million in 2021. Comparatively lower cost of online education, appreciable growth in internet and mobile devices penetration and escalating demand of working professionals have helped the growth of online education in India. Among the other Asian countries, the Chinese online education market has developed exponentially due to government support and a national curriculum. Universities have been providing lessons via satellite to thousands of remote schools and broadband internet connections have reached remote corners of the country. Challenges in the growth of online learning in the Middle East have been described due to the lack of educational resources in the Arabic language and low public esteem for online education. The Open University of Australia in collaboration with other leading Universities have become the national leader in online education. However, the lack of high bandwidth connectivity in remote locations has been reported as a principal factor preventing the growth of online learning. In contrast to other countries of the world, mobile-based learning has reached significant growth in Africa despite the lack of significant increase of information technology capacity [4–8].

2. COVID-19 pandemic and online learning

During the COVID-19 pandemic, schools and higher education institutes chose to temporarily cease face-to-face classes and remote learning was promoted by the administration. By the end of April 2020, 186 countries implemented nationwide closures. Schools for more than 168 million children were completely closed for face-to-face classes [9]. Behind the black cloud, there is always a promise for bright sun rays. To cope with the extraordinary situation, countries with centuries of lecture-based teaching and related institutional biases were forced to pursue creative approaches on relatively short notice. Various strategies were used to deliver remote learning (**Figure 1**).

During the crisis period, a large amount of online teaching started in various formats and many interfaces were used to deliver the content. From primary to tertiary education, the institutions attempted to develop an expectation that the students should take responsibility for their own learning. Often the teachers put an Increased emphasis on compliance with the technical needs and requirements at the expense of the student-centeredness and engagement. These changes had a significant impact on the students' learning system. Both synchronous and asynchronous online learning from the Learning Management System (LMS) are accessed by the students, using the internet via smartphones, iPads, laptops, or desktops. Most of the students in the developing countries rely on the computer and free internet in the schools due to the existing socio-economic conditions Students and instructors with

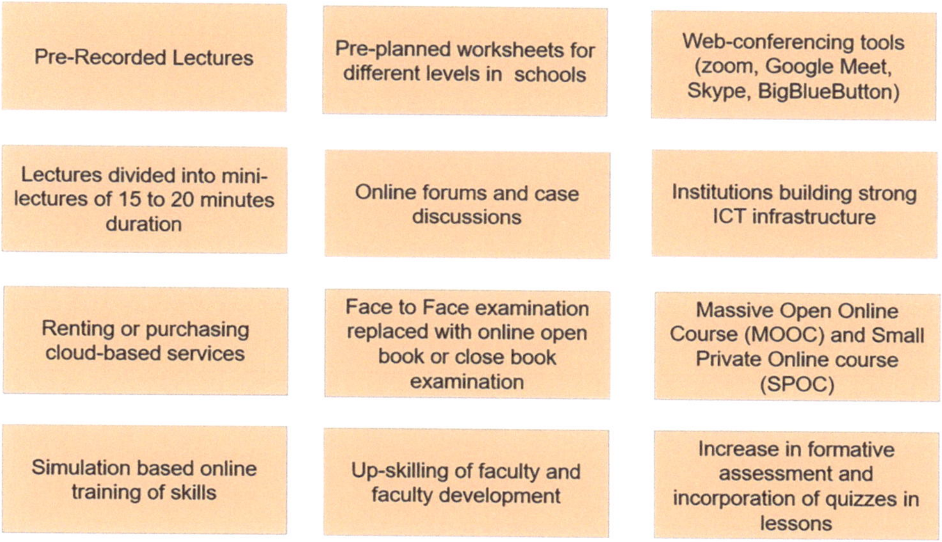

Figure 1.
Strategies used in online learning during COVID-19 pandemic.

poor internet connections in their residences were denied continuous access to the resources. Provision of the technological devices posed challenges to parents, institutions, Government, and non-governmental organizations. The appearance of family members and pets during the online teaching and learning caused a distraction to the attention of online learning participants. Students experienced more workloads as appropriate assessments were not introduced to match the level of coverage of the syllabus and the delivery of the lessons [10]. A study conducted in Poland in April 2020, among 2408 teenagers, found that half of the surveyed adolescents felt an increase in the requirements imposed by the teachers. About one-third of the teenagers opined about poor organization of remote learning at the schools and observed problems in consulting the teacher when they had problems in understanding the material [11]. A qualitative study was held with 79 faculty from 19 countries using Polarity Approach for Continuity and Transformation (PACT). The faculties worked in small groups to determine the pros and cons of face-to-face and distance learning. The warning signs identified in distance learning for continuous monitoring included dissatisfaction of students with faculty engagement, mentorship programs showing lack of significant engagement, failure of one-third of students to submit timely assignments and decrease in mean scores of formative assessments among 30% of the students. A reduction of 10% score in Objective Structured Clinical Examination (OSCE) stations on topics taught online was also observed [12].

3. Instructional design to improve engagement in online learning

With the studies reporting disengagement of the students in the online learning, educational institutions should plan to design appropriate learning activities and improve the learning environments. e-Learning Engagement Design (ELED) is a framework which can be added as common step in instructional design models to incorporate best practices for student engagement in online learning (**Figure 2**) [13].

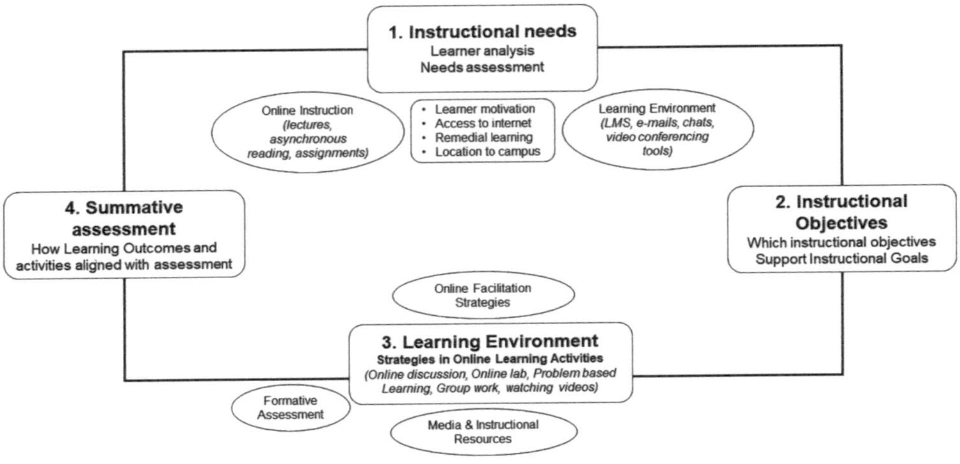

Figure 2.
Instructional design framework for increasing engagement [13].

Instructional design tasks start with identifying instructional needs of the learner and constructing a learner profile with all strategic information related to the learner. An analysis of the learning environment and the components of the online instruction along with the learner profile would enable the instructor and instructional designer to find out the problem in the instruction and the performance problem. The second phase starts with analyzing the instructional objectives and instructional goals which the students need to achieve to demonstrate their understanding. The third phase of the ELED framework is where most design and development tasks are performed. Both active and passive online learning activities should be investigated to plan strategic changes to improve levels of interaction and engagement. However, the most critical component in the student engagement is the role of the facilitator and how the online facilitation in different learning activities are carried out. Media selection is also a key task in the design process. The selection of the media for online student engagement requires consideration of interaction between the learners and the technology and, the role played by the media elements in the learner-learner, learner-course material and learner-instructor interactions. Formative assessment integrated with each type of online instruction helps to identify learner misunderstandings, misconceptions and mistakes and should be closely associated with the quality of feedback to be provided to the students. The fourth and final phase ends with the analysis of the summative assessment activities covering both learning and instructional effectiveness. Investigation of the alignment between the learning outcomes, online learning activities and tools of the summative assessment would indicate the gaps in the administration of the suitable online learning activities. To improve the student engagement in the online learning, engagement indicators of the academic challenge (i.e., learning strategies, reflective learning, higher order thinking), learning with peers (i.e., collaborative learning, group discussions), faculty experience of the student (i.e., teaching practices, student-faculty interaction) and campus environment (i.e., supportive campus environment, quality of interactions) should be investigated. Apart from the planning of strategic changes in the online instruction, administrators should also plan for developing the overall learning environment.

DOI: http://dx.doi.org/10.5772/intechopen.102576

4. Engagement in online learning

4.1 Creating effective interaction using CCAF model

Traditionally interactivity in the teaching-learning process has been described in 4 levels.

- Passive (images, non-interactive video, or audio).
- Limited participation (animation, test questions, drag and drop interactions, clickable menus).
- Moderate interactions (simulations, branching scenarios, gamifications).
- Full immersion (learners control the interaction e.g., virtual reality, augmented reality).

In the CCAF (Context, Challenge, Activity, Feedback) model of e-learning design, the intention and outcome of the learning focus on creating immersion, even if the context is simple. Context (C) provides a real-world environment where the results of the challenge (C) can seem to be real. Activity (A) provided by the gesture represents actions to be taken in the real world in the form of meaningful behavior. Feedback (F) provided allows the learner to reflect on intrinsic components of learning based on the context (**Figure 3**) [14]. The components of CCAF guide the structuring of the learning events and should not be confused with learning phases.

4.2 Structuring learning interactions in 'Flow Channel'

Learning experiences in the modules contain increasingly newer information. If the learning experiences are structured in an uphill channel and the equilibrium

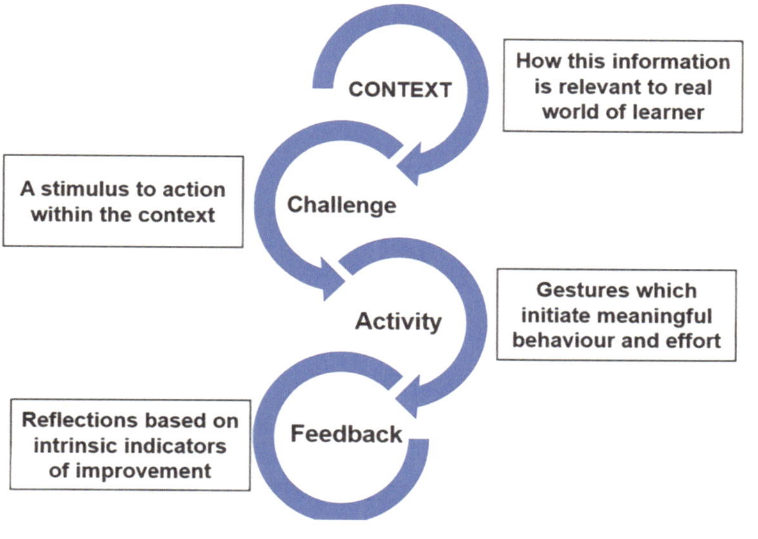

Figure 3.
CCAF model of instructional design [14].

between the learner's ability and the learning challenge is not considered in designing the modules in either fully online or blended learning, the experience would be exhausting for the learner. When the challenge is too easy compared to the ability, it does not motivate the learner. On the other end, the challenge being too hard compared to the ability brings frustrating experience. A challenge of a new learning experience that is 'slightly hard' brings a sense of motivation to complete the learning task. The principle of 'Flow channel' brings a balance between challenge and satisfaction (**Figure 4**).

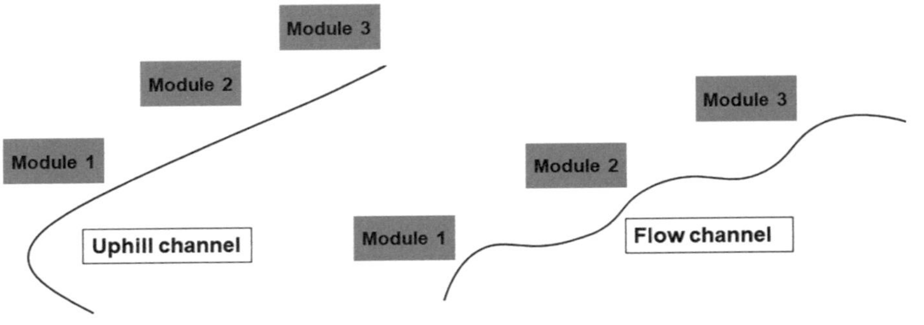

Figure 4.
Flow channel allows balance between the ability and challenge.

4.3 Tips on student engagement in asynchronous online learning

Creating a learning environment in online learning is a challenging task. The following examples of the application of the principles of online pedagogy [15–17] would help plan asynchronous online teaching sessions in the discussion boards of the Learning Management System (LMS) or Google group emails or blogs (**Table 1**).

4.4 Tips on student engagement in synchronous online learning

4.4.1 Cognitive presence in online teaching can be improved using the following principles

- Gain attention
  Gain attention by a case-scenario or a short video and ask questions to stimulate inquiry. Compared to the face-to-face lecture, the strategy to prepare the students for online lecture should differ and should be planned earlier by posting a small number of quizzes for the students to self-assess along with a short video reviewing the topic of the lecture.

- Learning outcomes
  Describe the goal by making clear statements on learning outcomes. Many a time, the outcomes from F2F teaching sessions are copied into online synchronous sessions without any alterations leading to increase in the cognitive load of the students. Choose the outcomes, which can be best delivered using the principle of microlearning (to keep the resources manageable) in the asynchronous learning resources (PDF/Video/links to web pages) component

Principle	Strategy
Student-directed learning	Chapter discussion by the students: Students are asked to start discussions by asking a critical thinking question from resources included in the lesson.
	Students as facilitators: Students to create a link to a website with summary of information and ask questions.
	Peer assistance: When a student has difficulty in completing a complex task, another student explains the concept in detail to him or her.
	Students grading their own assignments: Using a rubric students mark their own assignment and then suggest their grade to the instructor.
	Case study analysis: Following a rubric of discussion, students discuss the case. Think-aloud triad can be used for the group interaction. The explainer will analyze the case, the questioner will challenge the explainer and the recorder will record. At the end, the recorder will make the presentation available in the discussion board.
Student-student and student-teacher interaction	*Collaborative research paper*: Students to write a research paper with a review of literature from web-based journal articles. The paper can be submitted after including the comments /additional ideas from the other students.
	Research proposal by a team of students: A team of students work collaboratively to create background information, research questions and experimental design. The completed proposal is submitted to a 'reviewer panel' consisting of another team of students.
Strive for presence (*Community of inquiry*)	The '*Community of Inquiry*' framework is a process model of online learning which propagates a constructivist theory explaining online educational experience arising from the interaction of social, cognitive, and teaching presence [16]. Online environment inhibits self-expression due to absence of appearance. Opportunity for inter-personal interaction can be enhanced by opening 'Bulletin board' or 'Private chat rooms' in the LMS. Inherent distance between the student and instructor infects the communication. In 'cognitive presence' interaction, while providing feedback, the instructor should use a tone of intimacy and immediacy rather than a detached note. 'Teaching presence' can be enhanced by encouraging, acknowledging, and reinforcing student discussions and creating a learning environment.
Role-play Simulations	*Preparation, Presentation and Analysis*: Students feel greater freedom to express themselves during the role-play in online environment relieved of the stage fright. A small group (4 or 5 students) is assigned a story to enact. Once the time comes for the 'virtual curtains up', a forum is opened, where the actors articulate with each other in serial order in the voice of their characters. The rest of the class participate as audience. In the final phase, student performers answer the questions from the rest of the class [17]. The role-play in the online environment stimulates creativity in the student-performers to compensate for the lack of visual and auditory cues of the physical act.

Table 1.
Strategies for student engagement in asynchronous learning [15].

of the module page in the LMS. A timely reminder in the chat box of the web-conferencing tool in a non-intimidating tone is often helpful in guiding the student learning.

- Prior knowledge
  Link the outcomes with the prior knowledge.

- Chunking of contents
  Explore the contents by chunking the contents into short segments under outcome 1, outcome 2, outcome 3 ... by explanation of the concepts using examples, metaphors, and asking student experience.

- Scenarios or Examples
  Integrate the concepts under different outcomes by the scenarios or examples which can connect the outcomes.

- Voice as a tool
  Some instructors find the concepts of 'using the voice as a tool of engagement' and 'marrying the number of outcomes with duration of the session' useful in delivering the online lecture. Using emotive words, varying the speaking rates and volumes and use of verbal signposts are often helpful.

- Interactive tools
  Elicit performance by using interactive tools like 'Poll Everywhere', 'Kahoot', 'Slido', 'Kahoot', 'Quizizz' and 'Mentimeter'.

- Summarization
  Summarize the key concepts of the topic and let the students know about the arrangement of the question-and-answer session (chat-box/forum/discussion board).

4.4.2 Teaching presence in online teaching can be improved using the following principles

- Lecture plan:

  - Heading and Sub-Headings, division into segments (with maximum time for each segment)

  - Text-based content in each slide, font size, number of diagrams in each slide, choice of diagram and its clarity, clear explanation (Instructor should plan the text, narration, and images in the presentation with suitable application of Mayer's cognitive theory of multimedia learning (**Figure 5**) [18].

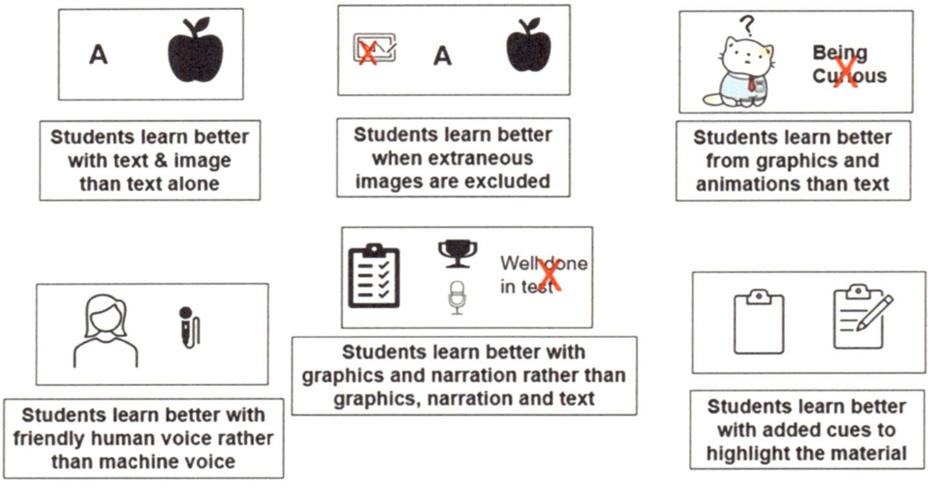

Figure 5.
Application of Mayer's cognitive theory of multimedia learning in presentation [18].

- Audio-visual components: pre-planned, simple to explain (not more than 50–60 seconds in one image), should facilitate change in sensory channel of the students

- Non-verbal aids:
  Pause, silence, hesitations, change of vocal quality like increasing tone to emphasize and then decreasing tone to continue, gesture/facial expression

- Common errors:
  Too quick speaking, failure to pause, explaining too much at one time, inaudible voice, not able to pitch the voice at comfortable level, not emphasizing key-points, use of long text without flow-chart/images/bullet points, not maintaining the timing to be given to sub-headings or parts of the lecture.

- Digital whiteboard:
  Use of digital whiteboard: an online whiteboard is used so that both the lecturer and students can write on the whiteboard and both sides can see it. Apart from sketches and calculations, video, audio can be displayed and used inside the whiteboard. Notes from the class can be digitized, saved, and shared with the students.

4.4.3 Social presence in online teaching can be improved using the following principles

- Trusting environment:
  Both teacher & students enter the online session few minutes before session so that icebreaking can be initiated by the teacher. In case of lack of attention from the students, the teacher should change the strategy and think about easier examples to explain the concept.

- Verbal feedback
  Teacher should consider students' verbal feedback (no student responds, or students respond with inadequate explanation) for improvement in the teaching session.

- Blended learning:

  - F2F driver: A struggling student is given online remedial assignment though the LMS, following the online teaching session.

  - ROTATIONS: In a station rotation model, students are organized into groups in the break-out rooms within the web-conferencing platform for the group work during the online session. These groups can be fixed (remain the same each day) or dynamic (change related to student skills/ needs).

  - FLEX: Blending online teaching session with traditional teaching methods. The assignments are completed by the students independently. Students work at their own pace through a predetermined set of material.

- Presence and social media:
  A teacher should have a virtual office to meet the students in online teaching-learning environment. Using social media, educators can have an opportunity to help students and blur the lines between informal and formal learning. The following social media can be used:

  - Twitter
  - Facebook
  - WhatsApp group
  - Google Hangout
  - Instagram

- Collaboration:
  Following online teaching session, teacher should create the sense of a learning community using appropriate platforms/tools e.g., forum in LMS and/or web-conferencing platform chat room

  - Frequent peer to peer communication (encourage students' interaction)
  - Be present as faculty to maintain student communication
  - Use video mode in synchronous activities to enhance the human connection

5. Conclusion

During the pandemic situation, online teaching-learning was initiated using various formats and many types of interfaces were used to deliver the content. A new-norm of online education is being delivered in the hybrid mode in many institutes, with a fraction of the students attending F2F being present in the campus and the remaining students attending online. Both online learning administered through the LMS in blended mode and hybrid learning have been accepted in most of the parts of the world to deal with the pandemic and to continue with the academic progress of the students. Educators need to meet the needs of the diverse learners and design the online learning experiences towards promoting a learning environment which should encourage engagement, promote interaction, motivate learners, and above all should facilitate learning both on campus and off-campus. Preparing web-based learning resources and administering online synchronous and asynchronous teaching require a great time and use of substantial resources. Educational institutes should invest on a sustainable information technology infrastructure that can support both the online resources and web-conferencing tools. The administrators should plan the budget for maintenance of cloud-based IT servers along with a stable LMS, suitable set of technological products, e-learning tools and a team of instructional designers, multi-media designers, content developers and web application programmer to run the online learning infrastructure. However, without a planned faculty development exercise aiming at educating the faculty in online learning pedagogy, instructional

DOI: http://dx.doi.org/10.5772/intechopen.102576

design skills and design of online learning activities, presence of technology alone will not ensure effective and engaging online learning capable of attaining the educational goals.

Acknowledgements

The author would like to acknowledge the motivation from Professor Vishna Devi Nadarajah and Professor Er Hui Meng of the Teaching and Learning Department of International Medical University, Malaysia in writing this book chapter.

Conflict of interest

The authors declare no conflict of interest.

Author details

Nilesh Kumar Mitra
Learning Resources Division, International Medical University, Kuala Lumpur, Malaysia

*Address all correspondence to: nileshkumar@imu.edu.my

References

[1] Fast Facts: Distance learning, Institute of Education Science, National Centre for Education Statistics. 2021. Available from: https://nces.ed.gov/fastfacts/display.asp?id=80

[2] Archibald D, Worsley S. The father of distance learning. TechTrends. 2019;**63**(2):100-101. DOI: 10.1007/s11528-019-00373-7

[3] Palvia S, Kumar P, Kumar A, Verma S. Exploring themes, trends, and frameworks: A meta-analysis of online business education research. AMCIS Proceedings. 2017;**16**

[4] Palvia S, Aeron P, Gupta P, Mahapatra D, Parida R, Rosner R, et al. Online education: Worldwide status, challenges, trends, and implications. Journal of Global Information Technology Management. 2018;**21**(4):233-241. DOI: 10.1080/1097198X.2018.1542262

[5] Popovich CJ, Neel RE. Characteristics of distance education programs at accredited business schools. The American Journal of Distance Education. 2005;**19**(4):229-240. DOI: 10.1207/s15389286ajde1904_4

[6] KPMG & Google. Online Education in India. 2017. Available from: https://assets.kpmg.com/content/dam/kpmg/in/pdf/2017/05/Online-Education-in-India-2021.pdf

[7] Mirza AA, Al-Abdulkareem M. Models of e-learning adopted in the Middle East. Applied computing and informatics. 2011;**9**(2):83-93. DOI: 10.1016/j.aci.2011.05.001

[8] Hillier M. Bridging the digital divide with off-line e-learning. Distance Education. 2018;**39**(1):110-121. DOI: 10.1080/01587919.2017.1418627

[9] Press Release: COVID-19: Schools for more than 168 Million Children Globally Have Been Completely Closed for Almost a Full Year, Says UNICEF, UNICEF for every child 75. 2021. Available from: https://www.unicef.org/press-releases/schools-more-168-million-children-globally-have-been-completely-closed

[10] Chand AA, Lal PP, Chand KK. Remote learning and online teaching in Fiji during COVID-19: The challenges and opportunities. International Journal of Surgery. 2021;**92**:106019. DOI: 10.1016/j.ijsu.2021.106019

[11] Korzycka M, Bójko M, Radiukiewicz K, Dzielska A, Nałęcz H, Kleszczewska D, et al. Demographic analysis of difficulties related to remote education in Poland from the perspective of adolescents during the COVID-19 pandemic. Annals of Agricultural and Environmental Medicine. 2021; **28**(1):149-157. DOI: 10.26444/aaem/133100

[12] Ahmed SA, Hegazy NN, Malak HW, Kayser WC, Elrafie NM, Hassanien M, et al. Model for utilizing distance learning post COVID-19 using (PACT)™ a cross sectional qualitative study. BMC Medical Education. 2020;**20**(1):1-3. DOI: 10.1186/s12909-020-02311-1

[13] Czerkawski BC, Lyman EW. An instructional design framework for fostering student engagement in online learning environments. TechTrends. 2016;**60**(6):532-539. DOI: 10.1007/s11528-016-0110-z

[14] Allen WM. Seven simple success strategies, In Michael Allen's guide to

e-Learning: Building interactive. In: Fun, and Effective Learning Programs for Any Company. 2nd ed. New Jersey: John Wiley & Sons; 2016. pp. 95-107. DOI: 10.1002/9781119176268.ch7

[15] Pelz B. (My) three principles of effective online pedagogy. Journal of Asynchronous Learning Networks. 2010;**14**(1):103-116. DOI: 10.24059/olj.v8i3.1819

[16] Garrison DR, Anderson T, Archer W. Critical inquiry in a text-based environment: Computer conferencing in higher education. The Internet and Higher Education. 1999;**2**(2-3):87-105. DOI: 10.1016/S1096-7516(00)00016-6

[17] Bender T. Role playing in online education: A teaching tool to enhance student engagement and sustained learning. Innovate: Journal of Online Education. 2005;**1**(4):5

[18] Mayer RE, Moreno R. A cognitive theory of multimedia learning: Implications for design principles. Journal of Educational Psychology. 1998;**91**(2):358-368

Chapter 3

Training Framework to Enhance Digital Skills and Pedagogy of Chemistry Teachers to Use IMFUNDO

Sibongile Simelane-Mnisi and Ntebogeng Mokgala-Fleischmann

Abstract

The purpose of this study was to develop a training framework to enhance digital skills, practice and pedagogy of Chemistry teachers to effectively use a learning management system (LMS). The Department of Chemistry has been unsuccessful in adopting and integrating technology in teaching since 2011 due to the lack of a framework for training teachers in skills and competencies required to successfully implement digitalization pedagogy, engage students and improve student success. The challenge was that Chemistry teachers used LMS as a repository. This observation was not in line with the newly approved study University's Teaching, Learning and Technology Strategy and did not support student-centered learning. Action research was employed. It was found that the teacher-training framework and the remote training of Chemistry teachers were developed and implemented. After training, the design and development of online modules significantly improved. COVID-19 lockdown accelerated the transition to fully online teaching.

Keywords: training framework, learning management system, pedagogy, digital skills, higher education Chemistry teachers

1. Introduction

The Learning Framework of 2030 stated that the world is facing unprecedented social, economic and environmental challenges driven by accelerating globalization and a faster rate of technological developments [1]. A case in point is the recent COVID-19 pandemic, which forced universities worldwide to suspend all on-campus activities and move to online learning or distance learning either with or without any digital tools [2]. Linney et al. [3] reports that while adapting to this new normal, universities have quickly evolved their digital tools and platforms to ensure uninterrupted educational delivery to their isolated students. Teachers were expected to transform the way they teach, moving from the traditional contact model to an interactive online learning model [3]. Due to the changing nature of learning and teaching, there is a growing need for ongoing professional learning to equip teachers with skills and competencies needed to adapt to the ever-changing student demographic and knowledge base, the speed of technological and societal changes [4].

In September 2015, the United Nations established the Sustainable Development Goals (SDGs), which serve as a road map for improving people's living situations, particularly in poorer nations [5]. The fourth of the Sustainable Development Goals pledges the international community to "provide inclusive and high-quality education for all and encourage lifelong learning" [5]. In realizing the National Development Plan's educational objectives (see Chapter 9), the study University's policy on Performance Management and Development [6] states that the employee and his or her line manager shall jointly develop an Individual Development Plan (IDP) to address any competency or other gaps that would impact on the employee's performance. This implies that upskilling teachers in the Department of Chemistry with competencies that would allow them to integrate technology in teaching for effective learning was part of the IDP that all teachers signed together with the line manager for 2020.

In 2011, the Nuffic-funded project intervention was introduced in the Department of Chemistry to train the teacher with the incorporation of technology in teaching. The Dutch teachers collaborated and assisted Chemistry teachers with developing a blended learning approach. In 2012, the department established the community of practice as Subject Groups. The purpose of the community of practice (CoP) was to facilitate collaboration, co-creating and sharing between Chemistry teachers. This CoP has been a success and still exists to date. Several teachers have also undertaken teacher training courses and workshops. Despite all these interventions, it was found that Chemistry teachers and students were still not using the learning management system known as IMFUNDO effectively for meaningful teaching and learning. For instance, more than half 56% of the teachers used the announcement tool to communicate relevant messages about the module to the students. Announcements were about changes to the teaching or assessment schedule, uploaded supplementary learning material such as videos, tutorials, etc.). However, the communication was one-way from the teacher to the students. More than half 53% of the modules used relevant learning resources such as PowerPoint presentations, notes or assessments. The PowerPoint presentations were, however, not interactive, not video presentations and did not have a voice recording of the teacher. Few of the modules used IMFUNDO for assessment purposes and used videos as a tool for anchored instruction. Based on these results, it could be argued that learning in the Department of Chemistry is largely teacher-centered based on the behaviorism learning theory [7]. The teacher-centered approach is perceived to have a negative impact on developing higher cognitive skills of students, encourages dependency on the teacher and memorizes content [8].

The challenge in this study was that Chemistry teachers used IMFUNDO as a repository, mainly for "dumping" PowerPoint slides of the learning unit, sending announcements to students and sharing the latest study guide. This observation is not in line with the newly approved study University's Teaching, Learning and Technology Strategy and does not support student-centered learning. If a teacher-centered approach and behaviorism continue in the teaching practice, it would be difficult for the institution to realize the University's 2020–2025 Institutional Strategic Plan Pillar 1: Future-ready graduates who make a positive societal impact and Pillar 4: Digitally-Advanced University.

Familiarity with subject knowledge alone is not enough for teachers to engage in effective and pedagogically meaningful instructional practices. Modern curriculum delivery requires teachers to do their best to find innovative ways that not only facilitate but also optimize students' learning to the greatest extent possible. The incorporation of technology in teaching is ubiquitous, therefore in considering the integration of technology in teaching, a potentially useful method is to consider what it is that needs to be addressed, and how technology can be used to assist [9]. In the current study, the Department of Chemistry has been unsuccessful in adopting and integrating technology in teaching since 201. This was due to the lack of a framework for training teachers in skills and competencies required to successfully implement digitalization pedagogy, engage students and improve student success.

The objective of this study was to develop a framework to improve the teaching of online modules using IMFUNDO, to ensure that students engage meaningfully with the online modules. Furthermore, it was critical that Chemistry teachers' digital skills, practice and pedagogy were effectively enhanced with the aid of IMFUNDO. To achieve the level at which Chemistry teachers adopted and integrated technology in teaching, a training framework based on Arena, Blended and Connected learning was developed and implemented via online webinars. The IMFUNDO reports were used to determine the number of modules developed and digital tools utilized.

2. Related literature

2.1 Technology-enhanced professional development of teachers

The importance of professional development in teacher education cannot be overstated [10]. Brown et al. [11], argued that there is no 'one size fits all' supply-driven or demand-led model of teacher professional learning. The Australian Government undertook an initiative called Teaching Teachers for the Future, to improve the preparation of future teachers by integrating technology into their practice [12]. The institution needed to support and upskill teachers if it desires to remain competitive in an increasingly uncertain global market, as most programs are only as successful as the people in charge of them [10]. In this study, the policy on Performance Management and Development [6], as well as the IDP, supports Li and Morris' opinion.

During the COVID-19 outbreak and national lockdown, the study university adopted the emergency multimodal teaching, learning and assessment strategy [2]. The strategy forced all the teachers to adopt and use IMFUNDO in their teaching practices to continue with learning and teaching in trying times [13]. Darling-Hammond et al. [10] argued that the nature of teacher development should be a continuous process of becoming and articulating an inner world of conscious choices made in response to the outward world of the teaching context. There are various approaches and strategies to teacher learning were established in higher education. At a study university in 2005, the Partners @Work empowerment strategy yielded positive results, but it was not sustained [14]. As indicated, the Nuffic-funded project as well as the eLearning Leaders intervention proved to be successful in introducing teachers to digital skills. However, the challenge remained of using the UMFUNDO to engage the students with the application of interactive tools. In an attempt to empower Chemistry teachers with the proposed professional development framework, the attention and emphasis were on including digital technology with various stages of curriculum delivery.

2.2 Transformative pedagogy

Transformative pedagogies include higher levels of pedagogical practice, are learner-centered, engage higher-order thinking skills and include a variety of interactions between learners, content and teachers [15]. To support pedagogy, teaching with a technology system should be capable of supporting a transformative learning pedagogy. This means it should allow for the integration of authentic learning activities as well as learning activities that support collaboration, discourse and reflective thinking by students [16]. This implies that the use of digital tools and resources in transformative pedagogies enhances deep learning [17]. DoBE [17] argued that the use of digital tools and resources in transformative pedagogies enhances deep learning. When implementing the DoE framework, thinking skills, information management and interactions between learners, teachers and content should be taken into consideration.

At the core of good teaching with technology, there are three core components: content, pedagogy, and technology. These three knowledge bases (content, pedagogy, and technology) form the core of the technology, pedagogy, and content knowledge (TPACK) framework [18]. The TPACK framework encourages teachers to design pedagogically sound learning activities that maximize the impact of both digital tools and content resources on teaching and learning in a given context [17]. Howard et al. [19] and Ngcapu et al. [13] support the use of the TPACK framework as it provided a focus on learning and pedagogy that is typically missing from conceptions of online learning. It would be safe to say that TPACK was the basis of effective teaching with technology [20] and was an essential component of transformative pedagogy [21]. Therefore, teaching successfully with technology requires continuous evaluation of the dynamic equilibrium among all TPACK components as well as continuous training of teachers and adequate ICT support by the university.

There is no perfect digital pedagogy model and there are always challenges and opportunities with the integration of technology in teaching. Some users of the TPACK model have criticized the model for lack of practical examples to explain knowledge required for the crossovers TCK and TPK and how technology fits into these crossovers [22]. A drawback of the TPACK model was that teachers who lacked training and information technology skills could not adopt the technology in their classroom and inadequate post-training support discouraged the use of technology. Challenges highlighted by teachers in a private higher institution in Malaysia with using ICT in teaching and learning environment were lack of TPACK teaching and learning skills and ICT support. These challenges were attributed to poor instructional design and 80% of the teachers not using ICT in their teaching and learning environment [23].

Constructivism is a learning theory central to transformative pedagogy. According to Bada et al. [24] central to the philosophy of constructivism is that learning is an active process. Hence, from a constructivist perspective, the primary responsibility of the teacher is to create and maintain a collaborative problem-solving environment, where students are allowed to construct their knowledge, and the teacher acts as a facilitator and guide. Furthermore, Hamlin et al. [16] adds another dimension that learning environments that are based on social constructivist learning principles can enhance transformative pedagogy. Donnelly et al. [25] implemented a constructivist learning approach in a blended problem-based learning module. Findings of the study indicate that some aspects of constructivist learning may be directly stimulated by using technology, the findings noted an increased level of collaboration and that involvement with content is often reinforced by technology use.

3. Research question

How can a training framework be developed and implemented to enhance the digital skills, practice and pedagogy of Chemistry teachers to teach effectively using IMFUNDO?.

4. Method

To respond to the question, action research was used to a better understanding of study problems. Action research is defined as an approach in which the action researcher and a client collaborate in the diagnosis of the problem and the development of a solution based on the diagnosis [26]. The process of action research involves, planning to initiate change, implementing g the change (acting) and observing the process of implementation and consequences reflecting on the process of change and replanning, acting and observing as well as reflecting [27].

On the 23rd of March 2020, a national lockdown in response to the COVID-19 pandemic was announced in South Africa [2]. To respond to the national lockdown regulation, the study university implemented a remote multimodal teaching, learning and assessment strategy from June 1, 2020. This required an unprecedented rapid transition from face-to-face teaching to online teaching and learning. To assist teachers with the design and development of online modules on IMFUNDO, the study university implemented Emergency remote teaching and empowerment [2]. For 3 months, the instructional designers conducted online teaching and empowerment. The emergency remote teaching and empowerments' purpose was to empower lecturers in transitioning from traditional teaching to online or remote teaching through the use of various tools on the IMFUNDO to benefit students [2]. Since technology alone does not guarantee a pleasant or effective learning experience, it was vital for instructional designers to ensure that pedagogy was given higher attention throughout [2].

To further ensure the training of teachers in the Department of Chemistry, the training that was scheduled for 4 months (March 1, 2020–July 31, 2020) was then reduced to 2 weeks (April 14–17, 2020 and May 11–15, 2020) to ensure that teachers have the necessary technical skills and competencies to teach remotely [15]. The Arena, Blended and Connected learning design approach was used for training teachers to develop online modules [2, 15]. The Arena, Blended and Connected (ABC) learning design, according to Young [28] is a quick way to (re)design programs and modules through a hands-on workshop where academic teams discuss and create storyboards of students' activities. A minimal version of the ABC learning design adapted from [28] was followed and consisted of the following elements:

- Pre-workshop: resources provided for teachers to engage with before each session
- Live session: daily using virtual conferencing tool IMFUMDO Collaborate for about 1 h 30 min
- Post-workshop: consisted of support provided through a community of practice WhatsApp chat group

To develop a successful framework that improves teaching and learning using digitalization pedagogy and TPACK principles, firstly, the chapter reflects on the findings of the preliminary study, which was conducted in 2019 to develop a plan that improved the teaching and learning practices. From the findings, it was evident that a systematic approach was required for the training of teachers to ensure that they possess skills, values and attributes central to transformative pedagogies that were student-centered, engage higher-order thinking skills and include a variety of interactions between students, content and teachers. Secondly, the teacher development framework and a framework for designing online modules were developed and implemented.

4.1 Participants

In this study, purposive, convenient and was used to select the participants. Purposive sampling means that the researcher selects individuals and sites for study because they can purposefully inform an understanding of the research problem and central phenomenon in the study [29]. Convenience sampling refers to the selection of settings, groups, and or persons who are readily available and eager to engage in the study [30]. In this case, the participants were 25 full-time teachers who taught 756 students, of which 711 were undergraduate and 45 postgraduates in the Department of Chemistry. Their age ranged between 32 and 65 years. In terms of qualification, 17 (68%) of the teachers hold a PhD in Chemistry, 7 (28%) hold a Masters in Chemistry and one holds a Bachelor degree in Pharmaceutical Sciences.

4.2 Instrument and procedure

Document analysis (Remote Multimodal Teaching, Learning and Assessment Strategy and Plan as well as the Faculty Emergency Teaching and Empowerment Plan), and learning management system reports, were employed to collect data in this study.

4.3 Document analysis

The Remote Multimodal Teaching, Learning and Assessment Strategy and Plan (RMTLAS&P) was used because during the second announcement of COVID-19 national lockdown in April 2020 and to comply with the directive by the Ministry of Higher Education, Science and Innovation, the study university adopted the RMTLAS&P. The RMTLAS&P's goal was to finish the 2020 academic year successfully [31]. This was contingent on the possibilities during the lockdown and when the measures were eased to enable contact learning and teaching to resume. The RMTLAS&P was implemented in two approaches. The first approach used was the digital delivery through the IMFUNDO and the second was the distribution of printed study material to students who may not be able to use the digital mode due to various reasons. For this chapter, the digital delivery with the aid of IMFUNDO is presented. The university teachers were given mobile devices and Internet connectivity as well as training in remote teaching and learning methods. The training was conducted by Instructional Designers.

To assist university teachers with the planning, design, and development of online modules, an emergency remote teaching and empowerment plan was also developed. In the Faculties, the Instructional Designers adopted the institution empowerment plan and customized it to suit the Faculty of Science needs [32]. Simelane-Mnisi et al. [2] argued that it was vital not to compromise the quality of the online material when preparing for online or remote instruction. The concept of constructive alignment was suggested to equip university lecturers to move their content online or remotely. Learning outcomes, learning material (content), learning activities, interactions (collaborations), feedback, and course technology can all benefit from constructive alignment. These ideas work together to guarantee that students attain the learning results they desire. Various instructional design models relating to Gagne's nine events of instructional design, backward design Revised Bloom taxonomy, and ADDIE model Analyze, Design, Develop, Implement and Evaluate were also used to ensure the design and development of online learning and teaching material on IMFUNDO.

4.4 Learning management system reports

The LMS report was used to determine the number of online modules developed and the tools used within the modules.

5. Results and discussion

5.1 Development of teacher-training framework

A teacher-training framework was developed to upskill university teachers in the Department of Chemistry with technological skills and TPACK pedagogical approaches to teaching online modules. The framework was designed and developed with the assistance of a Senior Instructional Designer in the Faculty of Science. The framework was adapted from the Faculty of Science training framework. This statement is supported by Sumer and Sim et al. [33, 34] who revealed that university teachers may or may not have prior experience with open, online, and remote learning during pandemics, so these authors emphasize that formal training on how the new system works and what teaching online looks like with adaptive frameworks supplied should be conducted.

It was critical that during this training session that the instructional designer ensured that pedagogy was taken into consideration. Instructional design principles relating to Gagne's nine events of instructional design, backward design Revised Bloom taxonomy, and ADDIE model Analyze, Design, Develop, Implement and Evaluate were considered during the facilitation of the online training sessions. Furthermore, the educational theories and models were also considered. The teacher-training framework was grounded by the ABC learning design, TPACK, Flipped learning approach, Revised Community of Inquiry and constructivism theory. These theoretical frameworks and models assisted the instructional designer and teachers to ensure that online modules provided quality in the online delivery of learning material, taking into cognizance the socio-economic backgrounds of the students. Summer and Sim et al. [33, 34] support these statements and further argue that to ensure that quality learning and teaching practices are established, appropriate pedagogical frameworks must be explicitly communicated to university teachers and just-in-time training be provided. The focus in this study was not only technology. However, incorporation of these strategies responded to the cry that often teachers fail to incorporate technology with pedagogy because training is mostly offered by facilitators who are technology experts, however, lack the pedagogy.

The study university serves the community from urban, rural, townships as well as informal settlements. It is not technology that matters, but teaching and learning to achieve the learning outcomes. In this regard, various teaching approaches were also used during the remote training relating to active learning design, scaffolding as well as matters of quality. It is critical to recognize the time required to adapt teaching to an online platform that is engaging, interactive and gives a positive student experience while transitioning to online [33, 34]. In this case, the Arena, Blended and Connected Approach provide the opportunity for teachers' transition from traditional teaching to remote teaching using digital technologies. The ABC approach assisted the lecturers in this process. This approach guided converting the conventional teaching and learning activities lecturers use with their students to use remotely, online with digital technologies. The ABC approach further assists lecturers to select various six learning activities that support six teaching methods that encourage engagement and interaction in the online environment. The learning activities include acquisition, collaboration, discussion, investigation, practice and produce.

A flipped learning approach was used. Flipped learning is the approach to learning where content delivery is assigned as homework or pre-classwork in a form of a video, online learning material or lecture notes and assignments are completed as classroom activities in-class as well as after-class [35]. Due to the pandemic and in the case of RMTLAS&P, in-class activities and after-class activities were completed online. This implies that the instructional designer encouraged teachers who were students to engage using IMFUNDO and other technologies to ensure that students engaged with the learning content. When the instructional designer conducted live classes on IMFUNDO Collaborate Ultra, it was guaranteed that students would be better prepared to engage in interactive and higher-order activities, such as critical thinking, problem-solving, discussions, and debates in class [36]. In this study, Chemistry teachers had access to the learning content and activities on IMFUNDO before the online session and could also engage the learning content at their own time and pace. The aim development of the flipped classroom was to fulfill students' needs, develop twenty first-century skills, and integrate technology into regular education [37].

Flipped learning was driven by the Revised Community of Inquiry theoretical framework to benefit teaching and learning. The Revised Community of Inquiry (RCOI) is one of the frameworks that was employed in a flipped learning approach. It is argued that in RCOI [38] knowledge construction results from the collaborative interaction between active students and lectures, particularly in the technology-enhanced environment. The community of Inquiry theoretical framework by Garrison et al. [39] is a widely researched framework representing a process of creating a deep and meaningful learning experience [40]. The interdependent elements of the learning process central to the framework are cognitive, social, and teaching presence, each of which represents different aspects of the inquiry-based learning process [40]. These elements contribute to successful learning as well as a student-centered environment [41]. This framework was used based on the fact that RCOI provides a collaborative-constructive perspective to understanding the dynamics of online learning.

5.2 Chemistry teachers training framework

Figure 1 shows the training framework for Chemistry teachers to enhance digital skills, practice and pedagogy. Due to the COVID-19 pandemic and national lockdown, training was conducted online, using IMFUNDO Collaborate virtual conferencing platform. The IMFUNDO online module named "Emergency Remote Support" was created for all the Faculty of Science lecturers. This module was also used by the Chemistry teachers. All the teachers were given students access to the online module.

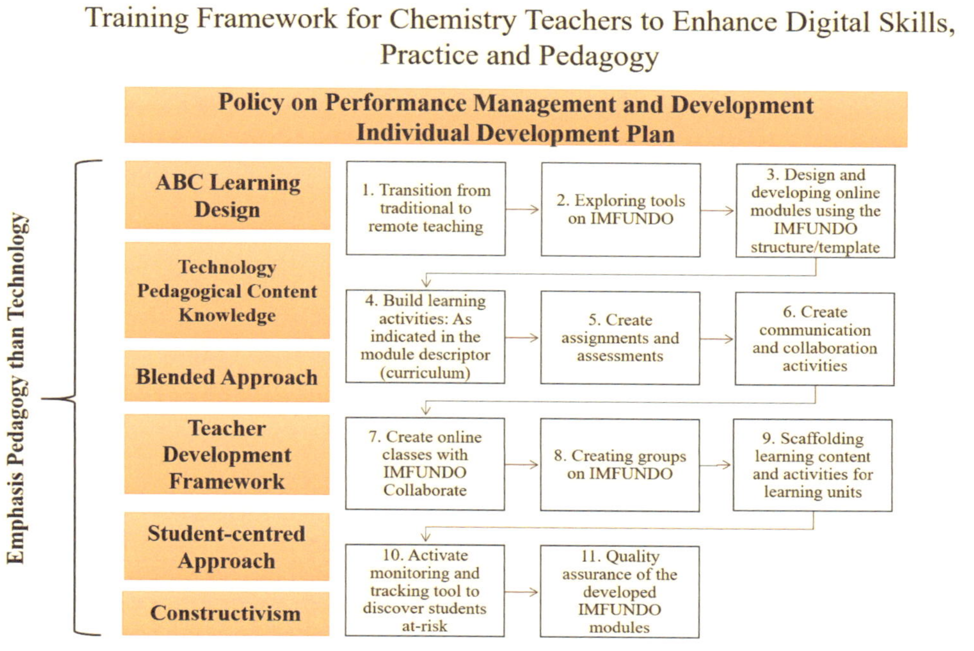

Figure 1.
The training framework for Chemistry teachers to enhance digital skills, practice and pedagogy.

Training took place twice daily (morning and afternoon) for 2 h over 2 weeks (April 14–17, 2020 and May 11–15, 2020), a link to the live session was sent daily to teachers using the announcement tool of the LMS and also using a WhatsApp chat group that was established for the teachers to stay connected during the lockdown. WhatsApp also serves as a safe environment as well as a community of practice where lecturers asked questions and share best practices about the development and implementation during the COVID-19 pandemic. The training framework consisted of 10 learning units with learning outcomes.

The aim of the transition from traditional to remote teaching was to create a safe environment for university teachers to learn more about the traditional learning activities that they provided in class on how they should use digital technologies. Gumede et al. [42], opined that it is essential for university teachers to acquire continuous support and skill development as they transition from face-to-face to online teaching and learning during the pandemic. To fulfill Gumede et al.'s [42]. opinion, the ABC learning activity was emphasized as it provided the fundamental of learning activities and methods. The literature revealed that the transition to online learning posed a big challenge to decide which online technology is best suited for university teachers [43]. In this study, teachers were introduced to interactive remote module development. Teachers prepared online teaching and learning material using a storyboard/course map using the approved university HEQSF curriculum. In this instance, the module descriptor and study guide supported this process to ensure the quality of online modules and to meet the standards as required by the professional and statutory and regulatory bodies. Namada et al. [44], argued that COVID-19 has compelled the education sector to adapt to the visible indicators of a new paradigm, our continuous experiences with online teaching and learning should frame our expectations of what will happen after the Covid-19 pandemic.

To understand the different functionalities of IMFUNDO, it was imperative to explore various IMFUNDO tools. The learning management system has the potential to facilitate both synchronous and asynchronous types of e-learning with the aid of a variety of digital tools [45]. In this study, the digital tools that were used to facilitate synchronous, asynchronous and binochronous learning were divided into seven categories namely, content, collaboration, communication, assessment, video conferencing, management and survey. Synchronous instruction occurs in real-time and requires the simultaneous participation of students and teachers [46]. Examples include test chats, audioconferencing, videoconferencing, whiteboards, and real-time break-out rooms. Asynchronous instruction on the other hand occurs in delayed time and does not require the simultaneous participation of students and teachers [47]. In an asynchronous setup, learning events are independently experienced by students and learning is not synchronized in time or space. Examples include discussion forums, emails, and surveys.

The content tools comprised of IMFUNDO server, folders, items, files. The collaboration tools included a discussion forum, the journal for reflection, groups, wiki and blogs. The communication tools included announcements, Chats (WhatsApp class group), email and calendar. The Assessment tool consisted of the IMFUNDO test, Microsoft Form, Respondus, assignment, rubric and plagiarism detective tool. The video conferencing tool is known and IMFUNDO Collaborate Ultra was used for live teaching or webinars. The management tools included reports, grade center, retention center for monitoring and tracking students-at-risk. The survey tool consisted of an Enterprise survey for student lecturer, evaluation. It can be seen that the LMS allows university teachers to use dynamic digital tools to make it what they want it to be to facilitate successful and efficient teaching and learning.

It was important to design and develop online modules using the IMFUNDO structured template. Research shows that to provide best practices for using technology for developmental education, the use of a common 'master' template in an LMS was observed at the College of the Mainland, Texas City, Texas [48]. In this study, the content structure was used which was aligned to the module descriptor and study guide. The structure assisted in providing the shell to build the online modules. The structure aimed to ensure to provide clear guidance to students as they were learning in isolation from their homes. Cho et al. [48] argued that the LMS common template/ structure was seen to be effective with 100% teachers' usage and student participation. Also, in this study, the structure was created in a manner that was user-friendly and appealing to students. The teachers were trained to create a welcome page that consisted of inserting the Department banner in the module landing page, creating a text welcome statement, recording a short welcome video using their smartphone and uploading it on IMFUNDO, uploading a headshot picture, add teacher details and consultation time. The teachers had to create a page that included a module overview with a module purpose statement, module outline and assessment plan. In addition, the teachers had to populate learning content on the IMFUNDO server. In this case, lecturers had to create folders and upload files in relevant folders. The usage of a common pre-built template was shown to be efficient in alleviating instructor frustration [48].

The teachers were also empowered on how to build the learning activities as indicated in the module descriptor or study guide. In this regard, lecturers used ABC learning approach to create interactive and engaging activities in an online environment. The activities encourage assessment for learning, formative assessment as well as continuous assessment. Student's engagement, interaction and participation were promoted by creating short quizzes and exercises using Microsoft forms, Respondus and IMFUNDO quiz tool. These engaging activities were created for each learning unit. Lapitan et al. [43] argued that teachers should transition from the old teaching paradigm to new teaching methods that are compatible with technology to teach online.

Concerning the design of assignments and assessments, the teachers had to design formative and summative assessments in a form of formal online tests and assignments. These assessments were used as predicate for the final examination. It was reported that university teachers had to adjust their teaching plans, teaching styles, and assessment methods as a result of the abrupt move to full online teaching [43]. In this study, the continuous assessment strategy was adopted in most of the modules. The reason was the COVID-19 pandemic lockdown and the shutdown of the universities. Undergraduate students and teachers did not have access to campus nor attend classes. The assessments were built with the aid of Microsoft forms, Respondus, IMFUNDO quiz tool and assignment. Lapitan et al. [43] revealed that self-assessment questions were made available for each topic on the LMS. The assignments were used with an online rubric which was opened to students, to see what was expected of them and how they will be evaluated. For the assignment, the SafeAssign tool to detect similarity for plagiarism check was used. Mbhiza et al. [44] contends that the shift to online technology-based teaching and learning means that traditional assessment methods were no longer sustainable.

Teachers needed to learn the tools to promote student engagement on IMFUNDO relating to communication and collaboration. According to Cho et al. [49], if implemented with appropriate pedagogical approaches, online learning environments improve student engagement and learning outcomes. Teachers were trained on how to create announcements, send emails to students and different class groups, create a calendar for the module. In this regard, Summer and Sim et al. [33, 34] indicated that the university teachers were required to quickly adapt and establish innovative communication channels that could be accessed by both domestic and international students. With regards to collaboration with students, lecturers create a discussion forum, used the IMFUNDO journal for student reflection after each learning unit.

Since classes were to be presented remotely, teachers were also empowered on the use of a virtual classroom known as IMFUNDO Collaborate Ultra as stated by Study University of Technology [31]. Mbhiza et al. [44] identified other virtual classrooms that were used in most of the South African higher education institutions to ensure learning continuity, provide support to students throughout COVID-19, and so improve online learning. In this study, teachers were trained on the functions of IMFUNDO Collaborate Ultra relating to recording the session, muting participants, video, chat, raising hands, creating breakaway rooms for group discussion. They also leant to record their lesson and later upload it on the IMFUNDO for students to access. Teachers were trained to set times and dates and release the link using IMFUNDO announcements or student's institutional email. The aim was for teachers to emphasize students' engagement and participation during live classes.

Various interactive tools to promote student engagement were also used. In this instance, teachers were empowered to create groups on IMFUNDO, use social media network tools such as Facebook, WhatsApp, Twitter, and YouTube Videos as well as create social media groups. These social media tools were linked on IMFUNDO.

After teachers were empowered on each technology tool on IMFUNDO, the concepts of scaffolding and chunking content were applied. Chunking is the process of breaking down a component into smaller "chunks" of related information [50].

These authors further indicate that chunking is utilized in circumstances where content can be broken into smaller groups or categories to improve meaning clarity. Scaffolding is the process of breaking down learning content into chunks and giving each chunk a structure [51]. The aim of using these strategies in this study was to ensure a better and user-friendly learning material and activities delivery. This was to ensure a better student learning experience while learning in isolation and their homes. In the study conducted by Chen et al. [52] at Victoria University, it is reported that the Online Interactive Activities was used in a blended approach where the chunking content into bite-sized chunks to increase the sustainability of the activities (smaller topic-specific activities are more likely to be cloned, adapted, and incorporated into a variety of subjects), which allows students to focus on their learning without being distracted by outside factors. To achieve scaffolding and chunking content, the university teachers designed and developed online learning units using folders. In the folder they presented learning unit topic with a brief description, the file with learning outcomes and assessment criteria, they uploaded learning and reading material using PowerPoint presentation with audio narration, add links to web resources, audio and video (Notes, Videos, PPT/Video PPT, Audio files, PDF, etc.) using links tool. Teachers linked the learning activities which foster students to engage and participate in the online modules. In this way, students tested their understanding, knowledge and skills. They included a link to the virtual class and the reflective journal was provided at the end of each unit. In this study, the Instructional Designer then helped teachers to chunk the content into topics or chapters, linking it to complimentary activities to engage students through interactivity, knowledge testing, or reflection and interaction [53]. Chunking and scaffolding of learning material and activities promotes student-centered, as it for participation and engagement and avoid distraction or boredom.

Teachers needed to monitor, track and discover students at-risk while learning in isolation and provide necessary support during the earning process. The Retention Center tool was activated and the criteria were set accordingly. Teachers were also empowered on downloading various reports on the system to monitor students in an online environment.

The training was hands-on, teachers were provided with step-by-step instructions on how to design and develop modules, how to choose the relevant technology and tools for their subject matter and how to integrate technology in teaching online modules. All training sessions were recorded, to monitor attendance and so that the teachers can revisit any session that they need to, at their own time. At the end of the training, an "online teaching toolbox" was developed and shared via email with all teachers to ensure that they engage with the training material at their own pace. The toolbox contained links to all the recorded training webinars, standard operating procedures of how to develop an online module using the standardized template, how to record audio over PowerPoint presentations, how to create online to check the quality of the design, developed of the online modules for remote teaching, teachers' self-evaluation on quality assurance were used. The quality assurance instruments were developed by the researchers.

5.3 IMFUNDO reports

A standardized template for IMFUNDO modules was developed using a blended approach of synchronous (live lectures online) or asynchronous (work at own pace). The blended approach often leads to deeper processing and retention of knowledge [54].

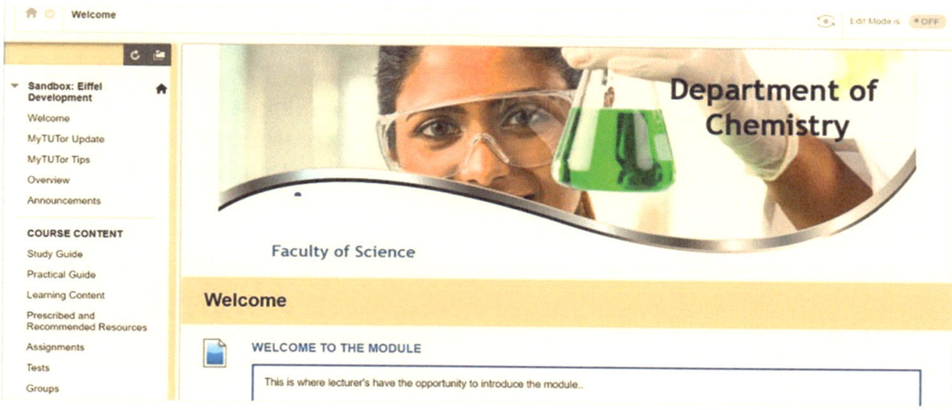

Figure 2.
An example of IMFUNDO online module.

People do not learn from interacting with content only, however, they learn from processing that content and through social interactions [54]. Learning content in IMFUNDO modules was structured to maximize retention and promote student success using the scaffolding and chunking design approach. All modules complied with this basic requirement. An example of an IMFUNDO online module with the standardized Department of Chemistry banner is illustrated in **Figure 2**.

A sample of data of 39 modules offered by the Department of Chemistry from June 1, 2020 to November 31, 2020 was retrieved from IMFUNDO on December 3, 2020. A quality rating using a descriptor Yes or No was applied to evaluate the module design. The IMFUNDO module design quality results from the 2019 development project were compared to those obtained in 2020 after the implementation of the digitalization pedagogy framework in the Department of Chemistry. The IMFUNDO results show the comparison of the statistics of the module design in 2019–2020. A significant improvement in the design and usage of the functionalities of IMFUNDO was observed after teachers in the Department of Chemistry were upskilled and gained relevant competencies to integrate technology in teaching. In 2020, 100% of the online modules had the latest study guide and timetable uploaded on the VLE, compared to 54% in 2019. The learning content was arranged in smaller easy to follow learning units in 79% of the modules in 2020 compared to 53% in 2019. The use of online assessments increased tenfold from 5% in 2019 to 55% in 2020. Similarly, asynchronous activities such as assignments and tutorials increased from 16% in 2019 to 50% in 2020.

6. Conclusions

In this chapter, the training framework to enhance digital skills and pedagogy of chemistry teachers to use IMFUNDO was developed and implemented. It was reported that the COVID-19 lockdown reportedly hastened the move to entirely online learning. For the university teachers to be able to transit from traditional to online or teaching remotely, professional development needed to be conducted to equip chemistry teachers with the necessary skills to teach online. It may be observed that the various pedagogical approaches ad well as the instructional design principles were taken into consideration to bridge the gap between the two. A standardized structure for IMFUNDO modules was created utilizing a hybrid approach of synchronous and asynchronous. The scaffolding and chunking of learning content were applied to ensure student engagement. All the online modules were created using a similar structure/template. There was a significant improvement in 2020 on the module created of LMS in the Department of Chemistry as compared to 2019. We observed an increase in the digital tools created that promoted synchronous and asynchronous learning in 2020. It was imperative to create such activities as students were learning from home.

Acknowledgements

We wish to show our appreciation to the Study University of Technology, Faculty of Science, Department of Chemistry Teachers to participate in the study and provide the Learning Management System.

Conflict of interest

The authors declare no conflict of interest.

Author details

Sibongile Simelane-Mnisi[1*] and Ntebogeng Mokgala-Fleischmann[2]

1 Tshwane University of Technology, Pretoria, South Africa

2 University of Venda, Tohoyando, South Africa

*Address all correspondence to: simelanes@tut.ac.za

References

[1] Organisation for Economic Co-operation OEC. The Future of Education and Skills Education 2030 [Internet]. 2018. Available from: https://www.oecd.org/education/2030/E2030%20Position%20Paper%20(05.04.2018).pdf [Accessed: January 26, 2020]

[2] Simelane-Mnisi S, Mji A. COVID-19 pandemic: Opportunities for online learning to unblock the minds of students during the lockdown period. In: Proceedings of the Education and New Learning Technologies Virtual Conference (EDULEARN '20); 6-7 July 2020; Spain. Palma de Mallorca; 2020. pp. 8621-8629. DOI: 10.21125/edulearn.2020.2124

[3] Linney S. How Universities are Embracing Online Learning during the Coronavirus Outbreak [Internet]. 2020. Available from: https://www.qs.com/how-universities-are-embracing-online-learning-during-the-coronavirus-outbreak/ [Accessed: April 1, 2020]

[4] Ngatoro M. The Value of a School Based Digital Learning Framework: Does It Offer the Support and Guidance Needed for Teachers of Varying Digital Capabilities [Internet]? Master of Applied Practice. Unitec Institute of Technology; 2018. Available from: https://unitec.researchbank.ac.nz/handle/10652/4641 [Accessed: March 31, 2020]

[5] United Nations. What are the Sustainable Development Goals [Internet]? 2021. Available from: https://www.undp.org/sustainable-development-goals [Accesses: July 14, 2021]

[6] Study University of Technology Policy on Performance Management and Development [Internet]. 2017. Available from: http://staff.tut.ac.za/sites/registrar/Legal/policies/Shared%20Documents/Forms/Alphabetical%20View.aspx [Accessed: March 31, 2020]

[7] Yilmaz K. The cognitive perspective on learning: Its theoretical underpinnings and implications for classroom practices. The Clearing House: A Journal of Educational Strategies, Issues and Ideas. 2011;**84**:204-212. DOI: 10.1080/00098655.2011.568989

[8] Kompa JS. Disadvantages of Teacher-Centred Learning [Internet]. 2012. Available from: https://joanakompa.com/2012/06/25/the-key-disadvantages-of-teacher-centred-learning/ [Accessed: March 31, 2020]

[9] Seery M. Technology Enhanced Learning in the Chemistry Classroom [Internet]. 2013. Available from: http://michaelseery.com/home/index.php/2013/11/technology-enhanced-learning-in-the-chemistry-classroom-paper/ [Accessed: March 30, 2020]

[10] Darling-Hammond L, Hyler ME, Gardner M. Effective Teacher Professional Development. Learning Policy Institute; 2017

[11] Brown M, Conole G, Beblavý M. Education outcomes enhanced by the use of digital technology: Reimagining the school learning ecology. European Expert Network on Economics and Education Analytical Report No. 38. 2019. pp. 1-54. DOI: 10.2766/965566

[12] Chittleborough G. Learning how to teach chemistry with technology: Pre-service teachers' experiences with integrating technology into their learning and teaching. Journal of Science Teacher

Education. 2014;**25**:373-393. DOI: 10.1007/s10972-014-9387-y

[13] Ngcapu SR, Mji A, Simelane-Mnisi S. The strategy as perspective for the integration of technology in education. In: Proceedings of the European Conference on e-Learning (ECEL '20); 29-30 October 2020; Berlin. Germany: ECEL; 2020. p. 570. DOI: 10.34190/EEL.20.084

[14] Simelane S. Stakeholder support during the implementation of web-based courses in higher education. In: Méndez-Vilas A, editor. Education in a Technological World: Communicating Current and Emerging Research and Technological Efforts. FORMATEX; 2011. pp. 406-413

[15] Mokgalaka-Fleischmann N. Improvement of teaching and learning of Chemistry through digitalization pedagogy [thesis]. Haaga-Helia Applied University of Applied Sciences; 2021

[16] Hamlin M. Technology in transformative learning environments. In: Halupa C, editor. Transformative Curriculum Design in Health Sciences. IGI global; 2015. pp. 126-140

[17] Department of Basic Education DoBE. Professional Development Framework for Digital Learning [Internet]. 2018. Available from: https://www.education.gov.za/DigitalLearningFrameworkJuly18.aspx [Accessed: April 1, 2020]

[18] Koehler M, Mishra P. What is technological pedagogical content knowledge (TPACK)? Contemporary Issues in Technology and Teacher Education. 2009;**9**:60-70

[19] Howard SK, Tondeur J, Siddiq F, Scherer R. Ready, set, go! Profiling teachers' readiness for online teaching in secondary education. Technology, Pedagogy and Education;**202**(30):141-158. DOI: 10.1080/1475939X.2020.1839543

[20] Koehler M. TPACK Explained [Internet]. 2012. Available from: http://tpack.org/ [Accessed: December 24, 2020]

[21] Jang SJ, Chen KC. From PCK to TPACK: Developing a transformative model for pre-service science teachers. Journal of Science Education and Technology. 2010;**19**(6):553-564. DOI: 10.1007/s10956-010-9222-y

[22] Reid A. A Critique of TPACK and SAMR [Internet]. 2016. Available from: http://reidswhatthetech.blogspot.com/2016/01/a-critique-of-tpack-and-samr.html [Accessed: January 16, 2020]

[23] Lye LT. Opportunities and challenges faced by private higher education institution using the TPACK model in Malaysia. Procedia-Social and Behavioral Sciences. 2013;**91**:294-305. DOI: 10.1016/j.sbspro.2013.08.426

[24] Bada SO, Olusegun S. Constructivism learning theory: A paradigm for teaching and learning. Journal of Research & Method in Education. 2015;**5**:66-70

[25] Donnelly R. Activity systems within blended problem-based learning in academic professional development. International Journal of Applied Educational Studies. 2008;**3**:39-60

[26] Bryman A, Bell E, editors. Business Research Methods. 3rd ed. Oxford University Press; 2011

[27] Dudovskiy J. Action Research [Internet]. 2020. Available from: https://research-methodology.net/research-methods/action-research/ [Accessed: 2020 December 24, 2020]

[28] Young C, Perović N. Designing Programmes and Modules with ABC

Curriculum Design [Internet]. 2018. Available from: https://www.ucl.ac.uk/teaching-learning/case-studies/2018/jun/designing-programmes-and-modules-abc-curriculum-design [Accessed: December 30, 2020]

[29] Creswell JW, editor. Research Design: Qualitative, Quantitative, and Mixed Methods Approaches. 3rd ed. Thousand Oaks, CA: Sage; 2009. 342 p

[30] Collins H, editor. Creative Research: The Theory and Practice of Research for the Creative Industries. AVA Publishing, Bloomsbury Publishing; 2010

[31] Study University of Technology. RMTLAS&P, Remote Multimodal Teaching, Learning and Assessment Strategy and Plan. 2020

[32] Simelane-Mnisi S. Faculty Online or Remote Teaching Support Plan. 2020

[33] Sumer M, Douglas T, Sim KN. Academic development through a pandemic crisis: Lessons learnt from three cases incorporating technical, pedagogical and social support. Journal of University Teaching & Learning Practice. 2021;**18**:1

[34] Sim KN. The use of learning management system (LMS): Are we using it right? Journal of Applied Learning and Teaching. 2021;**4**(1):100

[35] Simelane-Mnisi S, Mji A. Student engagement in the flipped classroom. In: Proceedings of the South Africa International Conference on Education; 19-21 September 2016; South Africa: African Academic Research Forum; 2016. pp. 111-123

[36] Thai NT, De Wever B, Valcke M. The impact of a flipped classroom design on learning performance in higher education: Looking for the best blend of lectures and guiding questions with feedback. Computers & Education. 2017;**107**:113-126. DOI: 10.1016/j.compedu.2017.01.003

[37] Adonu CJ, Nwagbo CR, Ugwuanyi CS, Okeke IO. Improving Students' Achievement and Retention in Biology using Flipped Classroom and Powerpoint Instructional Approaches: Implication for Physics Teaching. International Journal of Psychosocial Rehabilitation. 2021;**25**(02):234

[38] Kim MK, Kim SM, Khera O, Getman J. The experience of three flipped classrooms in an urban university: An exploration of design principles. The Internet and Higher Education. 2014;**22**:37-50. DOI: 10.1016/j.iheduc.2014.04.003

[39] Garrison DR, Akyol Z. The community of inquiry theoretical framework. In: Moore MG, editor. Handbook of Distance Education. 3rd ed. Routledge: Taylor and Francis; 2013. pp. 122-138

[40] Stenbom S, Jansson M, Hulkko A. Revising the community of inquiry framework for the analysis of one-to-one online learning relationships. The International Review of Research in Open and Distance Learning. 2016;**17**:36-53. DOI: 10.19173/irrodl.v17i3.2068Copied

[41] Simelane-Mnisi S, Mji A. Students' perspective on technology-engagement teaching strategy using clickers in a mathematics course. In: Proceedings of the International Conference on eLearning; 1 June, 29-30 October 2017; United Kingdom: Academic Conferences and Publishing International Limited; 2017. p. 205

[42] Gumede L, Badriparsad N. Online teaching and learning through the students' eyes–uncertainty through the

COVID-19 lockdown: A qualitative case study in Gauteng Province, South Africa. Radiography. 2021;**28**(1):193. DOI: 10.1016/j.radi.2021.10.018

[43] Lapitan LD Jr, Tiangco CE, Sumalinog DA, Sabarillo NS, Diaz JM. An effective blended online teaching and learning strategy during the COVID-19 pandemic. Education for Chemical Engineers. 2021;**35**:116-131. DOI: 10.1016/j.ece.2021.01.012

[44] Mbhiza HW. Shifting paradigms: Rethinking education during and post-COVID-19 pandemic. Research in Social Sciences and Technology. 2021;**6**(2):279-289. DOI: 10.46303/ressat.2021.31

[45] Namada JM. Learning management systems in the era of e-learning. In: Gulza Z, Leema A, editors. Machine Learning Approaches for Improvising Modern Learning Systems. IGI Global; 2021. pp. 169-190. DOI: 10.4018/978-1-7998-5009-0

[46] Dorsah P. Synchronous versus asynchronous: Pre-service teachers' performance in science formative assessment tests. Open Access Library Journal. 2021;**8**:1. DOI: 10.4236/oalib.1107193

[47] Branon RF, Essex C. Synchronous and asynchronous communication tools in distance education. TechTrends. 2001;**45**:36

[48] Goomas D, Czupryn K. Using a learning management system common template in teaching adult basic education: Opportunities and challenges. Community College Journal of Research and Practice. 2021;**45**:227-230. DOI: 10.1080/10668926.2019.1669229

[49] Cho HJ, Zhao K, Lee CR, Runshe D, Krousgrill C. Active learning through flipped classroom in mechanical engineering: Improving students' perception of learning and performance. International Journal of STEM Education. 2021;**8**:1-3

[50] Sinnayah P, Salcedo A, Rekhari S. Reimagining physiology education with interactive content developed in H5P. Advances in Physiology Education. 2021;**45**:71-76. DOI: 10.1152/advan.00021.2020

[51] Alber R. 6 Scaffolding Strategies to Use With Your Students [Internet]. 2014. Available from: https://www.edutopia.org/blog/scaffolding-lessons-six-strategies-rebecca-alber#:~:text=Scaffolding%20is%20breaking%20up%20the,and%20discuss%20as%20you%20go [Accessed: December 30, 2020]

[52] Chen L, Manwaring P, Zakaria G, Wilkie S, Loton D. Implementing H5P online interactive activities at scale. In: Proceedings of the ASCILITE 2021, Armidale: University of New England; 2021. pp. 81-92. DOI: 10.14742/ascilite2021.0112

[53] Razeed A, Werkhoven T. Design and development of a large Business School core interdisciplinary unit to foster blended learning during the Pandemic. In: Proceedings of the ASCILITE 2021, Armidale: University of New England. 2021. pp. 257-266. DOI: 10.14742/ascilite2021.0138

[54] Dalto J. Blended Learning Basics: Using Asynchronous and Synchronous Training Activities [Internet]. 2020. Available from: https://www.elearninglearning.com/activities/examples/synchronous/?open-article-id=14673020&article-title=blended-learning-basics--using-asynchronous-and-synchronous-training-activities&blog-domain=convergencetraining.com&blog-title=convergence-training [Accessed: December 22, 2020]

Chapter 4

The Impact of Academic Discipline on Student's Engagement in Online Learning: An Extension of the Technology Acceptance Model

Ka Long Chan, Roy Kam and Man Sing Wong

Abstract

Tertiary education has dramatically changed after the outbreak of COVID-19. The use of the Learning Management System (LMS) in online learning has become popular. Many researchers are trying to investigate its features that influence the degree of acceptance and usage of learners among those techniques. However, some of their acceptance is not behavioral, but more on mental and abstract, which would be considered as engagement. In addition, academic disciplines would have a different focus on the integration of technology into their teaching and learning, thus, it would influence students' acceptance of the technology. This research addressed this gap by studying university students in Hong Kong about the Technology Acceptance Model (TAM), and behavioral, agentic, cognitive, and emotional engagement. The findings extended the previous literature of TAM by adding engagement and academic discipline into the model. The current study demonstrates that LMS displays the potential of delivering learning and teaching materials amid the pandemic.

Keywords: iBeacon/BLE technology, COVID-19, learning management system, technology acceptance model, engagement

1. Introduction

The sudden outbreak of COVID-19 in China in 2019 during the Spring Festival, has spread rapidly worldwide [1]. The disease spread relatively fast and affected the whole world [2]. The COVID-19 has now become a global issue [3]. Several measures have been taken to prevent physical contact during the pandemic and contain the spread of COVID-19. The most stringent step for epidemic prevention is lockdown [4], which aims to restrict the movement/mobility of people. Colleges and universities are also facing unprecedented challenges. The pandemic has forced the closure of schools, and more and more universities have to turn to online learning [5]. Several studies indicated that online learning displays the potential of overcoming course delivery difficulties during the pandemic of COVID-19. For example, Guo [6] found that physics students have a better performance in introductory calculus class as attending the online sessions than those absent in online sessions and only rely on self-learning materials. More students attending online sessions believe that synchronous online sessions are the same as face-to-face teaching compared to their counterparts since those sessions allow students to interact with the teacher. This implies that engagement during lectures will be an important factor to facilitate students' study.

2. Literature review

2.1 Research on students' technology acceptance of LMS

The use of LMS in online learning become famous during COVID-19. Many researchers are trying to investigate features that influence learners' and educators' degree of acceptance among those technologies [7]. The literature has shown that the Technology Acceptance Model (TAM) is the most adopted theory to investigate the students' technology acceptance. Davis [8] suggested the TAM examine the determinants of users' acceptance for using the technology. Originally, TAM postulated that *perceived usefulness* and *perceived ease of use* are two main factors associated with user acceptance. Perceived usefulness is the degree to which the user believes that it would enhance their performance by using a specific system. Perceived ease of use refers to the degree to which the user believes that it would cost less effort by using a specific system. TAM also posits that the actual use of a specific system is determined by *behavioral intention to use*, determined by both perceived usefulness and *attitude toward using technology*.

After the publication of Davis [8], in several studies, it is argued that the attitude toward the use of technology would be removed to simplify the model without losing the explaining power [9, 10]. Therefore, the extended model, TAM2 [11], and another subsequent model, UTUAT [12], removed the attitude toward using technology.

Šumak, Heričko [13] conducted a meta-analysis to summarize the TAM-related studies. They found that perceived usefulness and ease of use are two significant factors affecting users' intention to use e-learning systems. For instance, Brunel University offered a series of online courses in LMS and examined the factors of increasing the use of the platform [14]. They found that both the perceived ease of use and the perceived usefulness have been significantly and positively associated with using the platform. During COVID-19, Siron, Wibowo [15] also found similar results. They used TAM to evaluate the use of e-learning platforms during COVID-19. They found that both the perceived usefulness and the perceived ease of use are the major factors affecting students' intention to use e-learning at several state universities in Indonesia during the pandemic.

However, using the actual usage of technology is not enough to capture the whole picture of their acceptance behavior. Some of the acceptance is not behavioral but mental and abstract, which is considered engagement. Also, academic disciplines would have different emphases in integrating technology into their teaching and learning; thus, it would influence students' acceptance. In the following sections, therefore, we will discuss the relationship between academic discipline, student engagement, and the actual use of LMS.

2.2 Engagement and LMS

Students' academic performance is primarily influenced by student engagement [16]. More recently, researchers have begun to conceptualize student engagement as a multidimensional phenomenon. The review by Fredricks, Blumenfeld [17] identified three dimensions of engagement: behavioral, emotional, and cognitive. Behavioral engagement refers to students' levels of involvement in the learning activity, including attention, participation, interaction with students and teachers, and spent effort and time. Emotional engagement is defined as students' presence of positive emotional reactions to learning in general, such as value, identity, interest, and happiness, and absence of adverse emotional responses such as anxiety. Cognitive engagement centers on students' self-regulation strategies to employ sophisticated rather than superficial learning strategies in their learning processes. Besides, another review by Kahu [18] used the integrative framework to emphasize engagement as a state influenced by a wide array of teacher and student factors. The framework also acknowledges that students learn through being engaged with their study; thus, learning is not only acquiring skills and knowledge. Build on the previous literature, Reeve [19] also proposed agentic engagement, which is defined as students' attempt to contribute to the learning environment to create for themselves a more motivationally supportive learning environment.

Several studies have found student engagement to be an indicator of students' higher academic achievement. Carini, Kuh [20] found that improvements in students' engagement improve their learning outcomes. Kahu and Nelson [21] assessed students' emotional and cognitive engagement and found that emotional and cognitive engagement can predict academic success. However, online/remote learning has been famous recently, and the question may raise whether students engaging in LMS would benefit academic achievement. For example, Wang [22] examined the relationship between behavioral engagement on Moodle and academic performance (defined as course grade) in a university in Taiwan. Wang found that engagement in problem-solving-related learning activities in Moodle has a direct effect on academic performance. In the studies of Hsiao, Huang [23] and Lee, Park [24], they defined academic performance by GPA and self-developed academic capability measurement, respectively. They also found that behavioral engagement positively correlates with academic performance. This study hopes to extend their findings by assessing whether another type of student engagement, cognitive, emotional, and agentic engagement, also predicts academic performance.

2.3 Academic discipline and LMS

Since the technology advanced, students gradually developed "the information-age mindset" over the three decades [25]. In the meantime, the Learning Management System (LMS) was developed in the 2000s to create a virtual learning environment and facilitate the implementation of online learning (Oblinger & Kidwell, 2000). Since the LMS is a teaching and learning tool, the discussion of LMS has to be informed by pedagogical considerations. As early as 2000, researchers were beginning to identify the influence of LMS on teaching and learning to form the theoretical framework. Coates, James [26] identified some practical problems when the teacher used LMS; one of the dominant problems is that LMS is only used to transmit the text. Teachers did not modify their teaching pedagogy; instead, they employed their traditional teaching approaches when using the LMS [27]. Sadaf, Newby [28] also found similar results in the group of pre-service teachers that use of the LMS would predict the intention to use LMS.

On the contrary, the successful use of LMS depends on the integration between LMS and the subject (including teaching material and learning objective). Research also suggests that different courses emphasize different learning outcomes by providing discipline-specific learning environments [29, 30]. For example, teachers from soft fields tend to focus on facilitating and developing students' ability to discuss alternative and critical perspectives [31]. Those in hard fields tend to focus on having students memorize and apply essential concepts [32]. Therefore, courses in the same academic discipline would have similar learning objectives; different academic disciplines would have a different level of integration with LMS. Smith, Torres-Ayala [33] investigate the academic discipline as a factor in the instructional design of e-learning. They found that mathematics and nursing/healthcare emphasize learning outcomes and utilization of e-learning tools differently. For example, mathematics focused on the abstract concept of mathematics, whereas nursing/healthcare focused on authentic assessment, which facilitates students to apply the skill and knowledge in real life. White and Liccardi [34] also used Biglan categorization [35] to categorize academic disciplines based on the degree of consensus about knowledge within them. Their categorization classifies disciplines into soft (a low degree of agreement) and hard fields (a high degree of agreement). They found that soft and hard fields have a difference in using LMS tools, which soft fields utilize discussion and simulated virtual environment (role play). In contrast, hard fields utilize real-time visualization tools and assessment.

2.4 Gaps in the literature and the present study

There are several gaps in the literature among students' engagement in online learning. First, the literature's findings focus on behavioral engagement only, which neglects cognitive, emotional, and agentic engagement. Second, previous studies do not differentiate the influence of academic discipline on engagement in e-learning.

This study seeks to address these gaps by combining TAM with engagement and academic discipline. Its theoretical framework is outlined in **Figures 1–4**. This study hypothesizes that 1) ease of use has a direct effect on the intention to use, 2) ease of use has an indirect effect through usefulness toward intention to use, 3) positive relationship between students' intention to use and their engagement is stronger in soft fields than in hard fields. Sharma et al. (1981) defined a moderating variable as influencing the relationship's strength and direction between predictors and outcome measures. A moderating variable is different from a mediating variable—the latter accounts for the relationship between

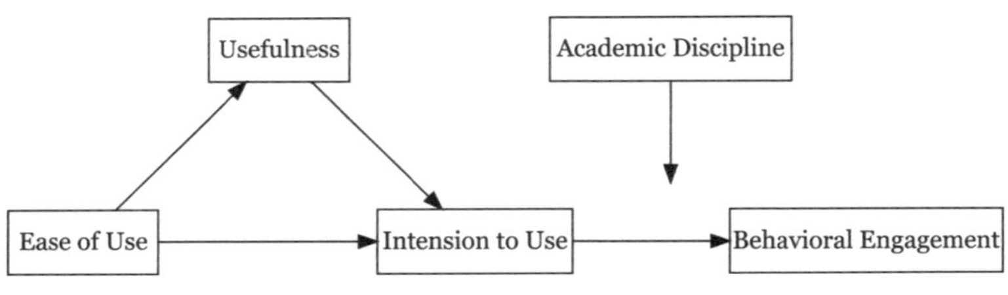

Figure 1.
Hypothetical model of behavioral engagement.

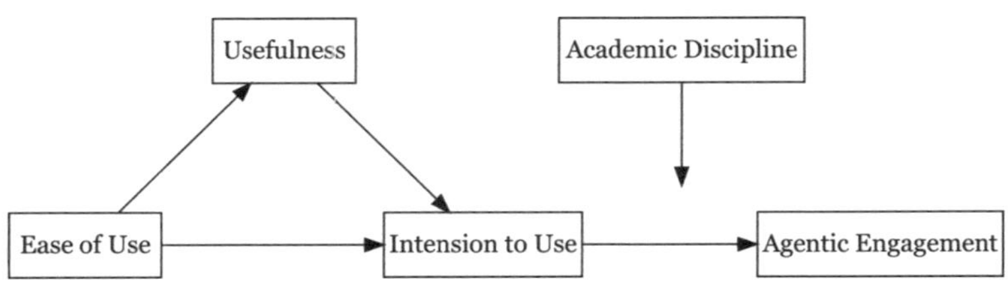

Figure 2.
Hypothetical model of agentic engagement.

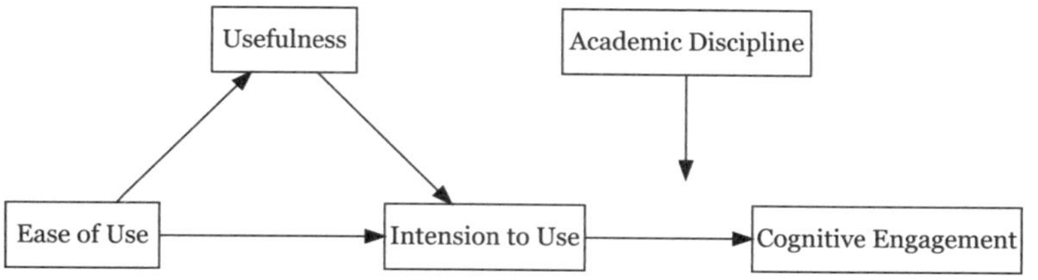

Figure 3.
Hypothetical model of cognitive engagement.

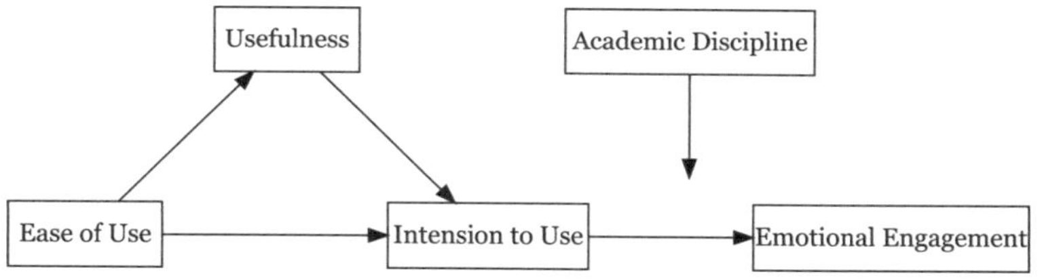

Figure 4.
Hypothetical model of emotional engagement.

predictors and outcome measures [36]. We used regression in our moderation analysis to include the interaction term for both predictors and moderators in our model [37].

3. Method and procedure

3.1 Participants

We recruited study participants from The Hong Kong Polytechnic University, The University of Hong Kong, and The Chinese University of Hong Kong between January and May 2021. A total of 6 courses participated in this study. The research team sent the online survey via Microsoft Form to students at the end of the semester. All of these participants were aged 21–23 years. They had a mobile phone, which shows that the participants were previously mobile users and can be good evaluators of any mobile application. Overall, 68 students responded to the questionnaire. More than 54% of students used the iOS System, and other students used the Android System.

3.2 In-campus and off-campus wholistic learning management system

To overcome the challenge of COVID-19, the project team had developed a system named "Augmented Teaching and Learning Advancement System (ATLAS)" to enhance the teaching quality and student learning experience in the university setting of Hong Kong. Students' mobiles install the app on their mobile phones and sign the written consent before participating in the study. More details are provided on the ATLAS website: https://www.atlas-learn.com/. The description of ATLAS is defined as below:

3.2.1 Location-based service

A standalone system for use in conjunction with iBeacon protocol to provide location-based features is being developed. The System is named ATLAS. The purpose of ATLAS is to empower teachers with the ability to open new streams of engagement, facilitate active participation and communication between students and instructors, and enhance the learning experience in general by providing a holistic platform for contents sharing, discussion, assessment, and engagement.

ATLAS has four main parts: a web-based portal for administration, a student/visitor mobile app for iOS and Android devices, a web-based content management system for instructors, and, lastly, server-side services for the central storage of educational information location-based data collected. The mobile app was developed to utilize an iBeacon-based system to facilitate questions and answers, attendance monitoring, seating location measurement for enhancing teaching and learning outcomes, and activity for "Contactless Learning and Teaching". To achieve "Contactless Learning and Teaching", the teacher set up several learning locations to deliver learning and teaching material. After the teacher set up the contactless learning and teaching activity in ATLAS, the mobile app would guide the students to different locations. It depends on the students whether to participate in the contactless activity, and it is a voluntary activity without affecting their final academic performance.

3.2.2 Online teaching and learning

Since there were difficulties in conducting the face-to-face classes under the COVID-19 pandemic, an additional function has been added to the System for teachers and students to use off-campus. Teachers and school administrators can create off-campus classes for the teaching activities. During the remote class, all the location-based features are disabled.

3.3 Measurement

3.3.1 Engagement

We assessed four aspects of student engagement— behavioral, agentic, cognitive, and emotional. We use the engagement scale developed and modified from Reeve's [19] confirmatory factor analysis study, which contained 4, 5, 4, and 4 items for behavioral, agentic, cognitive, and emotional engagement. The items were rated using a five-point Likert scale (1 = strongly disagree and 5 = strongly agree), where Cronbach's alphas were 0.95, 0.92, 0.92, and 0.91, respectively for behavioral, agentic, cognitive, and emotional engagement.

3.3.2 TAM

The usefulness, ease of use, and intention to use were adopted by introducing the Technology Acceptance Model (TAM). Three constructs were modified to fit our System (ATLAS), which contained 9, 4, and 3 items for usefulness, ease of use, and intention to use. The items were rated using a seven-point Likert scale (1 = strongly disagree and 7 = strongly agree), where Cronbach's alphas were 0.97, 0.88, and 0.94 respectively for usefulness, ease of use, and intention to use.

3.3.3 Academic discipline

We used Biglan [35] classification to divide the academic disciplines into soft (code = 1) or hard fields (code = 2). The categories classify the disciplines into soft (a low degree of agreement) and hard (a high degree of agreement).

4. Data analysis

We performed a path analysis in R studio with the PROCESS macro, version 3.5.3 beta0.6 [38]. **Figures 1–4** display the hypothetical model being tested in the current study. Age and gender were set as covariates. Maximum likelihood (ML) was used to estimate the parameter, and the robust test statistic was reported. To examine the moderated serial mediation effect, we specified 5000 bootstrap samples based on 95% confidence intervals (CIs). A significant conditional indirect effect can be found when the 95% CIs do not include zero. We used a simple slope analysis to visualize the significant interaction between variables [39]. All alpha was set at 0.05, two-tailed.

5. Results

As shown in **Table 1**, participants' average engagement score was 3.92, 3.34, 3.77, and 3.88 for behavioral, agentic engagement, cognitive engagement, and emotional engagement, respectively. About 70% of them were hard fields, and 57.4% of them were female. Nearly 60% of them came from Hong Kong Polytechnic University. The mean scores of usefulness, ease of use, and intention to use were 4.11, 4.78, and 3.84, respectively.

	Mean / N	SD / %
Age	20.838	2.477
Gender		
Male	29	42.65
Female	39	57.35
TAM		
Usefulness	4.112	3.118
Ease of Use	4.756	4.022
Intention to Use	3.840	3.055
Engagement		
Behavioral	3.915	0.771
Agentic	3.338	0.822
Cognitive	3.772	0.725
Emotional	3.882	0.770
Academic discipline		
Soft field	20	29.41%
Hard field	48	70.59%
University		
The Chinese University of Hong Kong	19	27.94%
The Hong Kong Polytechnic University	40	58.82%
The University of Hong Kong	9	13.24%

Table 1.
Participant characteristic.

Figures 5–8 show the results of our path analysis. Results showed that "Ease of Use" was significantly associated with "Usefulness" (ß range from 0.863 to 0.864) and "Intention to Use" (ß range from 0.298 to 0.302) in all models. "Usefulness" was also significantly associated with "Intention to Use" (ß range from 0.777 to 0.781) in all models. "Intention to Use" was also significantly associated with behavioral engagement (ß = 0.274), agentic engagement (ß = 0.320), cognitive engagement (ß = 0.253), and emotional engagement (ß = 0.324). Significant interaction effect between students' "Intention to Use" and their academic discipline can predict their emotional engagement scores only (ß = −0.236), there were no significant interaction effect was found in behavioral engagement (ß = −0.171), agentic engagement (ß = −0.169), and cognitive engagement (ß = −0.162). Thus, we performed a simple slope analysis to probe the significant interaction effect. The simple slope analysis revealed no significant relationship between students' "Intention to Use" and their engagement scores in hard fields (β = 0.094) but a significant relationship between these two variables in soft fields (β = 0.252) (**Figure 9**).

Regarding the bootstrap moderated serial mediation analysis, significant conditional indirect effect was found from "Ease of Use" to "Usefulness" to "Intention to Use" to emotional engagement only (Index of moderated mediation = −0.161, 95% CI [−0.293, −0.035]), there were no significant effect was found in behavioral engagement (Index of moderated mediation = −0.119, 95% CI [−0.244, 0.012]), agentic engagement (Index of moderated mediation = −0.118, 95% CI [−0.260, 0.041]), and cognitive engagement (Index of moderated mediation = −0.109, 95% CI [−0.247, 0.024]). Similar to simple slope analysis in emotional engagement, no significant conditional indirect effect was found in hard fields (β = 0.062, 95% CI [−0.029, 0.162]) but a significant effect in soft fields (β = 0.223, 95% CI [0.117, 0.332]).

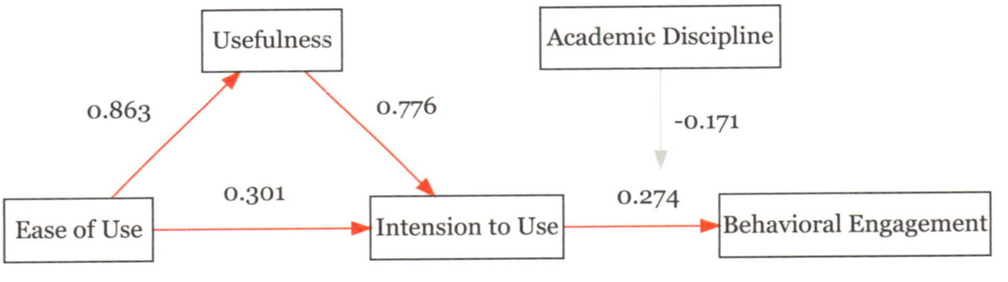

Figure 5.
Path analysis of TAM, academic discipline, and behavioral engagement. Lines in red color indicated significant paths.

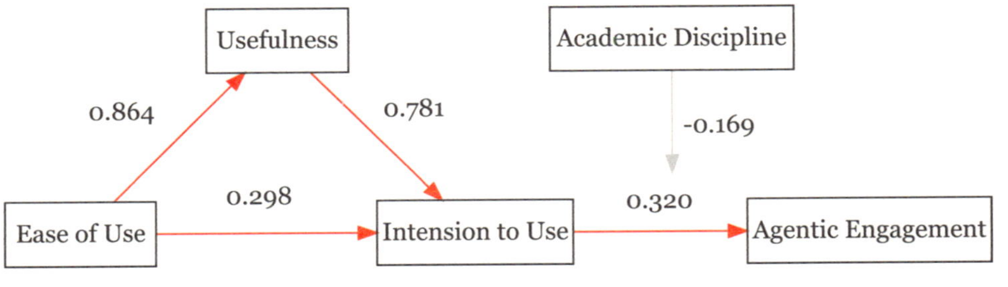

Figure 6.
Path analysis of TAM, academic discipline, and agentic engagement. Lines in red color indicated significant paths.

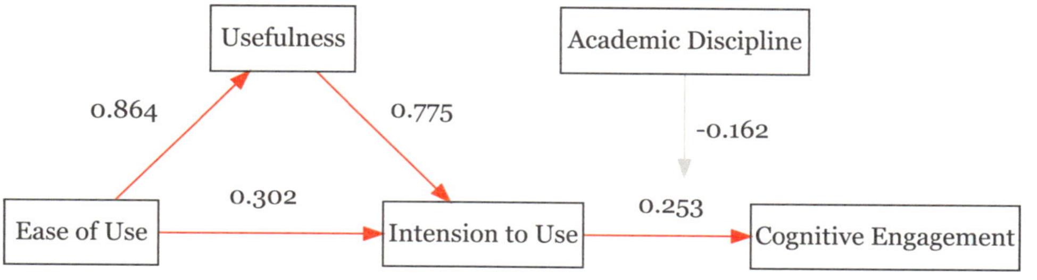

Figure 7.
Path analysis of TAM, academic discipline, and cognitive engagement. Lines in red color indicated significant paths.

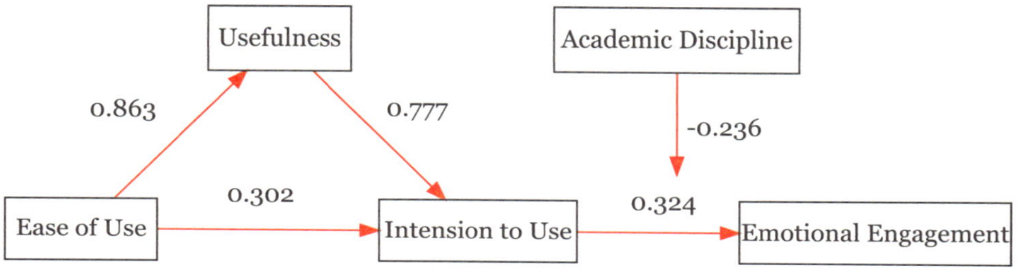

Figure 8.
Path analysis of TAM, academic discipline, and emotional engagement. Lines in red color indicated significant paths.

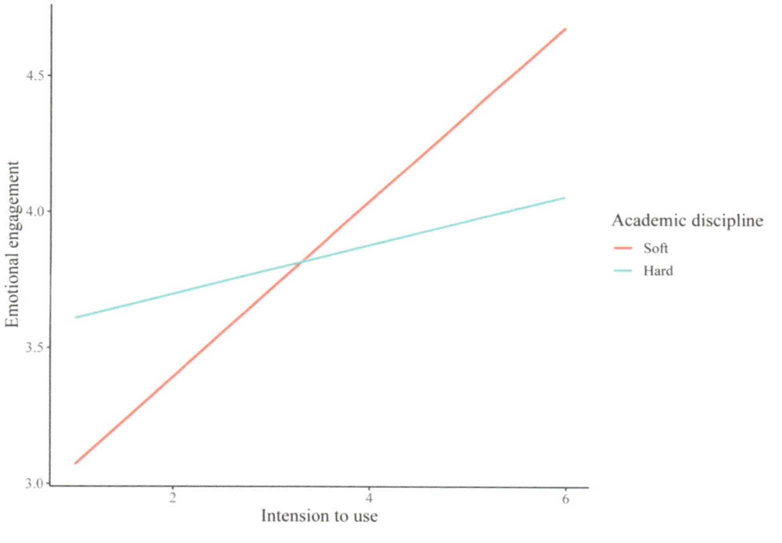

Figure 9.
Relationship between intention to use and emotional engagement among students with the soft and hard field in the academic discipline.

In summary, students from soft fields had higher emotional engagement scores when they had the higher intention to use ATLAS in the future. Students from hard fields' emotional engagement scores did not vary significantly by their "Intention to Use". Regarding behavioral engagement, agentic engagement, and cognitive engagement, the relationship between students' "Intention to Use" and their engagement scores did not vary significantly by their academic discipline.

6. Discussion

The literature presents many studies where student engagement has been studied from the perspective of behavioral engagement. However, the relationship between agentic, cognitive, and emotional engagement and LMS is an understudied topic. In COVID-19, the use of LMS has become common in the higher education sector, and it has become essential to study it currently. This study explored the relationship between technology acceptance of LMS and engagement with a moderating role for academic discipline.

Study findings add to the literature on the technology acceptance model and students' engagement. Our results are consistent with those of Marangunić and Granić [40] and Al-Emran, Mezhuyev [41]. They noted that ease of use is positively related to the usefulness and intention to use. Aligned with TAM, we expected the usefulness is the mediator from the ease of use to intention to use. Our results align with Tawafak, Romli [42], who found that students with high perceived ease of use among the LMS show higher perceived usefulness. The perception of usefulness leads to a higher intention to use LMS in the future.

Another exciting aspect was that this model operates through the fully online learning platform. Previous studies had investigated the technology acceptance of e-learning platforms [43–45]. Before COVID-19, students used an e-learning platform combined with face-to-face teaching at the same time. The learning does not become highly dependent on the platform and only serves as a supplement. However, face-to-face teaching is suspended and entirely depends on those platforms. Therefore, there is a question of whether the TAM would be applied in this situation. The results align with the above literature on e-learning. Our study recruited participants in a fully online learning undergraduate program, which is different from the previous literature. Therefore, the current study fills the gaps that the experience in a fully online learning program would explain using TAM.

Our study also showed a significant implication in the different types of engagement. Our results were consistent with previous literature [13] that intention to use was associated with the usage of the technology. Also, our current study extended the engagement from behavioral to cognitive, emotional, and agentic. The findings indicate that students without behavioral engagement would also have a high engagement level in other aspects. While comparing the different types of engagement, emotional and agentic engagement had higher effects than behavioral engagement. The results indicate that some of the engagement during the class would be implicit and non-observable. The study makes a case for teachers to be more sensitive toward engagement during the class.

The current study also found a significant moderation effect through academic discipline. The result is aligned with previous literature that there are discipline differences in student engagement [46]. We found that students with the soft field in academic discipline had a stronger relationship between intention to use and emotional engagement than their counterparts. The results were partially consistent with the study of Espejo [47]. Espejo [47] investigated the different types of engagements between classroom characteristics. They found that a learning environment with enough support would facilitate students to engage emotionally and behaviourally.

Our result indicates that students with soft fields are more affected by intention to use and might become more engaged emotionally. However, there are no moderation effect would be found in behavioral, cognitive, and agentic engagement. The insignificant moderation effect would explain that academic disciplines have various effects on the different types of engagement. Different academic disciplines would lead to different learning environments, for example, it is most likely that teachers from the soft field would lead to a person-centered learning environment (reference). Under this learning environment, students would work enthusiastically and enjoy their involvement during the class, even though there are no face-to-face interactions [48]. On the contrary, students would engage in their class behaviorally, cognitively, and genetically at a similar intensity no matter their academic field. This is consistent with the finding that students would engage more with greater teacher support [49]. Therefore, teachers in the hard field could also provide a supportive and interactive learning environment. In aligning with the benefit of an autonomy-supportive learning environment [50], teachers are critical in developing appropriate strategies to heighten the intention to use LMS toward such students and become an autonomy-supporter in facilitating the use of LMS.

This study's findings can provide university administrators and teachers with several important insights and recommendations regarding how to use and redesign the LMS to engage the student. For example, researchers in the University of Hong Kong compared different e-quiz platforms during the class, which the selection of the platform was based on the TAM [51]. They found that the platforms would enhance engagement through friendly competition. The immediate feedback also was perceived as another important component in engaging students to learn since students would perceive the platform as useful for their learning. Researchers at the Chinese University of Hong Kong also examined the impact of digital support on students' engagement [52]. During the learning in LMS, several difficulties about learning materials would be faced by students. In traditional classroom teaching, teachers would provide support for the needs of students. However, the teachers cannot support students all the time when students learn in LMS. Therefore, redesigning the LMS to include digital support based on the TAM would engage students better. Our study and preceding studies mentioned here suggest that several components should be added or platforms should be selected based on the TAM. The more ease to use and usefulness, the better.

7. Conclusion and limitation

The present study extended the TAM by adding cognitive, emotional, and agentic engagement as the outcome; students' acceptance of the ATLAS is associated with the behavioral, cognitive, emotional, and agentic engagement. Academic discipline also modifies the relationship between the acceptance of the ATLAS and emotional engagement. However, it has several limitations to overcome by future researchers.

First of all, since we employed the cross-sectional study design for current research, the relationship between different types of engagement and user acceptance may not be generalized [53]. Future researchers might use a longitudinal study design to understand better the underlying mechanisms driving our theoretical model.

Second, in the present study, the issue arising from the discipline difference in the engagement is not addressed. Our findings still beg the question of what the underlying mechanisms are, which drive this moderating effect. Future studies will cover several related factors, e.g., classroom characteristics, pedagogical approach, or learning environment.

Acknowledgements

The study was supported by the "Augmenting Physical Learning Spaces with Location-based Services Using iBeacon Technology for Engaging Learning Experiences" project from the UGC Funding Scheme for Teaching and Learning Related Proposals (2016–2019 Triennium), University Grants Committee, Hong Kong.

Conflict of interest

The authors declare no conflict of interest.

Author details

Ka Long Chan[1], Roy Kam[2] and Man Sing Wong[1*]

1 Department of Land Surveying and Geo-Informatics, The Hong Kong Polytechnic University, Hong Kong

2 Educational Development Centre, The Hong Kong Polytechnic University, Hong Kong

*Address all correspondence to: lswong@polyu.edu.hk

References

[1] Huang C, Wang Y, Li X, Ren L, Zhao J, Hu Y, et al. Clinical features of patients infected with 2019 novel coronavirus in Wuhan, China. The Lancet. 2020; **395**(10223):497-506

[2] Singhal T. A review of coronavirus disease-2019 (COVID-19). The Indian Journal of Pediatrics. 2020;**87**(4):281-286

[3] Sohrabi C, Alsafi Z, O'Neill N, Khan M, Kerwan A, Al-Jabir A, et al. World Health Organization declares global emergency: A review of the 2019 novel coronavirus (COVID-19). International Journal of Surgery. 2020;**76**:71-76

[4] Lonergan M, Chalmers JD. Estimates of the ongoing need for social distancing and control measures post-"lockdown" from trajectories of COVID-19 cases and mortality. European Respiratory Journal. 2020;**56**(1):2001483

[5] Pokhrel S, Chhetri R. A literature review on impact of COVID-19 pandemic on teaching and learning. Higher Education for the Future. 2021;**8**(1):133-141

[6] Guo S. Synchronous versus asynchronous online teaching of physics during the COVID-19 pandemic. Physics Education. 2020;**55**(6):065007

[7] Sharin AN. E-learning during Covid-19 a review of literature. Journal Pengajian Media Malaysia. 2021;**23**(1):15-28

[8] Davis FD. Perceived usefulness, perceived ease of use, and user acceptance of information technology. MIS Quarterly. 1989;**13**(3):319-340

[9] Szajna B. Empirical evaluation of the revised technology acceptance model. Management Science. 1996;**42**(1):85-92

[10] Davis FD, Bagozzi RP, Warshaw PR. User acceptance of computer technology: A comparison of two theoretical models. Management Science. 1989; **35**(8):982-1003

[11] Venkatesh V, Davis FD. A theoretical extension of the technology acceptance model: Four longitudinal field studies. Management Science. 2000;**46**(2):186-204

[12] Venkatesh V, Morris MG, Davis GB, Davis FD. User acceptance of information technology: Toward a unified view. MIS Quarterly. 2003;**27**(3):425-478

[13] Šumak B, Heričko M, Pušnik M. A meta-analysis of e-learning technology acceptance: The role of user types and e-learning technology types. Computers in Human Behavior. 2011;**27**(6):2067-2077

[14] Abu-Al-Aish A, Love S. Factors influencing students' acceptance of m-learning: An investigation in higher education. The International Review of Research in Open and Distributed Learning. 2013;**14**(5):82-107

[15] Siron Y, Wibowo A, Narmaditya BS. Factors affecting the adoption of e-learning in Indonesia: Lesson from COVID-19. Journal of Technology and Science Education. 2020;**10**(2):282-295

[16] Krause KL, Coates H. Students' engagement in first-year university. Assessment & Evaluation in Higher Education. 2008;**33**(5):493-505

[17] Fredricks JA, Blumenfeld PC, Paris AH. School engagement: Potential of the concept, state of the evidence. Review of Educational Research. 2004;**74**(1):59-109

[18] Kahu ER. Framing student engagement in higher education. Studies in Higher Education. 2013;**38**(5):758-773

[19] Reeve J. How students create motivationally supportive learning environments for themselves: The concept of agentic engagement. Journal of Educational Psychology. 2013;**105**(3):579-595

[20] Carini RM, Kuh GD, Klein SP. Student engagement and student learning: Testing the linkages. Research in Higher Education. 2006;**47**(1):1-32

[21] Kahu ER, Nelson K. Student engagement in the educational interface: Understanding the mechanisms of student success. Higher Education Research and Development. 2017;**37**(1):58-71

[22] Wang FH. An exploration of online behaviour engagement and achievement in flipped classroom supported by learning management system. Computers & Education. 2017;**114**:79-91

[23] Hsiao CC, Huang JCH, Huang AYQ, Lu OHT, Yin CJ, Yang SJH. Exploring the effects of online learning behaviors on short-term and long-term learning outcomes in flipped classrooms. Interactive Learning Environments. 2018;**27**(8):1160-1177

[24] Lee J, Park T, Davis RO. What affects learner engagement in flipped learning and what predicts its outcomes? British Journal of Educational Technology. 2018

[25] Frand JL. The information-age mindset changes in students and implications for higher education. Educause Review. 2000;**35**:14-25

[26] Coates H, James R, Baldwin G. A critical examination of the effects of learning management systems on university teaching and learning. Tertiary Education and Management. 2005;**11**:19-36

[27] Zanjani N, Edwards SL, Nykvist S, Geva S. LMS acceptance: The instructor role. The Asia-Pacific Education Researcher. 2016;**25**(4):519-526

[28] Sadaf A, Newby TJ, Ertmer PA. Exploring factors that predict preservice teachers' intentions to use web 2.0 technologies using decomposed theory of planned behavior. Journal of Research on Technology in Education. 2012;**45**(2):171-196

[29] Smart JC, Ethington CA, Umbach PD, Rocconi LM. Faculty emphases on alternative course-specific learning outcomes in holland's model environments: The role of environmental consistency. Research in Higher Education. 2009;**50**(5):483-501

[30] Smart JC, Umbach PD. Faculty and academic environments: Using Holland's theory to explore differences in how faculty structure undergraduate courses. Journal of College Student Development. 2007;**48**(2):183-195

[31] Gaff JG, Wilson RC. Faculty cultures and interdisciplinary studies. The Journal of Higher Education. 1971;**42**(3):186-201

[32] Smart JC, Ethington CA. Disciplinary and institutional differences in undergraduate education goals. New Directions for Teaching and Learning. 1995;**64**:49-57

[33] Smith GG, Torres-Ayala AT, Heindel AJ. Disciplinary differences in E-learning instructional design: The case of mathematics. International Journal of E-Learning & Distance Education. 2008;**22**(3):63-88

[34] White S, Liccardi I, editors. Harnessing insight into disciplinary differences to refine e-learning design. In: Proceedings Frontiers in Education 36th Annual Conference. San Diego, CA: IEEE; 2006

[35] Biglan A. The characteristics of subject matter in different academic areas. Journal of Applied Psychology. 1973;**57**(3):195-203

[36] Baron RM, Kenny DA. The moderator–mediator variable distinction in social psychological research: Conceptual, strategic, and statistical considerations. Journal of Personality and Social Psychology. 1986;**51**(6):1173-1182

[37] Sharma S, Durand RM, Gur-Arie O. Identification and analysis of moderator variables. Journal of Marketing Research. 1981;**18**(3):291-300

[38] Hayes AF. In: Little TD, editor. Introduction to Mediation, Moderation, and Conditional Process Analysis: A Regression-Based Approach. Second ed. New York: The Guilford Press; 2018

[39] Hayes AF, Rockwood NJ. Regression-based statistical mediation and moderation analysis in clinical research: Observations, recommendations, and implementation. Behaviour Research and Therapy. 2017;**98**:39-57

[40] Marangunić N, Granić A. Technology acceptance model: A literature review from 1986 to 2013. Universal Access in the Information Society. 2014;**14**(1):81-95

[41] Al-Emran M, Mezhuyev V, Kamaludin A. Technology acceptance model in m-learning context: A systematic review. Computers & Education. 2018;**2018**(125):389-412

[42] Tawafak RM, Romli AB, Arshah RBA. Continued intention to use UCOM: Four factors for integrating with a technology acceptance model to moderate the satisfaction of learning. IEEE Access. 2018;**6**:66481-66498

[43] Tarhini A, Hone K, Liu X, Tarhini T. Examining the moderating effect of individual-level cultural values on users' acceptance of E-learning in developing countries: A structural equation modeling of an extended technology acceptance model. Interactive Learning Environments. 2016;**25**(3):306-328

[44] Tarhini A, Hone K, Liu X. Measuring the moderating effect of gender and age on E-learning acceptance in England: A structural equation Modeling approach for an extended technology acceptance model. Journal of Educational Computing Research. 2014;**51**(2):163-184

[45] Hayashi A, Chen C, Ryan T, Wu J. The role of social presence and moderating role of computer self efficacy in predicting the continuance usage of e-learning systems. Journal of Information Systems Education. 2004;**15**(2):139-154

[46] Leach L. Exploring discipline differences in student engagement in one institution. Higher Education Research and Development. 2016;**35**(4):772-786

[47] Espejo N, editor. Difference in academic engagement among college students as a function of learning environment. In: DLSU Research Congress Proceedings. Manila, Philippines: De La Salle University; 2018

[48] Reeve J, Lee W. Students' classroom engagement produces longitudinal changes in classroom motivation. Journal of Educational Psychology. 2014;**106**(2):527-540

[49] Jang H, Kim EJ, Reeve J. Why students become more engaged or more disengaged during the semester: A self-determination theory dual-process model. Learning and Instruction. 2016;**43**:27-38

[50] Reeve J, Cheon SH, Jang H-R. A teacher-focused intervention to enhance students' classroom engagement. In: Handbook of Student Engagement Interventions. Cambridge, MA: Academic Press; 2019. pp. 87-102

[51] Zainuddin Z, Shujahat M, Haruna H, Chu SKW. The role of gamified e-quizzes on student learning and engagement: An interactive gamification solution for a formative assessment system. Computers & Education. 2020;**145**:103729

[52] Chiu TKF. Digital support for student engagement in blended learning based on self-determination theory. Computers in Human Behavior. 2021;**124**:106909

[53] Sedgwick P. Cross sectional studies: Advantages and disadvantages. BMJ. 2014;**348**:g2276

Section 2

Technology Integration

Chapter 5

Strategy as Plan for Technology Integration to Reposition Lecturers for the New Normal in Higher Education

Sibongile R. Ngcapu, Sibongile Simelane-Mnisi and Andile Mji

Abstract

This chapter reports on the strategy as plan using ICT policy that could impact on repositioning the lecturers for the integration of technology for the new normal in education. Global, the COVID-19 pandemic distinctly exposed the unpreparedness of lecturers to integrate technology in teaching and learning when the shutdown of the higher institutions was announced. The participants consisted of 37 lecturers from four departments in the School of Education at a university of technology in South Africa. A qualitative case study method was used. An open-ended questionnaire, individual interviews and document analysis were used to collect data. Atlas.ti was used to analyse data. The findings revealed that the study University does not have the eLearning policy to enforce technology integration. Hence the unpreparedness of lecturers to integrate was discovered during Covid-19. It is recommended the study university develops an ICT policy, involving lecturers as stakeholders to promote ownership and conformability.

Keywords: ICT policy, repositioning, integration technology, COVID-19

1. Introduction

The unpreparedness of lecturers to integrate technology for teaching and learning was distinctly exposed when the shutdown of the higher institutions of learning was announced in March 2020 due to the COVID19 pandemic [1] and the lockdown regulations to facilitate social distancing, as a measure to control the spread of the virus [2]. The pandemic brought an enormous transformation in the way we live, learn and work [3]. These factors resulted in the new normal in all the sectors including education [4]. Global, education institutions provided a speedy adaption to the way learning and teaching were conducted [3]. To save the 2020 academic year, online teaching and learning were opted for Simelane-Mnisi and Mji [2]. In the study conducted in 20 countries on the online adoption for teaching and learning, the results reveal that very few countries were prepared to swiftly move to online learning instantly [5].

In South Africa, out of fourteen universities, only four universities were able to switch to online learning immediately [6]. This posed a challenge to both the lecturers and the students in the study university, as they were not able to continue with learning and teaching during this period. The emergency remote workshops were put in place to prepare lecturers for remote teaching [7]. Emergency remote technology-enhanced development programs were adopted to support lecturers with the design and development of online modules [8] by the instructional designers as experts [9, 10]. However, not all lecturers were on board. Furthermore, students were affected by digital divide as not all of them had access to a strong network connection. Hence the study university had to adopt the multimodal teaching and learning to save 2020 academic year [6]. These barriers were also observed with the University students in Nigeria who did not have computers and Wi-Fi to move their studies online [3]. It is worth noting that in the study university professional development programs on technology integration in education including Partners@work and eLeaders had been in place, but the buy-in remained low as the lecturers reverted to traditional methods of teaching [11].

This chapter reports on the strategy as a plan, ICT policy that could support in repositioning lecturers for the integration of technology for the new normal in Education. The question posed in this study is "*How can the strategy as plan, ICT policy, be utilized to promote technology integration to reposition lecturers for the new normal in the School of Education?*" To respond to this question, literature on the strategy as plan, ICT leadership role, stakeholders and the ICT policy processes were reviewed, the document analysis on the school of Education policies, relating to Internet access policy, strategic plan, consolidation plan and institutional strategy 2014–2019 was conducted. Furthermore, to establish lecturers' perceptions on the promotion of ICT in the School of Education, open-ended questionnaires and individual interviews were conducted.

2. Strategy as plan

To overcome lecturers' challenges in this study, the strategy as a plan which is one of the strategies in the Mintzberg 5Ps strategic Model [12] used in the business sector was explored to reposition the lecturers. According to Simelane [13], the strategy as plan in the business sector is a policy of the organization intended to regulate how business is run. In education, the ICT policy is defined as the plan of actions or rules set by the institution to integrate technology in teaching and learning [14, 15]. The ICT policy determines the culture of teaching and learning. The integration of technology has been applauded for enhancing teaching and learning among other factors. Proponents of technology integration argue that the development of the ICT policy is the prominent step towards successful technology integration [14]. Furthermore, it is asserted that schools that are successful in technology integration are regulated by the ICT policy. Parry et al. [16] argue that for the policy to translate into results it must be planned, developed, implemented, monitored and reviewed. However, the development of the ICT policy requires ICT leadership with a distributive approach that is "diffused and dispersed" within the institution of learning [17]. It is also asserted that the involvement of all the stakeholders throughout the phases of the policy processes positively impacts the adoption and implementation of the policy [18]. Hence all the stakeholders must be involved in the planning, development, monitoring and reviewing of the policy.

2.1 The leadership role in the ICT policy process

Cross and Adam [19] and Nath [20] perceive the ICT leadership as an important and precondition for successful development and implementation of the ICT policy. These authors posit that effective leadership must establish the steering committee which must, in turn, establish the working committee. The working committee is responsible for reviewing the ICT policy draft and ensuring that all the stakeholders are involved and are in agreement with the stipulations [21]. They must also ensure that there are experts such as instructional designers to advise the working committee. The ICT policy from another institution can also be useful as an example. The steering committee is responsible for ensuring that the policy is approved by all the stakeholders before its implementation.

2.2 Stakeholder' role in the integration of ICT policy in HEIs

According to [18, 22, 23] stakeholders in the university includes anyone who is influenced or influences the innovation including the knowledge industry, academia, designers, policymakers and other institutions involved in higher education. The stakeholders consist of internal and external members. The internal members relate university admission board, governing council, undergraduate and postgraduate students, government, academic and non-academic staff, university administrators. Whereas, external stakeholders involve the National university commission, NGOs, industries, private companies, parents, development agencies and trade unions [20].

2.2.1 The university administrator

The Vice-Chancellor as the administrator, his assistants, including deputy vice-chancellor, registrar, the deans of faculties, directors of institutes and heads of departments has the responsibility to set the academic tone of the institution. This is accomplished when there is a collaborative approach in problem-solving and decision-making. This creates a healthy relationship between the stakeholders. Rana et al. [24] assert that a distributed approach influences the quality of education.

2.2.2 Government and university governing board

The government owns and funds the universities. It is their responsibility to ensure that there are relevant resources including the ICTs to influence the quality of education. Usman [25] argues that effective policymaking requires an enlightened governing board that has a broad view of the impact of higher education on society and is conscious of the strategic directions and resources for achieving institutional missions. Additionally, the governing council also must ensure the continuous improvement of the quality of university education, define strategic visions, formulate and monitor policies, contribute to the university decision making, ensure that the academic staff is of good quality. Goodson [18] posits that the governing council must collaborate with external stakeholders in improving academic standards and quality in the university.

2.2.3 Students

Students are primary stakeholders in the education industry [26]. The participation of students in taking decisions positions the students to play a responsible role in their learning. It is argued that students must be involved in academic decisions including the integration of ICT for teaching and learning as they are part of the academic community and clients of the university [27].

2.2.4 Council of Higher Education (CHE)

The regulating body responsible for all the universities in South Africa is the Council of Higher Education (CHE). Its responsibility includes ensuring that all the programs that are run in the university are credited, setting the standards for qualifications, the quality of teaching and learning determining the number of students to be admitted to each university [27]. The involvement of this council as stakeholders influences the decisions that would enhance the quality of teaching and learning.

2.2.5 University admission board

The admission board has a responsibility of ensuring that all the students admitted and enrolled meets the admission requirements as this has an impact on the quality of education in the university. Furthermore, this board must ensure that the environment in the university is conducive for teaching and environment including the relevant ICTs [18].

2.2.6 Academic and non-academic staff

Lecturers are the academic staff and play a very prominent role in enhancing the quality of teaching and learning. As the facilitators in the teaching and learning environment, they are responsible for ensuring a conducive environment that has relevant ICTs for students to engage meaningfully for learning to take place. Lecturers as professionals, are responsible for guiding, planning and evaluating the students [18].

2.2.7 The non-governmental organizations (NGOs)

For the government to accomplish the goals in the national development plan (NDP), it needs the NGOs that will assist by aligning their work with the NDP. For instance, the NGOs can mediate intervention programs, which will connect the department of education, and universities, other partners and industry. Moreover, NGOs can bring innovations that can benefit the institutions of learning. Additionally, the involvement of NGOs has a positive impact as they can influence collaboration, advocate excellence, assist in policymaking at the university level, to the attention of policy developers. The NGOs can solicit the 1% of net profit as the Broad-Based Black Economic Empowerment (BBBEE) code to be spent for socio-economic development [28].

2.2.8 Parents

Parents as stakeholders in education are responsible to ensure that the students have all the resources needed to enhance the quality of education. They are to ensure that there is food, accommodation, offer counseling to the student by encouraging them to attend classes [29]. The policy process is discussed next and illustrated in **Figure 1**.

DOI: http://dx.doi.org/10.5772/intechopen.102078

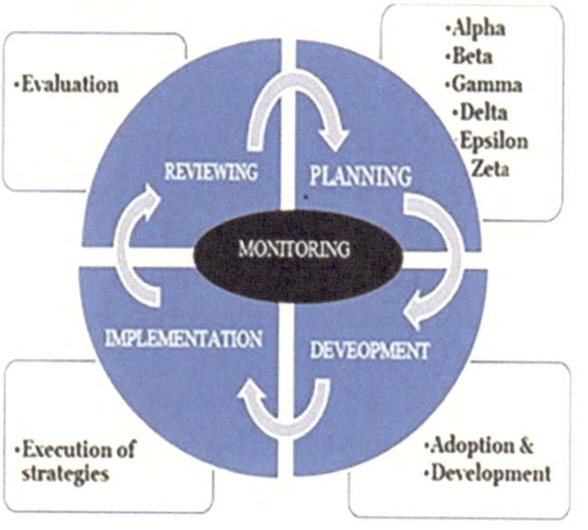

Figure 1.
Framework for ICT policy process.

2.3 Policy process

The ICT policy process as illustrated in **Figure 1** entails the planning, development, Implementation, reviewing phases. Monitoring is also an integral part of the cycle and runs throughout all the phases.

2.3.1 Planning phase

The planning phase is the initial phase of the policy cycle. This phase is sometimes referred to as the needs analysis. To conduct the needs analysis system approach is often used [30]. It consists of six levels relating to alpha, beta, delta, gamma, and zeta.

Alpha as the first level entails identifying the needs of the institution or clearly articulating the main objective to the stakeholders. In the case of changing the culture of instruction, the main objective would be integrating technology for teaching and learning to enhance students' engagement.

Beta involves establishing issues that are associated with the main objectives that can lead to its accomplishment. The baseline data is collected where the use of instruments including, survey questionnaires, document analysis, observations and interviews are employed. The data collected is analyzed. All the issues that have the agenda status that is, clearly defined are compiled in the agenda-setting. Which leads to the next phase. In Gamma as the third step, these items on the agenda are deliberated and solutions are identified, deliberated, and agreed upon. This step leads to Gamma, where the strategies to address issues raised in the first step are developed. Delta as the fourth level consists of the final report of the needs analysis which involves the compilation of the strategies to be used. The Epsilon level of the analysis entails the summative evaluation of the strategies employed to establish if they will work. For ICT integration, ICTs would be piloted [31]. The ultimate level is the Zeta level of analysis, the final level where amendment is done if needed. This level entails the compilation of a report to be submitted to the steering committee leading to the development of the ICT policy [30]. However, when the members of the working committee are not skilled, they may bring unrealistic recommendations that will hinder the implementation of the ICT policy. ICT policy [32].

2.3.2 Developing an ICT policy

The lack of a clear ICT policy poses major snags to effectively integrate ICT for teaching and learning in the universities [32, 33] argue that the school-based ICT policy planning must be in the context of curriculum reform and suggest that the ICT policy should possess the features including the institution ICT policy description that is in line with the ICT National policy. It must have a vision that serves as the blueprint or a guidepost to keep the institution focused [34]. It should include a mission statement on how the institution's vision will be achieved, objectives and subobjectives to be realized in teaching and learning an o. Have an overview of the ICT services relating to administration, education, research, a description of the university's infrastructure with the details of the hardware and the software to be installed in the lecture halls. Furthermore, the type of hardware and software general standards of how the ICT services are to be managed and supported and a plan regarding the implementation of the policies in the institution and the envisaged budget. However, the development of an ICT policy is not without challenges. These hindrances result from the lack of the stakeholders' involvement, skills and knowledge transfer that is required for a sound vision and a comprehensive ICT policy [35]. Furthermore, the incompetency of the leadership to promote the participation of the stakeholders affects the integration of technology [31–36].

2.3.2.1 Guidelines for a successful ICT policy

Fishman & Pinkard [37] postulate that the guidelines for the ICT policy should be grounded in a shared vision of teaching and learning [38, 39]. Secondly, the ICT policy must be aligned with the curriculum content and enhance the student's learning [40] in [41]. Thirdly, technology is ever-evolving therefore an ICT policy must be frequently reviewed and updated [38]. Lastly, the ICT policy development required the collaboration of all the stakeholders to be successful. However, its success depends on its implementation [42]. It is, therefore, asserted that the strategic plan developed in the planning phase should include strategies to implement the ICT policy [43].

2.3.3 Implementing the ICT policy

Implementing the ICT policy denotes the integration of the ICT to enhance teaching and learning for a meaningful engagement in the learning institution as stipulated in the ICT policy [44]. There are four dimensions of implementation relating to smart policy design, inclusive stakeholder engagement, conducive context and a coherent implementation strategy [45]. According to Aziz [46], a smart policy design consists of logical and feasible solutions to identified needs. Inclusive stakeholder engagement implies the involvement of the relevant, skilled stakeholders throughout the stages of the ICT policy. The conducive context denotes the implementation that is supported by an environment where there are relevant ICTs for students and lecturers to interact. Finally, there must be a coherent implementation strategy that outlines all concrete measures for the successful implementation of the ICT policy [47]. The implementation can be hindered by inefficient leadership, non-involvement of stakeholders, unskilled stakeholders, financial constraints, over-dependence on donors and students and lecturers' resistance [47].

2.3.4 ICT policy monitoring

Policy monitoring entails tracking the progress of policy implementation, observing the activities during the policy implementation, and identifying obstacles [48]. To allay some of the challenges associated with the policy process, it is suggested that stakeholders' participation; monitoring and evaluation with mechanisms for learning should be integrated into all the phases of the policy process [31]. Benner [49] and Maski Rana [50] assert that observations during the implementation of the ICT policies are scarce in the institutions of learning. This is due to the lack of expertise to assess the progress of strategies and activities, funding and human resource to effectively monitor the progress of the implementation of ICTs [48, 51] argue that there must be at least three units that assess different aspects of the ICT integration relating to the progress of the integration in general, activities in the classrooms, the skills and resources.

2.3.5 Reviewing the ICT policy

Reviewing the ICT policy implies evaluating the catastrophes or accomplishments of the implementation of the policy to come up with actionable outcomes [5]. According to Bratton & Gold [47] the three phases entailed in the review of the ICT policy include preparing the ground for the review, carrying out the review and finalizing the review report and disseminating the results.

'Phase 1: Preparing the ground for the review entails clearly defining the objectives to be reviewed and compiled a list of the aspects to be reviewed before the policy experts can be consulted. It is suggested that to effectively identify aspects to be assessed, previous research and reports of similar projects can be used to identify similar aspects to be evaluated. After the relevant information is identified, aspects to be reviewed may be handed over to the policy experts for consideration. It is also indicated that aspects may be assigned to stakeholders to be consulted and attend meetings where the mission will be discussed [47]. Phase 2: Carrying out the review, involves swotting the key policy components of the institution's ICT master plan and their implementation, examining the availability of human resources and ICT skills; assessing the institutional framework, scrutinizing implementation mechanisms and the roles of different stakeholders [6]. Phase 3: Finalizing the review and disseminating of the results relate to compiling a written report and distributing it to the relevant stakeholders to view and come up with the way forward [47].

For successful reviewing of the policy process, the leadership direct the reviewal and assign roles to the other stakeholders and report the progress of the ICT integration, ensuring that the stakeholders are capacitated with the necessary skills to review policies and there are relevant resources to conduct the process of reviewing and there is enough budget for the process. Furthermore, the leadership must encourage stakeholders' involvement in reviewing the ICT policy to avoid the process being the responsibility of certain individuals. If the stakeholders are not capacitated with negotiation skills, conflicts arise which results in disagreements [47].

For the ICT policy to work in the higher learning institution, stakeholders including lecturers, instructional designers, student teachers, subject heads, and ICT specialists have to collaborate in its planning and development [11]. The involvement of all the stakeholders during the development of the ICT policy promotes ownership and conformability in integrating technology [14, 52]. The collaboration of all the stakeholders is equally important in the implementation of the ICT policy [53]. In Vietnam, for instance, COVID-19 has resulted in the development of ICT policy to support blended learning [54]. Furthermore, it is posited that technology integration is more likely to succeed when the lecturers understand and share the value of ICT policies [55]. Furthermore, it is argued that many benefits could be obtained by giving students freedom of learning anytime and anywhere as education compared to traditional learning [11].

3. Method

A qualitative case study method was used to answer the question "*How can the strategy as plan, ICT policy be utilized to promote technology integration to reposition lecturers for the new normal in the School of Education?*" Imenda and Muyangwa [56] argued that in a qualitative case study, qualitative methods should be utilized and the research method should be located in the interpretive tradition. Hence in this study document analysis, an open-ended questionnaire and individual interviews were used to collect data. Atlas.ti was used to analyze data. From these instruments, 188 codes were created. These codes were clustered into 12 categories. These categories were grouped into the theme of ICT promotion to make an in-depth understanding of these categories.

3.1 Participants

Convenient and purposeful sampling was used to select the participants. Convenience sampling is a group of subjects selected based on being accessible and may represent specific types of characteristics [57]. Purposeful sampling allows one to select people or events because they are interested, relevant and suitable for the research [58]. Participants comprised of 37 lecturers, 25 females and 12 males from the four departments in the School of Education, Department of Technology and Vocational Education [21], Educational Foundations [4], Mathematics Science and Business Education [8] and Primary Education [40]. Most of the participants' age groups range between 41 years – 50 years and 51 years – 60 years. In terms of employment type, 24 were full-time and 13 were part-time.

3.2 Instrument and procedure

The instruments that were used to obtain data in this study were document analysis, open-ended questionnaires and individual semi-structured interviews. The procedure utilize to gather data is briefly explained.

3.3 Document analysis

Document analysis is a systematic procedure used to review and evaluate documents in qualitative research which includes text and images [59]. In this study, documents that were examined were Internet access policy, strategic plan curriculum development, institutional strategy, consolidation plan, technology stations policy, policy on electronic resource centres, and Internet centres policy and audit report on ICT.

3.4 Open-ended questionnaire

An open-ended questionnaire comprises questions that allow the respondents to express their opinion without being channeled to the alternatives provided by the researcher. The open-ended questionnaire was divided into two parts [60]. The first part allowed the participants to indicate gender. The second part comprises of five questions to find out more about the Strategy as Plan. The researchers developed these questions. The open-ended questionnaire aimed to establish if the lecturers were aware of the study university ICT, Teaching and Learning (T&L) and e-Learning policies. Furthermore, to find out if the T&L policy incorporates technology-enhanced teaching and learning. Also establishing if the lecturers participated in the development of the policies. Typical examples of items from this section included "Were you involved in the development and the reviewing of these policies? Yes/No. Explain" and "Does the teaching and learning policy incorporate technology-enhanced teaching and learning? Yes/No. If yes, elaborate."

3.5 Individual interview

In this study, individual semi-structured interviews were conducted with 18 lecturers. Interviews are referred to as the tools that yield an in-depth understanding of a subject at hand [60, 61]. The individual interviews consisted of one question. This question was: Were you involved in the development of the ICT policy? If yes explain. This question serves as the follow-up and verification of the responses provided on other instruments.

4. Findings and discussion

To determine the technology integration in teaching and learning, in terms of the Internet Access Policy, it was found that the provision of the Internet is clearly stated. The policy stipulated the Internet and connectivity would be provided to staff and students. It was also found that the rule on access to the Internet was available on the policy. Payne and Payne [62] support this policy and argued that the Internet is a fundamental need for technology integration to take place.

It was also found that the policy stated that, the institution's Internet connectivity and bandwidth shall be primarily intended for use by staff and students for teaching, learning and conducting research." It may be argued that the study university planned for the ICTs to be used for the benefit of teaching, learning and research. In this case, Rana and Rana [32] argued that in the strategic plan of the HEIs, ICTs intended to be incorporated to enhance the quality of teaching and learning as well as to create a platform for multimodal.

The findings show the update to the Internet would be undertaken by the ICT Services department. The policy indicated that the ICT Services is responsible for updating of policy as and when changes are required and ensuring compliance with this policy." It was also found that at a study university ICT Services department took accountability for the supervision of the execution of the policy by staff. In this regard, the policy stated that "the ICT Services is responsible for monitoring and reporting any breach of policy."

Concerning the strategic plan, findings revealed that the objectives of the strategic plan emphasize the quality of teaching and learning as well as the student-centered approach. The objectives relevant to this study included: to enhance the quality of teaching and learning for holistic student success as well as prepare diverse students for rewarding careers and responsible citizenry by providing a student-centered learning experience that is underpinned by a scholarship of teaching and learning. The student-centered approach highlights innovation in diverse learning environments [63, 64].

About the consolidation plan, it was found that this plan emphasized the strategy to capacitate the staff with the incorporation of technology in teaching and learning using the multimodal approach. The statement relating to a strategy to empower staff to integrate educational technology in T&L to achieve optimal results; introduce multimodal teaching. The multimodal approach played a significant role during pandemic at a study university to support the socio-economic background of the students, the role of study packs or printed material supported the students without access to technology and the Internet [64] and have access to the information anytime and anywhere [12]. The findings revealed that the study university had a plan to establish computer laboratories on all campuses. The university's infrastructure should be described in depth in the policy [64].

Concerning the curriculum development document, it was found that the document stipulated that all programs should incorporate technology. The document stipulated that all the new and existing programs must in addition to the particular focus of the learning area, also address areas of development in computer skills, technology innovation and technology transfer strategy and research skills. It may be argued that the curriculum development document supports 21st –century skills. In this regard, Suleiman et al. [64] argued that the 21st -century skills are necessary for the successful integration of technology.

In terms of the Study University Strategy 2014–2019 the findings reveal that technology integration was intended to support postgraduate studies by providing a conducive environment. The document stated the encouragement and promotion of postgraduate studies, research and innovation in current and emerging niche areas. The lack of relevant technologies in the teaching, learning and research environment is one of the primary hindrances for technology integration [65].

It was also found that postgraduates would be provided with technology to support the research projects. The document ensured an enabling and supportive environment through technology-based postgraduate studies, research and innovation. These findings are supported by the theory of the zone of proximal [66], where the appropriate resources are made available and accessible for the construction of knowledge.

The findings also revealed the improvement of quality of teaching and learning as well as student success. The document revealed the enhancement of the quality of teaching and learning for holistic student success. It was also found that the document promised to provide the utmost quality service to all the stakeholders. It was stated that to deliver the highest quality service to internal and external clients and stakeholders.

To establish lecturers' perception on the promotion of ICT in education to reposition them for the integration of technology in the new normal, in terms of the availability of the ICT policy, the findings revealed that the majority of lecturers were not aware of the ICT policy in the School of Education. Miss Koto and Dr. Lebelo indicated that they were not aware of the ICT policy and they were not sure if there was an ICT policy. Mrs. Tsotetsi disputed the availability of ICT policy and said, no, there was no ICT policy. However, Mr. Nyoni said, yes, there was an ICT policy. The lecturers as stakeholders would be aware if they took part in the development of the ICT policy [36].

Regarding the lecturer's awareness of e-Learning policy, the findings revealed that most lecturers were not aware of the availability of the eLearning policy. Mrs. Tsotetsi said there was no eLearning policy. Whilst Miss Pelle said she was not sure if there was an e-Learning policy. Mr. Ndlozi indicated "he had never seen the e-learning policy. Mrs. Ntanzi said she was not aware of the e-Learning policy. Mr. Nyoni indicated otherwise and stated, yes, there was an e-Learning. Lecturers must be involved in the development of eLearning policy, to increase awareness among the academic staff [36].

Pertaining to the awareness of the availability of the Teaching and Learning policy, the findings show that the lecturers attest to its availability. Mr. Nyoni, for instance, argued, "Yes, it was there we access it through the staff portal. Ms. Pelle also indicated that they always refer to it. It may be observed in this study that when lecturers are implementing the policy, their chances of awareness and utilization improve because of the collaboration of all the stakeholders [38].

Concerning the incorporation of technology-enhanced teaching and learning, the findings show that most lecturers were ignorant of this policy. For instance, Mr. Ndlozi posited, he did not know whether the teaching & learning policy incorporates technology. Mr. Pule indicated, he was not sure if the teaching & learning incorporates technology. However, Mr. Nyoni and Mrs. Nkosi posited, yes, the teaching & learning policy incorporates technology. To raise awareness of this policy, the emphasis should be made that technology is not meant to replace the teachers, but it is used as an add-on to harness teaching and learning [67].

In terms of the lecturers' involvement in the development and reviewing of policies. The findings indicate that most lecturers were not involved except for two lecturers. Mr. Booi and the rest of the lectures said, no, we were not involved in the development and reviewing of policies. Whereas Mr. Nyoni indicated, the draft was circulated, and we made inputs. Ms. Pelle indicated, yes, she was involved in the development and reviewing of policies. Ngcapu et al. [68] argue, that a bottom-up approach, is a more effective way to the policy change, in the long run, acceptance is aided by a democratic component.

Regarding the awareness of the constant development and reviewing of policies. It was found that most lecturers were not aware of the constant reviewing and development of policies except for one lecturer. Mr. Ndlozi stated, no, the institution does not constantly revise the policies. Mrs. Ntanzi indicated, "She did not know if the institution constantly revises the policies. Whereas Mr. Nyoni stated, yes, the institution constantly revises the policies. Van Der Mars [69] argues that the lack of advocacy of the policies negatively impacts its implementation.

5. Conclusion

In conclusion, the strategy as plan using ICT policy that could impact on repositioning the lecturers for the integration of technology for the new normal in education was explored. It may be observed in this study that indeed lecturers were not prepared before the COVID-19 pandemic to incorporate technology in their teaching practice. The new normal was the rapid online adoption of teaching and learning. Even though various policies were applied to the study university, it was clear during the pandemic that their implementation was not realized and was not advocated the lecturers.

During the first phase of the national lockdown, many universities in South Africa were not ready to immediately switch to remote teaching. Due to various challenges relating to lack of implementation of ICT and e-learning policies, the involvement of all stakeholders in the policy development, the unpreparedness of lecturers to teach online, digital divide, lack of network data. It was reported that emergency remote workshops serve to mitigate some of the challenges. It was indicated that the study university adopted multi-modal teaching, learning and assessment strategy to cater to the socio-economic background of the students.

It is worth noting that there was no evidence of the E-Learning policy or ICT policy. Hence, the majority of lecturers were not aware of these policies in the School of Education. However, lecturers ignored the integration of technology to enhance teaching and learning as there were training programs provided in the school of education. The lecturers were aware of the teaching and learning policy and they ensured to implement and constantly refer to it.

6. Recommendations

It is recommended that the strategy as plan using ICT policy be fundamental and populated in higher education institutions. This will enable the involvement of all stakeholders from the planning phase of the ICT policy, throughout the policy process. If this is considered The ICT policy implementation could prove successful. The involvement of the lecturing staff as the primary stakeholders can influence them to embrace the use of technology in teaching practices and prepare them to assume responsibility. Lecturers should be involved in the reviewing and the revision of the ICT and eLearning policies as they are the custodians of teaching and learning and they have more insight on what works and not with regards to technology integration in education.

Author details

Sibongile R. Ngcapu, Sibongile Simelane-Mnisi* and Andile Mji
Tshwane University of Technology, Pretoria, South Africa

*Address all correspondence to: simelanes@tut.ac.za

References

[1] Bozkurt A, Jung I, Xiao J, Vladimirschi V, Schuwer R, Egorov G, et al. Global outlook to the interruption of education due to COVID-19 pandemic Navigating in a time of uncertainty and crisis. Asian Journal of Distance Education. 2020;**15**:1-126. http://www.asianjde.org/

[2] Simelane-Mnisi S, Mji A. COVID-19 pandemic: Opportunities for online learning to unblock the minds of students during the lockdown period. In: Proceedings of the Education and New Learning Technologies Virtual Conference (EDULEARN'20); 6-7 July 2020; Spain. Palma de Mallorca; IATED Publications. 2020. pp. 8621-8629. DOI: 10.21125/edulearn.2020.2124

[3] Amrane-Cooper L. The New Normal of Online Learning in a Post COVID-19 World. University of London; 2020. Available from: https://london.ac.uk/news-opinion/london-connection/q-and-a/online-learning-post-covid-19. [Accessed: October 10, 2020]

[4] Tria JZ. The COVID-19 pandemic through the lens of education in the Philippines: The new normal. International Journal of Pedagogical Development and Lifelong Learning. 2020;**1**(1):2-4

[5] Crawford J, Butler-Henderson K, Rudolph J, Malkawi B, Glowatz M, Burton R, et al. COVID-19: 20 countries' higher education intra-period digital pedagogy responses. Journal of Applied Learning & Teaching. 2020;**3**:1-20. DOI: 10.37074/jalt.2020.3.1.7

[6] Mhlanga D, Moloi T. COVID-19 and the digital transformation of education: What are we learning on 4IR in South Africa? Education Sciences. 2020;**10**:180. DOI: 10.3390/educsci10070180

[7] Sangster A, Stoner G, Flood B. Insights into accounting education in a COVID-19. World. Accounting Education. 2020;**1**:132. DOI: 10.1080/09639284.2020.1808487

[8] Simelane-Mnisi S. Faculty Online or Remote Teaching Support Plan. Tshwane University of Technology; 2020

[9] Vlachopoulos D. COVID-19: Threat or opportunity for online education? Higher Learning Research Communications. 2020;**10**:2. DOI: 10.18870/hlrc.v10i1.1179

[10] Simelane-Mnisi S, Mji A. Preparing lecturers for remote teaching and flexible learning during COVID-19 pandemic. In: The Proceedings of the ICERI Virtual Conference (ICERI'20); 9-10 November 2020; Spain. Saville: IATED; 2020. pp. 8621-8629

[11] Siagian S, Sinambela PN, Wau Y. Effectiveness and efficiency of e-learning in instructional design. World Transactions on Engineering and Technology Education. 2020;**18**:73-77 http://www.wiete.com.au/journals/WTE&TE/Pages/Vol.18,%20No.1%20(2020)/13-Siagian-S.pdf

[12] Mintzberg H. Five Ps for strategy. In: Mintzberg H, Quinn JB, editors. Journal of Applied Learning & Teaching. Vol. 3. 1992. pp. 1-20 https://www.mindtools.com/pages/article/mintzberg-5ps.htm

[13] Simelane S. Success indicators and barriers in implementing technology enhanced courses during a professional development programme. In: Proceedings of the 3rd International Conference on e-Learning (ICEL '08); 26-27 June 2008. Cape Town, South Africa: ICEL. 2008. pp. 425-432

[14] Thurlings M, Evers AT, Vermeulen M. Toward a model of explaining teachers' innovative behaviour: A literature review. Review of Educational Research. 2015;**85**(3):430-447. DOI: 10.3102/0034654314557949

[15] Khanapurkar R, Bhorkar S, Dandare K, Kathole P. Strengthening the Online Education Ecosystem in India. ORF Occasional Paper. Observer Research Foundation; Vol. 182020. p. 282 https://www.orfonline.org/wp-content/uploads/2020/11/ORF_OccasionalPaper_282_OnlineEducation.pdf

[16] Parry K, Bryman AI, Clegg SR, Hardy C, Lawrence T, Nord WR. The SAGE Handbook of Organization Studies. 2nd ed. London: Sage Publication; 2006. 447-465. DOI: http://www.worldcat.org/oclc/64555407

[17] Asiyai RI. Improving quality higher education in Nigeria: The roles of stakeholders. International Journal of Higher Education. 2015;**4**:61-70. DOI: 10.5430/ijhe.v4n1p6

[18] Goodson IF. Professional Knowledge, Professional Lives. UK: McGraw-Hill Education; 2003

[19] Cross M, Adam F. ICT policies and strategies in higher education in South Africa: National and institutional pathways. Higher Education Policy. 2007;**20**:73-95. DOI: 10.1057/palgrave.hep.8300144

[20] Nath S. ICT integration in Fiji schools: A case of in-service teachers. Education and Information Technologies. 2019;**24**:963-972. DOI: 10.1007/s10639-018-9803-6

[21] Freeman RE. Strategic Management: A Stakeholder Approach. Cambridge: Cambridge University Press; 2010. 280p. DOI: 1034588229

[22] Sife A, Lwoga E, Sanga C. New technologies for teaching and learning: Challenges for higher learning institutions in developing countries. International Journal of Education and Development Using ICT. 2007;**3**:57-67 https://www.learntechlib.org/p/42360/

[23] Spillane JP, Diamond JB, editors. Distributed Leadership in Practice. New York: Teachers College, Columbia University; 2007

[24] Rana K, Greenwood J, Fox-Turnbull W. Implementation of Nepal's education policy in ICT: Examining current practice through an ecological model. The Electronic Journal of Information Systems in Developing Countries. 2020;**86**(2):e12118. DOI: 10.1002/isd2.12118

[25] Usman S. Governance and higher education in Pakistan: What roles do boards of governors play in ensuring the academic quality maintenance in public universities versus private universities in Pakistan? International Journal of Higher Education. 2014;**3**:38-51. DOI: 10.5430/ijhe.v3n2p38

[26] Mainardes EW, Alves H, Raposo M. An exploratory research on the stakeholders of a university. Journal of Management and Strategy. 2010;**1**:76. DOI: 5430/jms.v1n1p76

[27] Short PM, Greer JT. Themes from Innovative Efforts. New Jersey: Merrill Prentice Hall; 2002. 218p. http://www.prenhall.com

[28] Volmink J, van der Elst L. The Evolving Role of 21st Century Education NGOs in South Africa: Challenges and Opportunities. Centurion, South Africa: National Education Collaboration Trust; 2017. pp. 1-8. DOI: 10.1080/09720502.2015.1127457

[29] Alghazo Y. The theory of planned behavior and parental involvement: A theoretical framework for narrowing the achievement gaps. International Journal of Science and Research. 2013;**5**:570-572. DOI: 10.21275/v5i4.nov162664

[30] Dorner DG, Gorman GE, Calvert PJ. Information Needs Analysis: Principles and Practice in Information Organizations. London: Facet Publishing; 2014

[31] Makoza F, Chigona W. Review of challenges in national ICT policy process for African countries. In: The Proceedings of ITU Kaleidoscope on Building Sustainable Communities; 22-24 April 2013. Kyoto, Japan: IEEE; 2013. pp. 1-7

[32] Rana K, Rana K. ICT integration in teaching and learning activities in higher education: A case study of Nepal's teacher education. Malaysian Online Journal of Educational Technology. 2020;**8**:36-47 https://ojed.org/jimphe

[33] Vanderlinde R, Van Braak J, Dexter S. ICT policy planning in a context of curriculum reform: Disentanglement of ICT policy domains and artifacts. Computers & Education. 2012;**58**:1339-1350. DOI: 10.1016/j.compedu.2011.12.007

[34] Ertmer PA. Addressing first-and second-order barriers to change: Strategies for technology integration. Educational Technology Research and Development. 1999;**47**:47-61. DOI: 10.1007/BF02299597

[35] Davis K. An empirical investigation into different stakeholder groups perception of project success. International Journal of Project Management. 2017;**35**:604-617. DOI: 10.1016/j.ijproman.2017.02.004

[36] Vanderlinde R, van Braak J. School-Based ICT Policy Planning in a Context of Curriculum Reform. [thesis]. Gent: Universiteit Gent; 2011

[37] Fishman BJ, Pinkard N. Bringing urban schools into the information age: Planning for technology vs. technology planning. Journal of Educational Computing Research. 2001;**25**:63-80. DOI: 10.2190/6HDY-88WM-2QHX-QY3D

[38] Lim CP, Chai CS, Churchill D. A framework for developing pre-service teachers' competencies in using technologies to enhance teaching and learning. Educational Media International. 2011;**48**:69-83. DOI: 10.1080/09523987.2011.576512

[39] Staples M, Niazi M, Jeffery R, Abrahams A, Byatt P, Murphy R. An exploratory study of why organizations do not adopt CMMI. Journal of Systems and Software. 2007;**80**:883-895. DOI: 10.1016/j.jss.2006.09.008

[40] Hew KF, Brush T. Integrating technology into K-12 teaching and learning: Current knowledge gaps and recommendations for future research. Educational Technology Research and Development. 2007;**55**:223-252. DOI: 10.1007/s11423-006-9022-5

[41] Odukoya JA, Bowale E, Okunlola S. Formulation and implementation of educational policies in Nigeria. African Educational Research Journal. 2018;**6**:1-4. DOI: 10.30918/AERJ.61.17.059

[42] Tarus JK, Gichoya D, Muumbo A. Challenges of implementing e-learning in Kenya: A case of Kenyan public universities. The International Review of Research in Open and Distance Learning. 2015;**16**:120-141. DOI: 10.19173/irrodl.v16i1.1816

[43] Mofarreh A, Ibrahim Y. Implementation of ICT Policy in Secondary Schools in Saudi Arabia,

Doctor of Philosophy [thesis]. Saude Arabia: University of Wollongong; 2016 https://ro.uow.edu.au/theses/4718

[44] Viennet R, Pont B. Education Policy Implementation: A Literature Review and Proposed Framework. Paris: OECD Education Working Papers. 2017. DOI: 10.1787/fc467a64-en

[45] Sesemane MJ. E-policy and higher education: From formulation to implementation. South African Journal of Higher Education. 2007;**21**:643-654. DOI: 10.4314/sajhe.v21i6.25666

[46] Aziz A. Digital inclusion challenges in Bangladesh: The case of the national ICT policy. Contemporary South Asia. 2020;**28**:304-319. DOI: 10.1080/09584935.2020.1793912

[47] Bratton J, Gold J. Human Resource Management: Theory and Practice. Six ed. London: Palgrave Macmillan; 2017

[48] Adeyeye M, Iweha CC. Towards an effective national policy on information and communication technologies for Nigeria. Information Development. 2005;**21**:202-208. DOI: 10.1177/0266666905057337

[49] Benner C. Digital development and disruption in South Africa: Balancing growth and equity in national ICT policies. Perspectives on Global Development and Technology. 2003;**2**(1):1-26. DOI: 10.1163/156915003322649608

[50] Maski Rana KB. ICT in Rural Primary Schools in Nepal: Context and Teachers' Experiences [Thesis]. New Zealand: University of Canterbury; 2018

[51] Ritchie J, Spencer L. Qualitative data analysis for applied policy research. In: Bryman A, Burgess RG, editors. Analyzing Qualitative Data. 1st ed. London: Routledge; 2002. pp. 187-208. DOI: 10.4324/9780203413081

[52] Vanderlinde R, Dexter S, van Braak J. School-based ICT policy plans in primary education: Elements, typologies and underlying processes. British Journal of Educational Technology. 2012;**4**:505-519. DOI: 10.1111/j.1467-8535.2011.01191.x

[53] Keijzer N, Klingebiel S, Scholtes F. Promoting ownership in a "post-aid effectiveness" world: Evidence from Rwanda and Liberia. Development Policy Review. California: California Management Review. 2020;**38**:O32-O49. DOI: 10.1111/dpr.12469

[54] Tondeur J, Van Keer H, van Braak J, Valcke M. ICT integration in the classroom: Challenging the potential of a school policy. Computers and Education. 2008;**51**:212-223. DOI: 10.1016/j.compedu.2007.05.003

[55] Pham HH, Ho TT. Toward a 'new normal'with e-learning in Vietnamese higher education during the post COVID-19 pandemic. Higher Education Research & Development. 2020;**39**(7):1327-1331. DOI: 10.1080/07294360.2020.1823945

[56] Imenda SN, Muyangwa MM. Introduction to Research in Education and Behavioural Sciences. Ernmed Publishers; 2000 239p

[57] Henning E, van Rensburg W, Smit B. Finding your Way in Qualitative Research. Pretoria: van Schaik; 2004. p. 179p

[58] Creswell JW. Research Design: Qualitative, Quantitative, and Mixed Methods Approaches. 4th ed. Thousand Oaks: CA: Sage; 2014 342p

[59] Bowen GA. Document analysis as a qualitative research method. Qualitative

Research Journal. 2009:27-40. DOI: 10.3316/QRJ0902027

[60] Babbie E, Mouton J. The Practice of Social Research. Cape Town: Oxford University South Africa; 2001

[61] Payne G, Payne J. Key Concepts in Social Research. Thousand Oaks, CA: Sage; 2004 36p

[62] Pujari V, Sharma YK, Jathar M. Role of ICT in higher education. International Journal of Advance and Innovative Research. 2020;7:VI

[63] Richardson JC, Ashby I, Alshamari AN, Cheng Z, Johnson BS, Krause TS, et al. Faculty and instructional designers on building successful collaborative relationships. Educational Technology Research and Development. 2019;**5**(48):55-80. DOI: 10.1007/s11423-018-9636-4p

[64] Suleiman MM, Yahya AT, Tukur ME. Effective utilization of ICT tools in higher education. Journal of Xidian University. 2020;**14**:588-594. DOI: 10.37896/jxu14.9/061

[65] Ngcapu SR, Mji A, Simelane-Mnisi S. Exploring the student teachers' technological knowledge for ICTs integration. In: European Conference on e-Learning (ECEL '18), 1-2 November 2018; Greece. Athens: ECEL; 2018. pp. 686-XVII

[66] Vygotsky LS, Cole M. Mind in Society: Development of Higher Psychological Processes. Cambridge: Harvard University Press; 1978. Available from: https://www.hup.harvard.edu/catalog.php?isbn=9780674576292

[67] Feeley N, Cossette S, Côté J, Héon M, Stremler R, Martorella G, et al. The importance of piloting an RCT intervention. Canadian Journal of Nursing Research Archive. 2009;**15**:84-99. DOI: 10.1097/NNR.0b013e3181900cb5

[68] Ngcapu S, Mji A, Simelane-Mnisi S. Exploring lecturers' technological knowledge toward the teaching of student teachers in the school of education. In: Proceedings 11th International Conference on Education and New Learning Technologies (EDULEARN'19); 1-3 July 2019; Palma. Spain: EDULEARN; 2019. pp. 1808-1817

[69] Van Der Mars H. Policy development in physical education: The last best chance? National Association for kinesiology in higher education 37th Dudley Allen Sargent commemorative lecture. Quest. 2018;**70**:169-190. DOI: 10.1080/00336297.2018.1439391

Chapter 6

Lessons Learned in a Hybrid Environment

Eugenia Kovatcheva

Abstract

In the last two years in isolation, the hybrid environment for education becomes the most normal way to deliver education. The well-known design techniques are not enough for new learners from distance. The common practice from face-to-face training is neither. A lot of lessons are learned. The new combined approach is based on e-learning in combination with nugget education. The design considers learning and personal users' styles. The learning experience design takes a significant role in rethinking the course/training design in the hybrid environment. Nowadays, understanding learners' needs is most important for training design and to motivate them.

Keywords: hybrid environment, nugget education, learning experience design

1. Introduction

In the last two years in isolation, our way of working has changed. The most significant changes are in education for both teachers and learners.

A lot of authors [1–3] share the educational results in a pandemic situation. Deloitte has made several reviews about the pandemic situation [4, 5]. They take into account several factors as shifting to remote learning and students' behavior. Now most of the learners prefer to stay closer to their homes, they prefer to delay their education. Before pandemic students ran away from home to the college. The final decision will be made at the last possible moment. The universities have to be ready for the final decision and have to be more flexible in terms of the management of the enrolment process.

The long-term lessons for high education institutions are made as:

- learning analytics in action because the online training provides easily captured data that can be analyzed and then the new discoveries could be implemented for future training.
- data-driven improvement of the interaction between university/educators and learners reducing gaps between generations.

The strategies for improving learners' success and motivation could be provided as:

- support for sustainable development
- virtual innovative methods for interaction with learners
- using learning analytics to identify the gaps between generations and obstacles to graduation

In the pandemic period, each of the players in the educational process goes out of the comfort zone in terms of the educational process and the mental state. The institutions, educators and learners have to adapt to the new situation – new normal [6]. Certainly, the deepest impact is for the youngest, it is the subject of another study. In this chapter, attention is paid to the teachers, the learning process and used tools.

The migration from in-person education to online express some misunderstandings in high education teachers of the nature of the learning process from one side and unexpected learners' reactions. Different methods are considered, which are not related to specific subjects, but general educational approaches.

2. Online environment challenges

Most of the training before the pandemic was face-to-face and a small amount, of course, were presented in the learning management systems fully designed. The real contact between educators and learners is irreplaceable. The education got together a lot of challenges in the pure online environment [4–9]. Uncertainty was in the first place. The migration from face-to-face to online learning meets unprepared players. In the beginning, there was no clear strategy: how to provide courses, what kind of tools to use, what were the Internet quality access, how to examine learners, how to be sure of their identity, and so on.

Each institution has made its own decisions.

The divide problems in the digital environment cleared:

- divide in terms of access—Internet access or computer ownership
- divide in terms of digital skills and use refers to digital fluency
- divide in terms of digital outcomes—there are correlations between level of digital fluency and learning outcomes [10–12].

The same symptoms are observed, but at different depths for universities around the gloub.

Learners' behavior:

- Passive
- Kept muted
- Kept cameras off
- Do not carefully read course instructions

	Digital natives	Digital immigrants
Process information	Quickly	Slowly
Multi-/single-tasking	Enjoy multi-tasking	One thing at a time
Learning	Gaming	Serious approach

Table 1.
Behavior gaps.

Teachers' problems with:

- digital equipment: computer/laptop, camera,
- internet access
- meeting environment
- learning environment
- digital tools for collaboration

Most learners do not answer the teacher's questions. There is a difference between bachelor's and master's. Younger learners try to remain "invisible" by keeping their cameras and microphones off. Older take more part in the classes. It is important from educators' perspectives. Another aspect is learner satisfaction [13] which varies.

In order to motivate learners, some additional pedagogical and technological approaches need to be used. There must be a gap [14–17] in the digital behavior of learners and teachers (**Table 1**). They fall into different groups: digital natives and digital immigrants in terms of digital fluency with respect to technology usage in general, rather than on any specific technology [16].

Having in mind these prerequisites, the educators have to design their e-learning courses appropriate for blended and/or hybrid modes. The next section goes deeper into the "learning" terms.

3. Common understandings

The term technology-enhanced learning is introduced to describe technologies for teaching and learning in the last few decades. It is a broader term which has a lot of branches as e-learning, online, blended, flipped learning and so on. On the other side the traditional education or so-called learning in-person, distance learning has a longer history. The main question is what design to use digital immigrants to motivate digital natives in the extreme situation as a pandemic?

To answer is necessary to establish a common language (**Figure 1**).

In-person education or traditional classroom- means synchronous learning in a physical classroom when everyone is present. The educators provide new knowledge.

Distance learning describes the asynchronous process of learning. There is no contact between learners and educators. In the beginning, there is no limit to media. In the last twenty years usually, it means that everything is done through a learning management system. The initial effort of design, development of this type of education is more time-consuming.

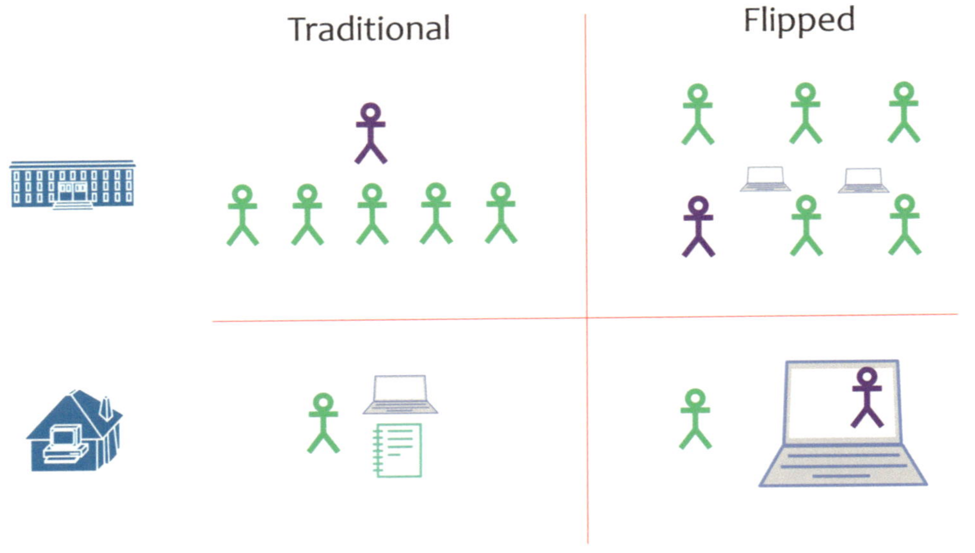

Figure 1.
From traditional to flipped education. Deliver mode: in-person or online.

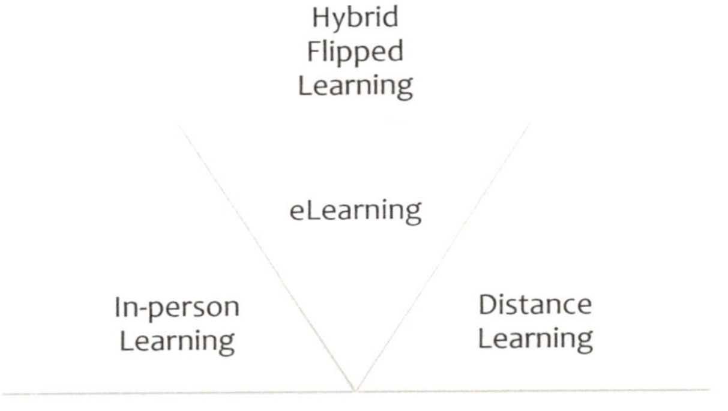

Figure 2.
Forms of education.

Online learning is a way of learning where most of the activities are done over the Net. In the pandemic days when most of the courses are online, this definition could be specified.

Blended learning is an approach to education that combine in-person and online modes. It was also known as hybrid learning. In the pandemic period, hybrid mode changes its meaning. **Hybrid learning** merges in-person and online learning synchronously. It happens when some of the learners are presented in the classroom and others are over the Internet.

Flipped learning and **Flipped classroom**– learners have direct access to knowledge, and they work at their own pace independent on time and place. Teachers serve

DOI: http://dx.doi.org/10.5772/intechopen.102575

Type of education		e-learning	In-person education	Distance learning	Online learning	Blended learning	Hybrid learning	Flipped learning	Hybrid flipped education
Type of classroom	Traditional	x	x	x	x	x	x		
	Flipped	x						x	x
Place dependent			x				x		x
Time frame	Synchronous	x	x		x	x	x	x	x
	Asynchronous	x		x		x		x	
Delivery type	In-presence	x	x			x	x	x	x
	Online	x			x	x	x	x	x
	Distance	x		x		x		x	
Learning management system		x	x		x		x	x	x

Table 2.
Forms of education and main indicators.

as mentors. Both have their contact moments in a classroom and educators can go deeper into the learning material [18–22].

The broadest definition of **e-learning** is learning facilitated by information and communication technologies, regardless of which stage of the process: preparation, implementation, delivery, management [23]. It is the more common term. Nowadays most common understanding is that a learning management system (LMS) is in use. In general, e-learning supports any form of education. The design of e-learning courses depends on the goal and abilities of educators.

All terms above are well-known. They are structured in **Figure 2**. The selected criteria from the left side relate to the conditions in the pandemic.

The last column describes the newly introduced form of education—Hybrid Flipped Education. It meets a different type of delivery and the most important support flipped classroom—the most motivating way of learning for digital natives according to the latest research (**Table 2**) [13, 18–22].

The learners' satisfaction increases in a flipped classroom. It is the phenomenon, observed by the author as well. The learning activities in flipped learning could be mixed project-based or case studies. They challenge the learners and develop their topic-oriented skills and knowledge as well as a wide-range of soft skills such as critical thinking and creativity.

In **Figure 2**, the most significant forms of education are presented. In the middle, the most supportive—e-learning. At the base of the triangle, there are two founders: in-present learning—footwear on the left and distance - footwear on the right. Going through the prism of e-learning and new approaches to motivate learners—the result in hybrid flipped learning.

Educators need to know their learners. Approaches in the learning process may be different, but the main thing is to strive to motivate learners with intriguing challenges. Working on real projects in a competitive environment is one of the most motivating [24]. Learners work at their own pace and teachers are just mentors. Creating such assignments requires effort on the part of the educators. Cooperation with business helps.

4. Course design

Course design starts with its syllabus and definition of learning outcomes. In the era of competency development, there are several standards as European Qualification Framework, e-CF and. At the beginning of the learning design process, the competence definition is the objective [25]. During the process of learning design, the competence behaviors are associated with the learning activities. During the assessment, the competence behaviors are used as the measurable indicators of learning progress. After the process, the learning outcome is the extent to which the competence is acquired (**Figure 3**).

After defining the competencies, accurate targeting with appropriate tools follows. The initial requirements for the course are defined, i.e. the minimum knowledge and skills before upgrading. The next step is knowing learners. In higher education, it can begin with knowledge of their personalities according to the Myers-Briggs methodology (**Figure 4**). There are 16 types, arranged in 4 groups. The test, which follows Myers-Briggs' methodology, returns four letters that determine whether a person is Introverted or Extroverted, Intuitive or Observant, Thinking or Feeling, Judging or Prospecting, Assertive or Turbulent.

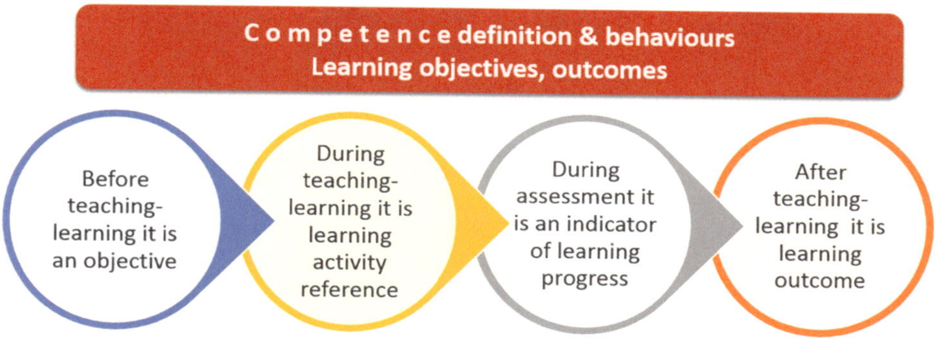

Figure 3.
Competence, learning aim, and outcome.

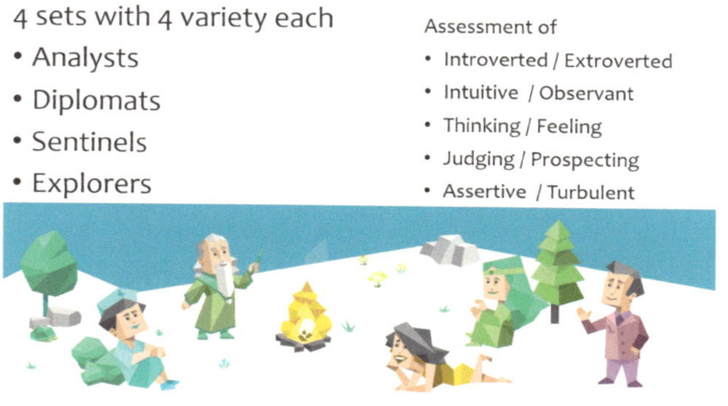

Figure 4.
16 personalities.

The main benefits of knowing the personality type are in group work and the distribution of learners according to their type in a group. The goal is to have a normal distribution of all types and especially not to have two or more leaders in a group, in opposite case collisions occur.

Equipping learners with appropriate tools and challenging them is next in the course.

Design thinking is a very powerful tool in various fields [26, 27]. It is a non-linear process with 5 stages (see **Figure 5**).

One of the tools wish to support the process is Bono's thinking heads (**Figure 6**), which can be associated with the stage of the design thinking process.

The tools especially for:

Empathy one as an empathy map. The responsibilities are to the Blue and Whitehats.

Define and Ideate stages could be covered by Green, Yellow, Red and White. Tools here are:

- Interview/questionnaires
- Observation/immersion

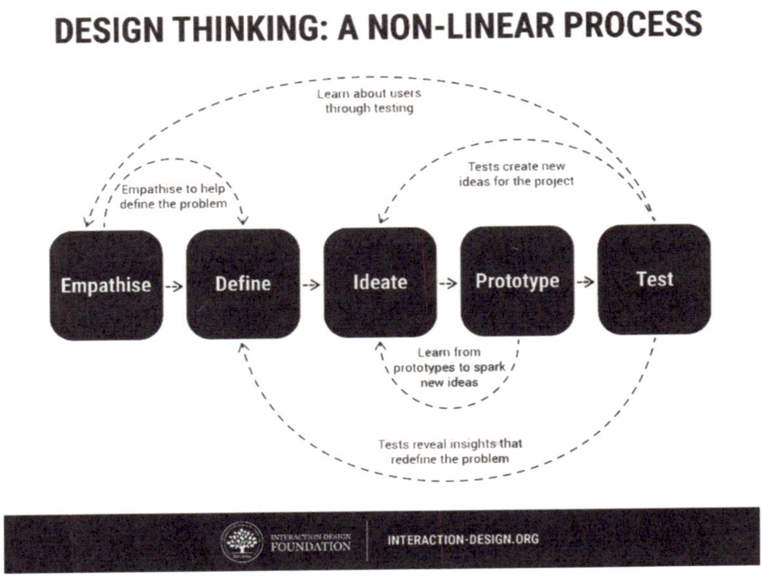

Figure 5.
Integrated design [26].

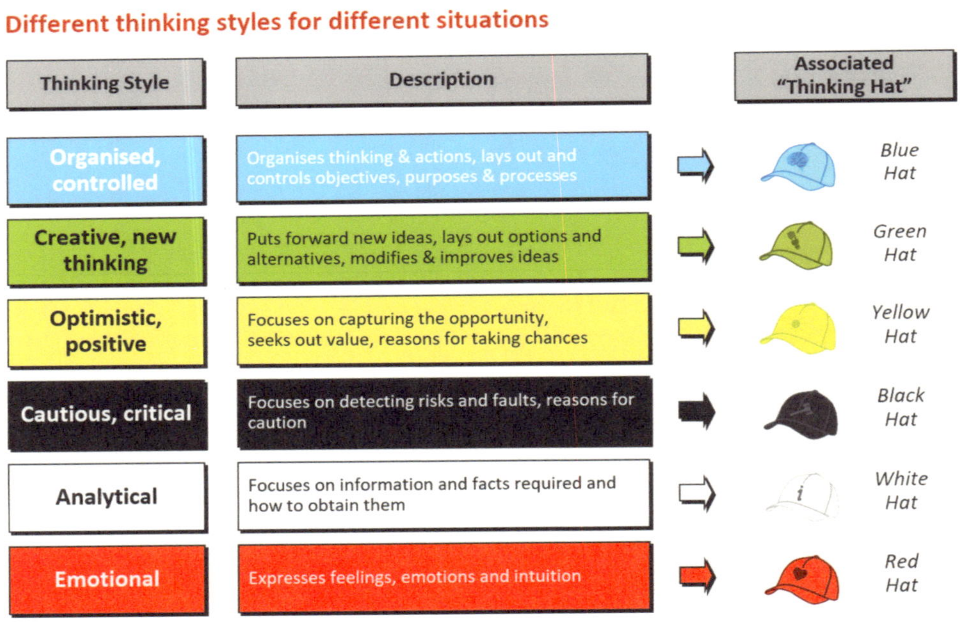

Figure 6.
Bono's thinking heads.

- Brainstorming
- Research

Prototyping—Blue, Black, White and Red hats. Possible tools are:

- Get visual
- Journey map
- Rapid prototyping
- Storyboard
- Role play
- Co-creation session
- Mindmap

Testing—Blue, Black and White. Tools could be:

- Live prototyping—a chance to run your solution for a couple of weeks out in the real world.
- Keep iterating—help you get a great solution to market and let you know where to push it when you do.
- Build partnerships—stakeholders/partnerships map.
- Roadmap—timeline and a plan of action to get your idea out into the world
- Sustainable Revenue—financial spreadsheets and forecasts on how the revenue of a certain product/solution/service would look like.
- Measure and evaluate—design the ways that you'll measure and grow it into your solution.

There are a lot of free or academic purposes tools for collaborative work. That means that learners can work together at the same place or from distance.

5. Activity design

The key to setting challenges is the clear instructions that learners need to receive: What the goal is, what is expected as a result, and how they will be assessed. It is important to see the real contribution, to be an important topic for them, to be able to empathize with it, regardless of their inner attitudes. And most of all to have fun in the process of work.

One example for Activity Design is presented in **Table 3**. The Abstract is not necessary to be. It is a summary of the full activity.

Efforts to design a course are great, the results are important in the eyes of motivated learners.

6. Conclusions

The isolation, the digital natives and the lack of in-person courses give birth to a new form of learning and teaching. The educators as digital immigrants have to see

Abstract	*Write a short (up to 60 words) description of the assignment, which should include: the topic, the age of the target group, the subject area, the style of work (individual or teamwork), the recommended time and the expected product.*
Title	If possible, write a challenging title!
Introduction	Write a motivating, short, challenging introduction.
Task	Write a short description of the task. Try to formulate it in a meaningful way for the pupil.
Goals	Formulate the learning goal/objectives (what is your goal as a teacher and/or what the pupils are expected to achieve by carrying out this assignment - with respect to subject knowledge, skills (ICT, cooperation, writing, etc.), attitudes.
Process	Describe the process step-by-step. Suggest the style of work (individual, teamwork)
Time	Give recommended time (in minutes, hours, days, weeks, ...)
Sources	Recommend appropriate sources for your pupils (websites, books, guides, activity planners)
Help	Recommend to your pupils what to do if they need help. Use instructions of the kind given below to stimulate pupils to attempt solving problems by themselves. Think about what you need to proceed further with the task. Look at the sources for help and ask your teammate for help. Only if you both do not know, ask your teacher for help.
Products	Formulate what you expect the pupils to produce.
Evaluation	Formulate the criteria to be used for evaluating the process and the product.
Appendices	Describe what needs to be developed or enclosed.

Table 3.
Examples for activity design.

insight into the situation and apply. The learning experience design takes a significant role in rethinking the course/training design in the hybrid environment. Nowadays, understanding learners' needs is most important for training design and to motivate them.

Thanks

Thanks to my sister-in-law, with whom we share similar cases in universities on both sides of the Atlantic, as well as to colleagues from the seminar on IT Innovation in Higher Education, Varna, Bulgaria October 2021, with whom we exchanged valuable ideas.

Author details

Eugenia Kovatcheva
University of Library Studies and Information Technologies, Sofia, Bulgaria

*Address all correspondence to: e.kovatcheva@unibit.bg

References

[1] Jordan K, Jones A. Editorial: Learning from lockdown special collection. Journal of Interactive Media in Education. 2021;**1**:6. DOI: 10.5334/jime.698

[2] Treve M. What COVID-19 has introduced into education: Challenges facing higher education institutions (HEIs). Higher Education Pedagogies. 2021;**6**(1):212-227. DOI: 10.1080/23752696.2021.1951616

[3] Reimers F. How can the university contribute to building a better future during the COVID-19 pandemic? Ibero-American Journal of Education. 2021;**86**(2):9-28. DOI: 10.35362/rie8624690

[4] Friedman S, Hurley T, Fishman T, Fritz P. COVID-19 Impact on Higher Education: Confronting Financial Challenges Facing Colleges and Universities, Deloitte Perspectives. 2020. Available from: https://www2.deloitte.com/us/en/pages/public-sector/articles/covid-19-impact-on-higher-education.html/#1

[5] Fishman T, Fleurimond B, Ludgate A, Peterson K, Malik N, Roberts R, et al. Five Strategies for Student Success, Deloitte Article 2021. Available from: https://www2.deloitte.com/us/en/insights/industry/public-sector/student-success-best-practices.html

[6] Shams SMR, Vrontis D. Covid-19 and the global higher education sector: In search of a new normal. In Proceeding: 13th Annual Conference of the Euromed Academy of Business: Business Theory and Practice Across Industries and Markets. EuroMed Press; 2022. pp. 1470-1472. ISSN: 2547-8516

[7] Cifuentes-Faura J, Obor DO, To L, Al-Naabi I. Cross-cultural impacts of COVID-19 on higher education learning and teaching practices in Spain, Oman, Nigeria and Cambodia: A cross-cultural study. Journal of University Teaching and Learning Practice. 2021;**18**(5):4-6. ISSN: 1449-9789

[8] Ivanova VR. Online training in higher education: An alternative during Covid-19. Strengths and Weaknesses of Online Training, Strategies for Policy in Science and Education-Strategii na obrazovatelnata i nauchnata politika. 2021;**29**(3):263-275

[9] Oliveira L, Silva P, Mesquita A, Sa Sequeira A, Oliveira A. Sadness, negativity, and uncertainty in education during COVID-19 on social media. International Journal of Online Pedagogy and Course Design. 2022;**12**(11):2-4. DOI: 10.4018/IJOPCD.2022010103

[10] Dewan S, Riggins FJ. The digital divide: Current and future research directions. Journal of the Association for Information Systems. 2005;**6**(12):298-337

[11] Wei K-K, Teo H-H, Chan HC, Tan BCY. Conceptualizing and testing a social cognitive model of the digital divide. Information Systems Research. 2011;**22**(1):170-187

[12] Zhao L, Lu Y, Huang W, Wang Q. Internet inequality: The relationship between high school students' internet use in different locations and their internet self-efficacy. Computers & Education. 2010;**55**(4):1405-1423

[13] Sáiz-Manzanares M-C, Casanova J-R, Lencastre J-A, Almeida L, Martín-Antón L-J. Student satisfaction with online teaching in times of COVID-19. Comunicar Journal 70. New challenges for teachers in the context of digital learning. 2022;**30**:33-34. DOI: 10.3916/C70-2022-03

[14] Prensky M. Digital natives, digital immigrants, Part 1. On the Horizon. 2001;**9**(5):2-3

[15] Prensky M. Digital natives, digital immigrants, Part 2. On the Horizon. 2001;**9**(5):1-6

[16] Wang QE, Myers MD, Sundaram D. Digital Natives and Digital Immigrants. Springer Bus Inf Syst Eng. 2013;**5**:409-419. DOI: 10.1007/s12599-013-0296-y

[17] Cut M, Digital Natives and Digital Immigrants—How are they Different, Digtail Reflections, Medium. 2017. Available from: https://medium.com/digital-reflections/digital-natives-and-digital-immigrants-how-are-they-different-e849b0a8a1d3

[18] Model Teaching, Flipping the Classroom Script: Flipped Learning Vs. Traditional Classroom Learning. 2020. Available from: https://www.modelteaching.com/education-articles/technology-in-the-classroom/flipping-the-classroom-script-flipped-learning-vs-traditional-classroom-learning

[19] O'Scanaill M. Flipped Classroom: A Blended Learning Model That Works. 2020. Available from: https://www.dyknow.com/blog/flipped-classroom-a-blended-learning-model-that-works/

[20] Kim NH, So HJ, Joo YJ. Flipped learning design fidelity, self-regulated learning, satisfaction, and continuance intention in a university flipped learning course. Australasian Journal of Educational Technology. 2021;**37**(4):6046. DOI: 10.14742/ajet.6046

[21] Meyliana, Sablan B, Surjandy, Hidayanto AN. Flipped learning effect on classroom engagement and outcomes in university information systems class. Education and Information Technologies. Springer; 2021. pp. 2-4. DOI: 10.1007/s10639-021-10723-9

[22] Al Mamun MA, Azad MA, Al Mamun MA, Boyle M. Review of flipped learning in engineering education: Scientific mapping and research horizon. Education and Information Technologies. Springer; 2021. pp. 4-5. DOI: 10.1007/s10639-021-10630-z

[23] Kovatcheva E. eLearning Horizons. Sofia: PH Demetra; 2013. p. 25 (appeared in Bulgarian Language)

[24] Vass V, Kiss F. Coherence Between Online Learning and Project-Based Courses in Higher Education. Lecture Notes in Networks and Systems. The Learning Ideas Conference, TLIC 2021. LNNS. Vol. 349. Springer; 2022. pp. 333-338. DOI: 10.1007/978-3-030-90677-1_32

[25] Nikolov R, Shoikova E, Kovatcheva E. Competence Based Framework for Curriculum Development. Za bukvite, O'pismeneh, Sofia. 2014. ISBN: 978-619-185-015-0, ISBN online: 978-619-185-016-7

[26] Friis Dam RF, Siang TY. 5 Stages in the Design Thinking Process. Interaction Design Foundation. 2021. Available from: https://www.interaction-design.org/literature/article/5-stages-in-the-design-thinking-process

[27] Kovatcheva E, Campos JA, Del Val Roman JL, Dimitrov GP, Petrova P. Design thinking in higher education. In: EDULEARN'19 Proceedings. DOI: 10.21125/edulearn.2019

Chapter 7

Improving Accessibility of e-Learning Templates for Students with Disabilities

Peter Čakš, Monika Ferk, Matjaž Debevc, Julija Bele Lapuh and Ines Kožuh

Abstract

Because of the effective development of contemporary technologies, also during the recent COVID-19 pandemic, students with disabilities have been increasingly integrated into the society, work, and academic environment. Accordingly, the question of how to provide accessible graphical design of e-learning materials for various categories of students with disabilities and how to comply with international accessibility standards is becoming more and more prominent. The purpose of the study was to propose recommendations for the design of e-learning materials to achieve the preparation of effective study materials for students with hearing and visual loss, as well as autism spectrum disorders. According to their needs and requirements, recommendations for the graphic design of accessible e-learning materials have been designed, developed, implemented, and evaluated. The findings revealed a higher level of acceptance of adapted material for all experimental groups and can be helpful for teachers and other professionals educating students with disabilities.

Keywords: e-learning, students with disabilities, accessibility, user interface design

1. Introduction

The spread of information and communication technology (ICT) in all parts of society and the increase of social awareness of the inclusion of persons with disabilities in the social, work, and pedagogical environment has enabled them to be more actively and effectively involved as equal actors in all areas of social activity [1].

Until recently, it was not a common practice for persons with disabilities (PWD) to publicly announce their forms of disability, but this has changed in recent years. For instance, in 2014, 27.1% of people in Europe declared having activity limitations [2]. Moreover, recent findings have revealed that over one billion people live with some form of disability [3]. Likewise, when students with disabilities (SWD) are in question, they are increasingly reporting on specific learning disabilities [4]. Over 10% of students have reported at least one special educational need (SEN), and over 5% have learning disabilities/disorders (LDs) (an overarching group of neurodevelopmental disorders that affect the development of primary and/or secondary academic abilities) [5].

The growing recognition of needs and requirements has also led to the adaptation of the accessibility of various contents, which was also recognized by UNESCO [6]. Assistive technology (AT) is deemed as 'any product whose primary purpose is to maintain or improve an individual's functioning and independence and thereby promote their wellbeing' [7]. Its implementation has the potential to improve functioning, reduce activity limitations, promote social inclusion, and increase participation in education, the labour market and civic life for PWD [8]. To be even more specific, in the study on the impact of AT use for SWD in higher education (HE), the use of AT was substantiated to increase social interactions, provide opportunities for learning support, promote active engagement with peers in course-related discussions, promote engagement in clubs or groups, and encourage the creation of a social group of AT users [8]. Moreover, the gap between assistive and general use technologies in internet tools, software, and hardware has been overcome and has allowed SWD access to a wide range of technologies [9].

Speaking about the learning process for SWD and the use of AT, the concept of e-learning must be considered. The definition of e-learning has changed through the years. Once a new type of training, can nowadays be deemed a web-based learning system for dissemination of information, communication, and knowledge for education and training [10]. E-learning, as a concept, covers a wide range of applications, learning methods, processes, and tools [5] and can be seen as an appropriate tool for SWD. The categorization of e-learning for SWD can be divided into two major groups. The first group refers to the use of AT (hardware or software, used to increase, improve or maintain capabilities of students with disabilities aimed to support and/or increase learning) [11]. The second group of e-learning, which is in the focus of this chapter, refers to a system of procedures, processes, and instructional materials that support learning [5, 12].

Today, computer-based learning management systems are the most used learning systems [13]. The reason is in its very nature. As Moore et al. [14] highlighted, all forms of e-learning could provide learning opportunities for individuals, and the incorporation of technology in education has undoubtedly improved learning for SWD [15]. Therefore, advances in computer-based education are seen as an effective way of remedying this situation by providing assistance and compensation for SWD [16].

The number of SWD attending universities is increasing [17]. Regardless of this fact, many HE institutions do not pay attention to disability, so students continue to face various barriers [9]. These include inaccessible digital course materials and websites, lack of training on how to use needed AT, poor compatibility between software used by the HE institution and students' AT, libraries that do not stock accessible digital textbooks or coursepacks, professors who do not allow students with disabilities to use their mobile technologies in class; procurement of inaccessible HE technologies that will affect teaching and learning for years, the high cost of some AT, and restricted access to computer labs [1]. SWD often report that learning and studying with ICT and related e-learning can help them [18]. It is also generally accepted that through the ICT they can overcome barriers to more successful education [19]. It cannot be overlooked that during recent COVID-19 pandemics, e-learning has been increasingly used to support students' learning processes, especially for SWD [5, 12].

Despite rich guidance and methods for the appropriate design of e-learning materials, which should enable successful accessibility for all, regardless of the type of disability [20, 21], the question arises as to how good graphic design of e-learning is. Do materials also consider the requirements and needs of SWD? The question is also whether there is an effective standardized e-learning course template for SWD. The final question that arises is how the graphic image or template of e-learning material affects the acceptance and effectiveness of the given content according to the type of disability of SWD. While general design guidelines are available [22, 23], there is, to our knowledge, a lack of studies and specific guidelines for the preparation of e-learning templates for SWD concerning different types of disabilities.

In the literature, the studies addressing the requirements of professors, disability service providers, post-secondary graduates, and assistive technologists prevail. At the same time, the problems of designing graphical user interfaces for SWD have still not been sufficiently covered [1]. In their systematic review of papers dealing with the impact of AT on educational and psychosocial outcomes for SWD in higher education, McNicholl et al. [8] found only one article dealing with autism and three with hearing impairments. A few studies have examined some dimensions of e-learning, for instance, learning mathematics [24] and distance learning during COVID-19 [5, 15, 25]. Likewise, Debevc [26] addressed the needs of students with hearing loss where the graphical image of the user interface for a website was developed. It provided the possibility of using a video sign language interpreter in the fixed and pop-up form on the website. However, in this study, there was no research on the acceptance and effectiveness of the user interface template and besides, it was designed for only one SWD category.

According to the literature, no specific standards and guidelines for graphical design of user interfaces for e-learning materials for SWD, in general, could be found, but only general rules for using additional utilities such as captions/subtitles, including an audio description of graphics, providing text-only versions and similar. These general guidelines are also set out in guidelines, such as the web content accessibility guidelines (WCAG), which are also linked to standards such as ETSI EN 301549 “Accessibility requirements for ICT products and services” [27] and other accessibility standards [28].

In the present study, which was part of a larger European Erasmus+ project Trans2Work [29] on transferring students to work environment, we examined whether the graphical design of e-learning course templates affects the acceptance of the given content according to the type of disability of SWD. We focused on the three groups of SWD, which are (1) blind and partially sighted (B&VI), (2) deaf and hard-of-hearing (D/HH), and (3) students with autism (only high functional autists with Asperger's syndrome – ASD). We designed, developed, implemented, and evaluated the effectiveness of our customized e-learning template. The study was conducted with the assistance of various national civil associations, NGO representatives, educational institutions, and medical institutions for PWD and SWD.

Based on the findings, we proposed an e-learning template to prepare appropriate e-learning materials adapted for individual types of disabilities in post-secondary education. The primary purpose was to identify the most suitable template for SWD, to design proposals of e-learning materials and to evaluate their efficiency.

2. Barriers and solutions in e-learning for students with disabilities

When preparing e-learning materials for SWD, first and foremost materials should be made accessible. Cooper [30] and Khazanchi [31] point out that e-learning materials should be designed without additional barriers for SWD, and the path to knowledge should be made easier for them. Every person, regardless of their disability, should have access to information through technology. Through the literature review, we first identified the problems that SWD encounter in the learning process and then sought appropriate solutions.

2.1 E-learning for blind or visually impaired students

Vision is the primary sense that is necessary for successful learning and development [32]. One of the main problems associated with low vision is access to information, which is only exacerbated using advanced technologies [33]. B&VI students are faced with barriers in daily life, and in their studies, they frequently require the use of assistive tools and technologies [34].

The barriers for B&VI students are different from those perceived by other people. Most e-learning environments are designed for students without vision problems. They are based on the use of visual images and interactive functions, which, however, cannot be used by students with acute visual impairments. As a result, they need to rely on applications that allow the translation of screen content and documents into more accessible formats [35].

The most common barriers for students with acute visual impairment are unavailability of websites, unavailability of learning materials, and special learning requirements related to their needs. To ensure an understanding of the concepts of teaching for B&VI students, additional learning resources created specifically for their needs are, therefore, needed [35]. In their work, Kesič et al. [36] emphasized the main barriers for B&VI students in the classical teaching approach. Based on the mentioned literature review, in **Table 1** we summarized essential e-learning solutions for B&VI, primarily relying on technology assistance.

Barriers in classical teaching	Solutions in e-learning for blind and visually impaired students
Fonts are too small.	Enlargement of the text in e-learning material.
Students need to sit close to a lecturer and in front of the blackboard to see clearly on blackboard.	Reading the e-learning material on a computer display and enlarging it accordingly.
Audible communication cannot be recorded.	Use of the dictaphone or other personal audio recorder.
Handouts are too small.	Enlargement of electronic handouts on the computer display.
Evaluation in a classical way by writing tests is difficult or even impossible.	Performing testing on a computer display.
Reading the written text is difficult or even impossible.	Use of audiobooks on different digital devices.
The lecturer must have a clear and strong voice without turning around so that the student can clearly listen to him.	Adjusting the speaking volume on a digital device accordingly.
Students cannot see clearly what is on the blackboard or the wall with the movie presentation.	Using audio description for figures or video in e-learning material.

Table 1.
Basic e-learning solutions for educating B&VI students.

2.2 E-learning for deaf or hard-of-hearing students

We defined four forms of support upon which an e-learning material could be designed for D/HH students [37, 38]: (1) sign language interpreting, (2) real-time speech-to-text transcription, (3) note taker's notes, and (4) printed or electronic saved copy of the text that was transcribed in the class. Some studies researched learning approaches for D/HH students, for instance, perspectives of AT [39], use of mobile technology, [40] and the use of AT for D/HH [38], where the SWD retained more lecture information with speech-to-text service in comparison to sign language interpreter support or studying note-taker notes or a hard copy of the text after the lecture.

When teaching D/HH students, the use of visual elements is strongly advised [36] as their problems in the learning process are defined by their disability. Therefore, photos, videos, charts, histograms, posters, sketches, etc., can be easily displayed in the e-learning material. Solutions for e-learning of D/HH are listed in **Table 2**.

2.3 E-learning for students with Asperger's syndrome

Children with ASD typically attend a regular school program because most of them do not have cognitive deficits. However, they need adjustment of lessons and help due to their other specific needs. They become very disturbed by noise, classroom, and schedule changes, so it is necessary to remove stimuli from the environment to which they are particularly compassionate, and to avoid surprises and unannounced changes [41]. With the help of e-learning, children with ASD can avoid disturbing stimuli in the classroom and learn at a distance. According to Žagar [41], computer learning is

Barriers in classical teaching	Solutions in e-learning for deaf and hard-of-hearing students
Students who use sign language as their first language need a sign language interpreter in class.	E-learning material uses pre-recorded sign language interpreter videos together with captions/subtitles.
The lecturer needs to be always facing the student so that he can read from his lips.	The student is always facing the computer display to see and read e-learning material.
The lecturer needs to have a clear and robust voice without turning around so that the student with a hearing aid can clearly listen to him.	Accordingly, adjusting the speaking volume on a digital device in case of direct connection to the hearing aid.
The student needs to sit close to the lecturer and in front of the blackboard to see clearly on the blackboard.	Reading the e-learning material on a computer display and enlarging it accordingly.
Students need mainly visual demonstration, which, however, is challenging to show in class on the blackboard alone.	E-learning material contains various graphic illustrations (photos, charts, etc.) or multimedia media (video, animation, etc.) together with captions/subtitles.
Disturbing sounds, background chatter and noises can occur in the classroom, causing problems for students who use hearing aids.	E-learning material on the computer can be listened directly using audio adapters connected to hearing aids. In this way, students do not hear noise and chatting in the background.
Students overhear important information during spoken lectures.	Audio description in the e-learning material. Important ones can be written at the end of each learning unit.

Table 2.
Basic e-learning solutions for teaching deaf and hard-of-hearing students through e-learning.

appropriate for people with ASD and among the advantages are the adjustment of difficulty and speed of progress according to the performance in solving tasks.

People with ASD are not interested in the whole subject matter provided for in the annual curriculum, but only in part. When a lecturer comes up with exactly this material, students with ASD ask a lot, which can be distracting for the rest of the students in the class. Also, time is limited by lecturers as they must stick to the curriculum and do not have time to address their questions fully. In the relevant literature, [42, 43] there is a solution to this problem. It can be solved with an avatar in e-learning material. A person with ASD can ask whatever he is interested in and for how long he wants because, according to the mentioned research, people with ASD sympathize very well and communicate with avatars. Another problem in education, which can be solved with the help of an avatar, is that it is difficult or impossible to predict in advance anything that a person with ASD will show a strong interest in. Therefore, we cannot predict which parts of e-learning materials will be interesting for them and consequently describe them in more detail. Thus, a person with ASD can ask the avatar only what interests him and avoid the learning material that does not interest him.

Based on the literature review and according to the detected barriers in classical teaching of ASD [36], we provide some essential solutions in e-learning as technology may assist these students to grasp the learning topics (**Table 3**).

It is possible to overcome frequent barriers in the classical teaching approach of SWD by using appropriate technology and applying a thoughtful approach tailored by the special needs of each SWD group. The key in the e-learning process is, therefore, the preparation of appropriate e-learning materials. Although e-learning materials are at first glance like printed ones, different solutions are needed in terms of design, development, and implementation procedures.

3. E-learning materials for students with disabilities

When dealing with e-learning materials, we do not only prepare the content (text), but we must include graphic and multimedia elements to ensure greater interactivity

Barriers in classical teaching	Solutions in e-learning for students with Asperger's syndrome
Students have difficulty in understanding the terminology or the meaning of words.	For harder-to-understand words, a hyperlink to a page that explains a particular word or phrase is included.
Students need mainly visual demonstration, which is challenging to show only on a blackboard.	E-learning material contains various graphic illustrations (photos, charts, etc.) or multimedia media (video, animation, etc.) together with captions/subtitles.
Students are confused by several instructions at once.	E-learning material contains each instruction as a visible list on handouts.
Students do not like social and/or eye contact.	Using a computer-based communication eye and social contact can be avoided.
Students do not know how to imagine alternative outcomes of situations and find it difficult to predict what will happen.	E-learning material contains a description of what was in progress before the chapter and what will follow it.
Students need a clear structure of the content.	At the beginning of the e-learning material, a clearly visible structure of the study material (index of chapters) is provided.

Table 3.
Basic e-learning solutions for teaching students with Asperger's syndrome.

and interest. E-learning materials must provide SWD with good orientation, sovereign use, transparency, accessibility, and encourage motivation to learn. E-learning material contains several types of media and comprises all the advantages provided by ICT. Namely, in addition to the text part, it can also include audio recordings, videos, animations, and simulations. A significant advantage is an interactivity allowing easy and quick feedback on exercises and tests. According to Lombardi et al. [44], professors often make online materials available on a course website, course management system or online education platform, which allows students to interact with learning materials outside the classroom. Interactivity can also be reached through interactive whiteboards (e.g., SMARTboard), study pods or via mobile technologies, which provides a wide range of learning tools, for instance, digital books with interactive elements [9].

Clark and Mayer [45] highlight two problems in designing e-learning materials. The first one is the fact that the potential of graphics in e-learning materials as visual media is underused. On the other hand, we encounter materials that authors overdecorate and overdesign because they try to achieve greater motivation. Such a design of materials can lead to inhibition of the learning process. When designing and adding graphics to teaching materials, it is fundamental that these graphics are relevant to the content.

Much of the printed learning material is unattractive to look at, does not hold an individual's attention, and does not arouse interest in reading further [46]. Therefore, Lockwood [46] believes that an essential goal in preparing materials should be to use as many resources as possible to create an environment that motivates the student. Apart from the topic, the writing process itself and the appropriate levels of difficulty, typography are also vital, which must bring high readability and make reading a pleasure. Of great importance are the design of entire pages, the placement of objects, and the application of rules. Graphic design is a vital component of texts, as it can significantly raise a student's level of motivation [46]. For instance, using a graphic organizer for students with learning disabilities [47] or students with ASD in teaching mathematics [48].

When using graphics, integration of text is very important, as a poor connection of these elements can lead to student confusion. A study has shown that poor integration of text and graphics can lead to distraction because visual elements take on attention that would otherwise be focused on important information [49].

3.1 Prototyping e-learning material for students with disabilities

Preparing e-learning material for SWD demands different preparation and design of e-learning materials. Accordingly, in the following subsections, we provide recommendations for B&VI, D/HH, and students with ASD. Recommendations are provided individually for each group of students, as their needs and requirements differ.

When providing recommendations for the accessibility of e-learning materials to SWD, we followed the recommendations on online accessibility and guidelines WCAG, as both e-learning materials and websites for SWD are accessed through the same user interface. WCAG defines [50] the following principles when designing e-learning materials for SWD: (1) perceivable, (2) operable, (3) understandable, (4) and robust. Each principle includes guidelines with success criteria. Standard ETSI EN 301549 [27], for example, specifies requirements for ICT to be accessible for people with disabilities, emphasizing that ICT must enable SWD to search for, identify and implement ICT and access the provided information, regardless of physical, cognitive, or sensory abilities. European standard ETSI EN 301549 was updated to adopt WCAG for information and communications technology (ICT), including web content, electronic documents, and non-web software, such as native mobile apps.

According to Cooper [30], it is recommended to all educators to include at least the following guidelines in the design of web or software course components:

- Allow for user customisation.
- Provide equivalent visual and auditory content and interface elements.
- Provide compatibility with assistive technologies.
- Allow access to all functionalities from the keyboard alone.
- Provide context and orientation information.

The above-listed recommendations were used as the main foundation in our prototyping for e-learning materials for SWD.

3.1.1 E-learning material for blind or visually impaired students

When preparing e-learning material for B&VI, we must pay attention to those who use screen readers and/or screen magnifiers. As to the use of screen readers, we must be careful to write all the information. We also need to write what we see in the pictorial material. It allows screen readers to pass on the information about what is in the image to blind people, as the computer program cannot describe the image material at this time.

Regarding those who use screen magnifiers, however, we need to pay attention to appearance and shape. It should not be taken for granted that all the information that is written and the pictorial material will be seen without difficulty. Instead, we must consider the following layout of the e-learning material:

- High contrast: Between the background and the foreground elements, such as text and graphic elements, there must be a high contrast for visually impaired people to distinguish the elements from each other. The most commonly used high contrast is black on white. The Iris Center recommends the use of the highest possible color contrast [51].
- Capital letters: Text must be larger than usual. The Iris Center recommends a font size of at least 18 pixels [51].
- Non-serif font: Letters must be easy to read, so a non-serif font is recommended, as it does not add ornaments on the letters, and the text is easier to read. The Iris Center recommends the Arial and Tahoma fonts [51].

In accordance with the recommendations for e-education of B&VI students, the following elements of e-learning material should be used (**Figure 1**):

1. Title (title of the lecture or chapter).
2. Text (we need to make the text visible, so we need capital letters and non-serif font).
3. Audio-audio recording of all information (all information recorded must also be available in audio form, despite the possibility that the person is using a screen reader).

DOI: http://dx.doi.org/10.5772/intechopen.101931

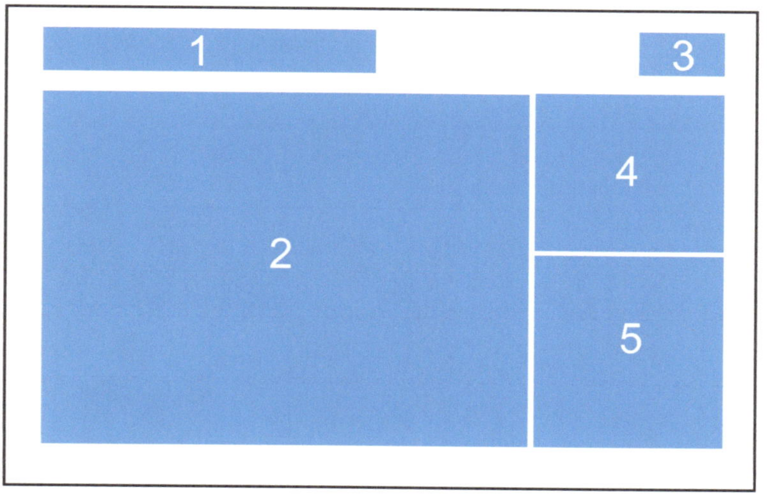

Figure 1.
Prototype of e-learning template for blind or visually impaired students.

4. Graphic element (if necessary, the text can be enriched with a graphic element).

5. Annotation to the graphic element (if we use a graphic element, we must describe in the caption what we see in the picture).

3.1.2 E-learning material for deaf or hard-of-hearing students

In the literature, two appropriate examples of e-learning materials for the D/HH were examined, and we followed the initial design. We immediately noticed that the examples of e-materials differ from other conventional e-materials, due to the video with the sign language interpreter and captions/subtitles. This is essential for e-materials for the D/HH, as we do not need it for the B&VI and people with ASD. Both examples also contain the title, text, and pictorial material, which are highly recommended for e-materials for the D/HH. Another example includes a video with a lecturer that D/HH can read from his lips, the possibility of multilingualism, which is needed only for international e-materials, and the possibility of sound, which is more important for the B&VI than for the D/HH persons.

Based on the recommendations for e-learning of D/HH described in the previous chapter and judging by two good examples of the proposal of e-learning material for D/HH (**Figure 2**), we can understand that we need to use the following elements of e-learning material (**Figure 3**):

1. Title (title of the lecture or chapter).

2. Text (all information must be written).

3. Graphic elements (it is recommended to support the text with pictorial material, as visual demonstration is recommended for D/HH).

4. Video of the lecturer (if possible, in addition to the text and pictorial material, include a video with a lecturer so that both D/HH can see his gestures and thus read from their lips).

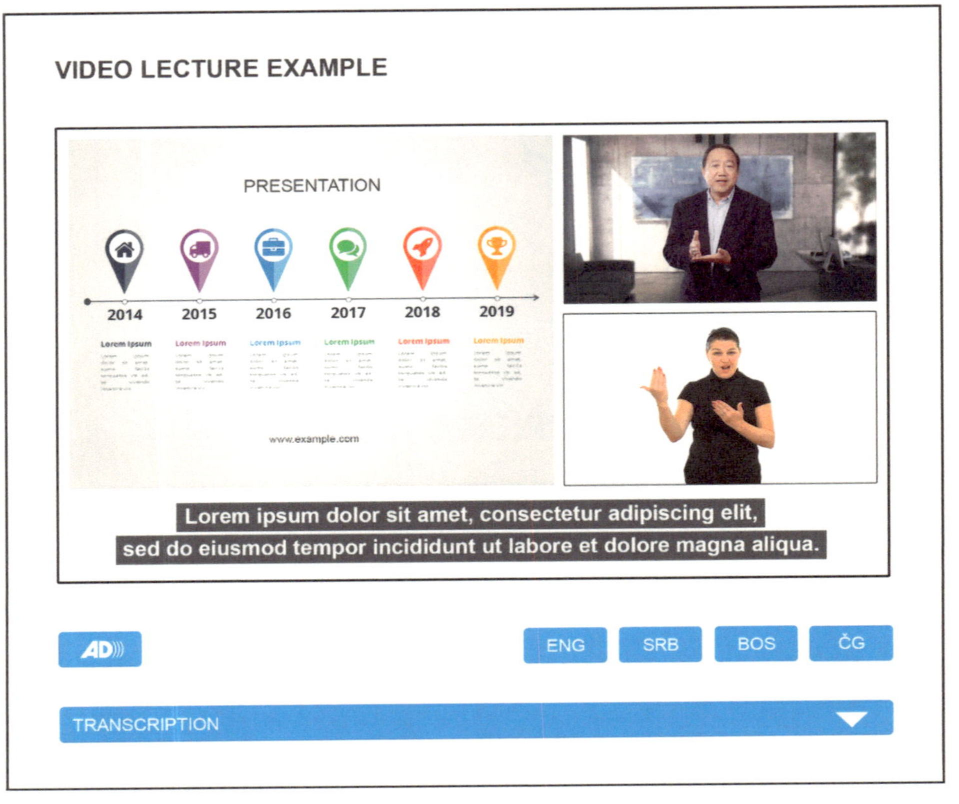

Figure 2.
Example of an e-learning template for deaf or hard-of-hearing students.

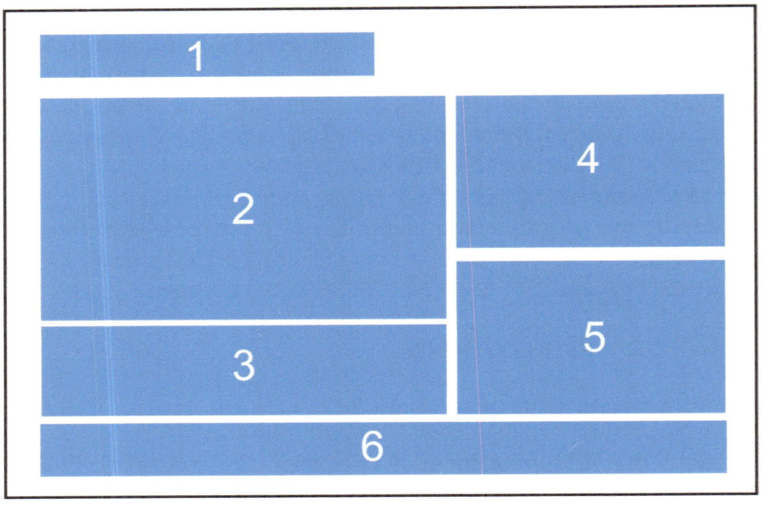

Figure 3.
Prototype of e-learning template for deaf or hard-of-hearing students.

5. Video with sign language interpreter (if possible, including sign language interpreter video, as some D/HH use sign language as their first language).

6. Captions/subtitles (under the video with a lecturer or with a sign language interpreter, we must add captions/subtitles so that D/HH can read what a lecturer or sign language interpreter is saying).

3.1.3 E-learning material for students with Asperger's syndrome

Persons with ASD are the most unpredictable of our three groups of SWD. Hearing problems are common to D/HH students, vision problems are common to B&VI students, and students with ASD have very different needs. Therefore, it is difficult for these people to make universal recommendations that would apply to everyone. Some are attracted to the blue color. Others would immediately close the e-learning material when looking at it. Even the pictorial material can be liked by someone, but someone else associates the motive in the picture with a bad experience and panics. Nevertheless, based on the literature some recommendations should be used for all people with ASD. It is advisable to stick to them when preparing e-learning material:

- At the beginning of the e-learning material, we prepare an index and present the structure of the learning material to acquaint the person with ASD what the course will be like so that there will be no surprises.

- Each page of the e-learning material must have navigation showing the previous and following chapters so that the person with ASD is not confused and knows what to expect.

- We use plenty of pictorial material, as people with ASD have a visual way of thinking and mostly describe their thoughts with pictures.

- Difficult words (terminology) and phrases need to be described in more detail. It is best to use a hyperlink for these words or, if this is not possible, at least a note where we write a word's meaning (definition). The same applies to phrases or proverbs, as people with ASD take them literally.

- For possible questions regarding a specific subject, we use an avatar, which, in addition to the presentation on the topic on the learning e-learning material, can also answer their questions.

The prototype website (WordPress) for people with ASD was created in 2015 as part of the European project Autism&Uni [52] and is intended for research, design, production, and evaluation of tools to help people with ASD during their studies (**Figure 4**). As we can see from our list of recommendations, it contains only a few graphic elements and content navigation. We can conclude that the prototype is poorly designed, does not solve the problems that people with ASD have online, and does not attract them.

From the recommendations for e-learning for students with ASD, we can understand that we need to use the following elements in e-learning material (**Figure 5**):

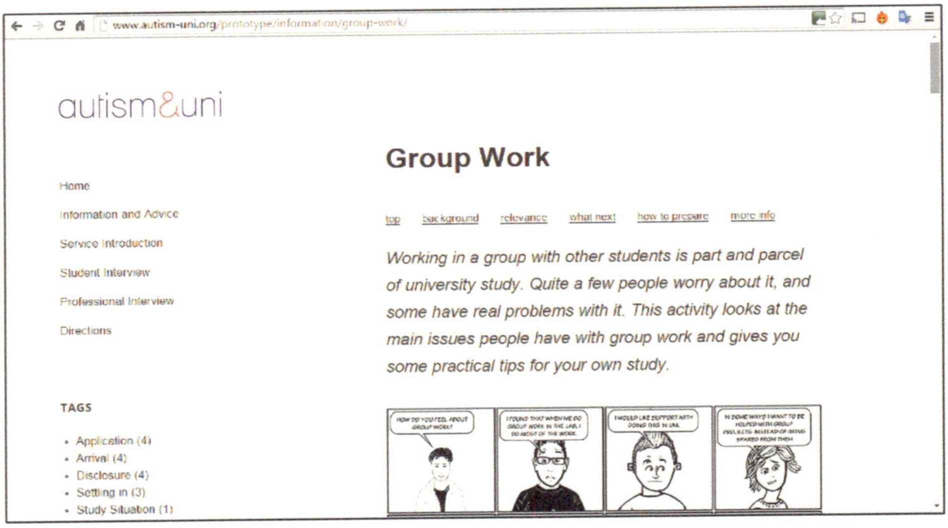

Figure 4.
Example of a website for students with Asperger's syndrome [52].

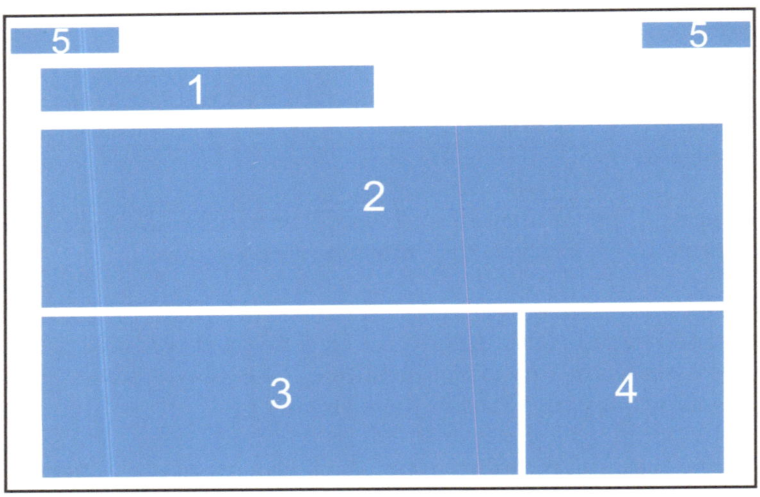

Figure 5.
Prototype of e-learning template for students with Asperger's syndrome.

1. Title (title of the lecture or chapter).

2. Lots of graphic elements (they need a lot of graphic elements as they visually memorize the material).

3. Text (we need to write clear and concise sentences that are complemented by graphic elements).

4. Avatar (use it so that people with ASD can ask what they are interested in. In addition to answering the questions, they can also describe the material on the

learning e-learning material and so people with ASD gain information through reading, visual demonstration, and sound, which dramatically affects the memorization of the given information).

5. Navigate with information about the previous and next chapters.

3.2 Evaluating prototypes: a case study

Our study was mainly intended to assess the approval of e-learning templates based on literature recommendations and prototypes. We created several examples of a PowerPoint presentation handout, namely one non-adapted disability (neutral handout), only based on the text, which we compared with a customized handout for an individual studied group of SWD. This was presented in the questionnaires only in the form of a captured image. Along with each handout, the survey also contained an attribution of the content elements represented on the handout.

3.2.1 The case

To explore the possibilities of e-learning materials, we have conducted a pre-survey of frequently used methods in the field of study. A review of several studies [53, 54] dealing with similar questions about SWD showed that a survey experiment method was used to investigate such questions. As a result, we also decided to collect data using the survey process, so that we would use the survey questionnaire as a measuring instrument.

Our study focused on three groups of SWD, namely (1) blind and visually impaired (B&VI), (2) deaf and hard-of-hearing (D/HH), and (3) people with ASD (only highly functional autistic people with Asperger's syndrome participated in the study). In connection with the latter, we aimed to find participants for each of the groups who met the following criteria: the person is computer literate, the person knows the education process, and the person has prior experience in using electronic material.

3.2.2 Research content design

In preparing the unadjusted disability handout, we followed the recommendations [55]. The neutral handout contained only the title and text with the recommended shape and font size. In contrast, the customized handouts were designed according to the recommendations and prototypes to produce e-learning material for SWD. The planned scheme of e-learning materials for individual observed groups is defined in **Table 4**.

As shown in **Table 4**, each experimental group of persons first evaluated the neutral and then the adapted e-material. According to the specific needs of each group, we prepared a separate customized handout for each of the groups, specific to them or their needs. The production of these e-learning materials is presented in the following sections.

We designed the text on the handout as simple, neutral, and understandable as possible. We followed the presentation at the annual Microsoft event, held on 26 October 2016. At the event, a fig tree was presented as an example of a presentation. In our case, we used the Slovenian symbol—a linden leaf. The material for the e-learning material was taken from the website [56]. An example of an unadjusted disability handout is shown in **Figure 6**.

Deaf and hard of hearing	Blind and visually impaired	Asperger's syndrome SD
E-learning material with written information.	E-learning material with written information.	E-learning material with written information.
E-learning material with video sign language interpretation.	Verbal-auditory conversion of visual communication e-learning materials.	E-learning material with content presented by multimedia media.

Table 4.
Planned scheme of e-learning materials for individual observed groups of persons with disabilities.

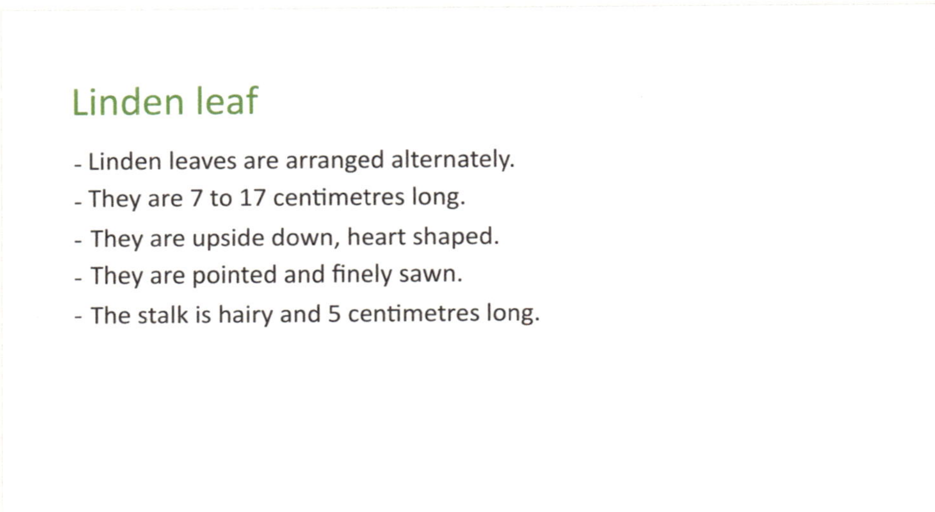

Figure 6.
Neutral handout.

3.2.3 E-learning material for blind or visually impaired students

According to the recommendations, it was necessary for visually impaired (VI) people to make the text visible, to enable audio-audio recording of information, and to add a graphic element, which also has a description of the content of the graphic. Based on these recommendations, we produced the handout shown in **Figure 7**.

In addition to basic information (title and text), the presented handout also contains a button—an audio recording (above right), which enables voice playback of recorded content, an image, and a caption to the image, which describes what we see in the image. The text differs from the text on the neutral handout, where only keywords are written, as whole sentences are written here for the case of a visually impaired person using a screen reader.

When creating the handout, we also followed the recommendations to produce materials for the visually impaired [51] and thus increased the font, and accordingly, used non-serif font and increased line spacing.

Figure 7.
Handout for blind or visually impaired students.

3.2.4 E-learning material for deaf or hard-of-hearing students

When preparing e-learning material for the deaf and hard of hearing, we wrote down all the information, added graphic elements and a video with a sign language interpreter on the handout, according to the recommendations. In doing so, we also included the video with the sign language interpreter and captions/subtitles so that

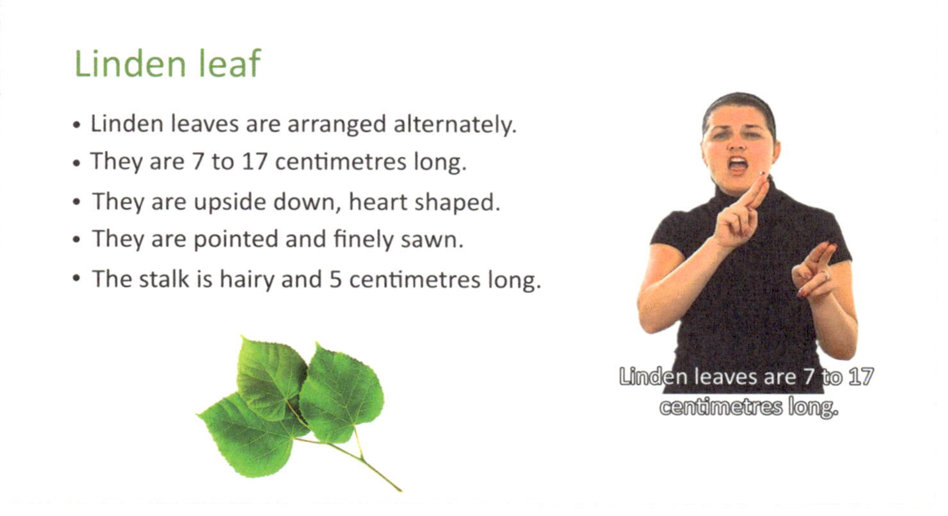

Figure 8.
Handout for deaf or hard-of-hearing students.

people can also read the content. Based on the mentioned recommendations, we designed the handout shown in figure (**Figure 8**).

It can be seen from **Figure 8** that the handout contains the entire text as presented by the lecturer. In addition to the text, it also contains visualizations with an image (bottom left), a sign language interpreter on the right who interprets the provided text in national sign language together with captions/subtitles.

3.2.5 E-learning material for students with Asperger's syndrome

The last experimental group in our study were people with ASD or Asperger's syndrome. Based on the recommendations, it is necessary, when teaching this group of SWD, to include as many graphic elements as possible, the text must be clear and concise, the handbook must contain straightforward navigation, and it must have an avatar, which allows students to access additional information on the selected topic. Based on the mentioned recommendations, we designed the handout shown in **Figure 9**.

According to the recommendations, our handout contains various visualizations with outlines of the information available in the text. The upper part provides additional information on navigation in the e-learning material, and the handbook also contains an avatar that allows accessing additional information whenever needed.

3.3 Participant recruitment

We found the respondents with the help of associations that connect PWD and organized meetings with them. Both paper-based and online surveys were applied. Although the survey was anonymous, anyone wishing to participate in the live survey signed a consent form to participate in the survey. If the participant was aged 18 or lower, the consent was signed by the parents or guardians. All participants in the survey process had the opportunity to withdraw from the survey process at any time or terminate their cooperation.

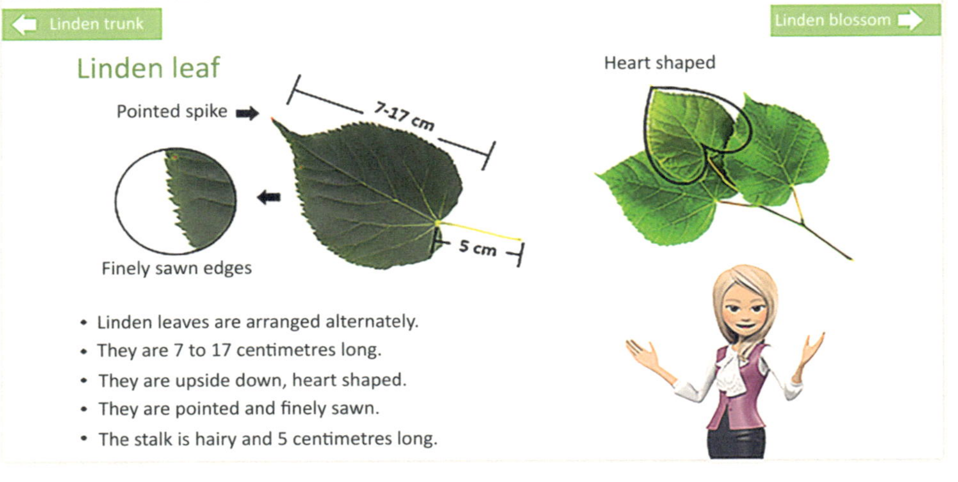

Figure 9.
Handout for a student with Asperger's syndrome.

The study was designed and implemented in line with the Declaration of Helsinki by the World Medical Association [57] and the Ethical Principles released by the American Psychological Association [58].

3.4 Measuring instrument

We prepared a questionnaire for each of the three experimental groups of SWD, as the adapted handouts of e-learning material differ from each other. The exception was a group of blind people, as they cannot see the handouts of the e-learning material. For this group, we removed the handouts from the survey questionnaire and left only questions that did not contain pictorial material. Because of the removal of handouts, we adjusted the survey a bit so that, despite the different forms of the questionnaire, we obtained enough information about their opinion on e-learning materials. The design of the survey was adjusted to the needs and requirements of B&VI [51].

The questionnaire contained two sets, namely the capture of demographic data and the evaluation of e-learning materials. The survey questionnaire consisted of explaining its intentions, one open-ended question, and six to nine closed-ended questions (depending on the type of questionnaire). We used closed questions with answer choices between the given answers and open-ended questions (age – a year of birth). For some close-ended questions, we used the Likert scale to answer questions, which is one of the most used instruments for measuring variables, such as motivation and self-efficacy [59].

The second part of the questionnaire was intended to evaluate e-learning materials, which was conducted so that the respondents (blind people were excluded here) evaluated the two handouts of e-learning materials presented in the previous subchapter. We had a problem in determining evaluation questions on elimination, as most of the evaluation questionnaires (user interface satisfaction questionnaire – QUIS, perceived usability and ease of use – PUEU, attributes of Nielsen usability – NAU, Questionnaire on computer system usability – CSUQ, Practical Heuristics usability – PHUE, and similar according to Edutechwiki [60]) are composed of assessing the actual performance of either a website, program, mobile application, or PowerPoint presentation. We used only the PowerPoint presentation handout for evaluation. As a result, we had to use questions that related only to our handouts and were not standard (the information on the handout is understandable, the handout is transparent, etc.).

To evaluate the given handouts, we identified nine five-point Likert type [61, 62] statements, based on which the respondents expressed their chosen level of agreement, namely:

1. The information on the handout is comprehensible,
2. The handout is transparent,
3. The handout provides sufficient information,
4. The handout is attractive
5. Nothing bothers me on the handout
6. The information is reasonably organized
7. With the help of a handout, I quickly learn something new

8. The handout is boring (reversed question)

9. The information is arranged in a meaningful way.

3.5 Procedure

The survey was conducted so that the respondents first assessed the handout that was not adapted to their disability. Then, in the same way, they assessed the handout of the adapted e-learning material. The questions, claims, and grading scales were identical on both handouts, which allowed us to compare respondents' agreement with the claims on the two given handouts. This answered the research question: Does the form of the e-learning template affect the acceptance of the given content of e-learning materials and the understanding of this content among people with special needs?

To verify with certainty whether the form of the e-learning template influences the acceptance of the given content of e-learning materials and the understanding of this content among people with special needs, we prepared an additional closed-ended question on the previous two questions. We wanted to get the opinion from the respondents on the importance of certain elements in the e-learning material. For each experimental group of SWD, we used statements with different elements in the e-learning material, which the respondents then rated with the Likert agreement scale.

B&VI respondents were asked about the importance of the contrast between the text and the background, the enlarged text, the use of images and graphs, and the captions to images describing the image in the e-material. We asked blind respondents about the importance of the audio recording in the e-learning material, the caption to the pictures with the audio description of the pictures, and the recording of the whole text as it would be read by the lecturer and not just keywords. Respondents with ASD were asked about the importance of using images and graphs, additional information, navigation, and a dictionary in the e-learning material. D/HH participants were asked about the importance of writing the entire text, images and graphs, sign language interpreters, video, and captions/subtitles in e-learning material.

3.6 Results

The D/HH survey results showed that, on average, respondents expressed neutral agreement with the unadjusted disability handout (3.0). In contrast, the adapted handout showed a higher acceptance rate, by as much as one level (1,1) to 4.1, which according to the five-point rating scale means that, on average, respondents from the group agree with the adapted template. An even significant difference was found in the handout boredom analysis, where the rate of agreement with the statement decreased from 3.7 to 2.0, representing a difference of 1.7 degrees. In this way, we substantiated that the adapted template for the D/HH group is much more interesting, which can affect the concentration and interest in the presented content (**Figure 10**).

When analyzing the importance of the participation of elements in e-learning materials, we also substantiated that all the proposed elements in e-learning materials are desirable, as at least 68% of respondents agreed with the presence of the given elements (use of whole sentences and captions/subtitles when using video), followed by using a video with an interpreter (84%) and the graphic elements (92%).

The next studied group were B&VI respondents. Because of the different abilities to perceive content (the difference between poor eyesight and blindness), we prepared two different questionnaires for this group. We did not include visual aids

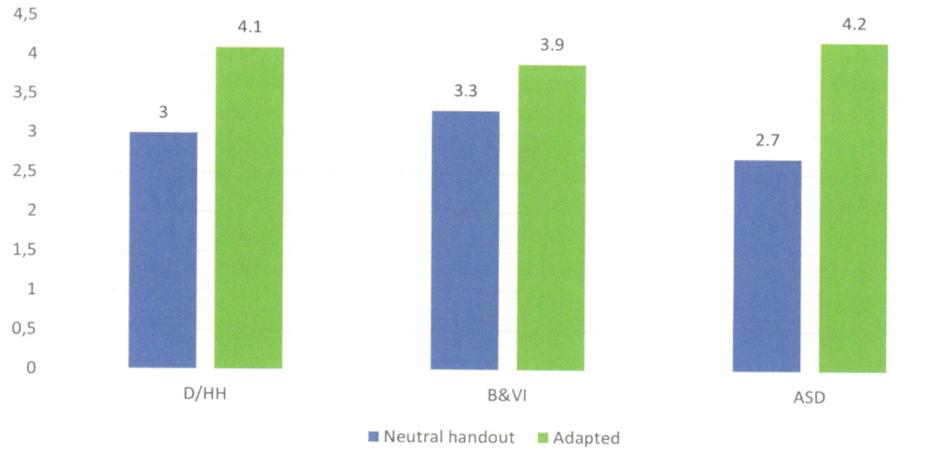

Figure 10.
Summary data of adapted handout assessment.

for the blind. The results for the visually impaired are described first, followed by the results for the blind.

In the visually impaired group of respondents, the results showed that the studied group agreed with the statements related to the unadjusted handicap of disability on average with a value of 3.3, which expresses neutrality. Compared to the neutral, the agreement with the adjusted handout increased on average by only 0.6 points to 3.9. We proved that the adapted proposal seems better to the mentioned group, but we did not achieve a significant difference.

The same applies to the claim related to the monotonous nature of the proposal, where the rate fell from 3.4 to 2.6, which also showed that although the adjusted yield was less tedious, it did not prove to be to a lesser extent reduce the boredom of the handout.

A minor degree of improvement can also be attributed to the results of claims related to the presence of elements in the e-learning material, where it was shown that for certain respondents some elements in the e-learning material were even undesirable. This was significantly evident in connection with the added visual materials, where 13% of respondents found it irrelevant to include graphic elements in the e-learning material, which can consequently be attributed to differences in the level of visual impairment, as it also depends on the ability to perceive such content. Despite the above, most respondents agreed with the given elements, namely 63% using images and graphs, 69% attributing information to them, and 86% with high contrast between text and background and increased text in e-learning material.

In the questionnaire, blind respondents assessed only the importance of the elements in the e-learning material. The results showed that the most important thing for this group is that the e-learning material contains a textual description and the pictorial material (76%), followed by the fact that the e-learning material contains the entire text and not just keywords (63%). However, a more significant difference is observed in the participation of the audio recording, where it turns out that 28% consider this option necessary. This result can be attributed to data on the use of screen readers, where the use of it was confirmed by 88% of blind people. As a result, we can conclude that they do not need audio content in e-learning materials, as they have already overcome this barrier by using a screen reader.

The last of the groups studied were respondents with ASD. Of all the groups studied, this group showed the most significant difference between the assessment of unadjusted and adjusted disability benefits. Respondents rated the unadjusted handout with an average level of 2.7, while they rated the adjusted handout with a grade of 4.2, representing a difference higher than 1.5 grade. This can also be attributed to the importance of visual elements in the materials for the mentioned group.

A similarly high difference was also shown in the analysis of the statement "Handout is boring," where the rate between handouts decreased from 4.2 by 2.5 to 1.7. It can be concluded that for respondents with ASD the adjusted handout proved to be much more appropriate than neutral.

ASD respondents also confirmed with a high degree the presence of the proposed building blocks in the e-learning material, namely two of the options (the use of graphic elements and the presence of definitions and a dictionary of words used) were 100% selected as an essential element. The possibility of asking for additional information seemed vital to 91% of respondents. The discrepancy was shown only in the case of the presence of navigation in the e-material, where this element was chosen as necessary by only 58% of respondents. We can conclude that of all the proposed elements, this one seems to be the least important.

3.7 Discussion and guidelines

In our study, we found that SWD face several problems when using e-learning materials, although they provide access to information and more opportunities to interact. There are quite some accessibility-related barriers in printed educational materials, which can be overcome by using e-learning materials. It is essential that e-learning materials can be understood by everyone, so they can navigate, interact, and co-create.

We expected the results of our study would show that the form of the e-learning template affects the acceptance of the given e-learning material content also on understanding the content among selected groups of SWD. The results of the analysis of the experimental groups showed that the form of the proposal in the case of all groups affects the acceptance of e-learning materials, where the biggest difference was shown in the case of ASD and the smallest in the case of B&VI.

Regarding the D/HH group, we expected that the template, which contains a written form of providing information or video interpretation with sign language, would affect the acceptance and understanding of the content. Our expectations were justified, as D/HH respondents confirmed that the form of the e-learning materials template influenced their acceptance of the given content of the e-learning materials and their understanding of the content. The information on the adapted handout was more understandable, sensibly organized, and distributed to D/HH than the non-adapted handicap. Also, the adapted handout was more transparent, interesting, and provided them with more information. In the survey questionnaire, D/HH respondents also confirmed that the video with sign language interpretation and the sharing of captions/subtitles are vital in the e-learning materials. Also important is the inclusion of graphic elements and entire sentences as if read by the lecturer and not just the keywords.

In the group of B&VI, we checked whether the written form of providing information or verbal-auditory transformation of visual communication of e-learning materials affects the acceptance of the given content and its understanding. The survey results confirmed the research question, as the B&VI confirmed that the form of e-learning templates influenced the acceptance of the given content and the understanding. Although the difference between the two handouts in this group was the most minor (0.6 degrees), (VI) respondents rated the adapted handout of e-learning material with a higher grade than the unadjusted handout of disability. The adapted handout was, in their view, more transparent, attractive, and provided them with more information. The information on the adapted handout was more understandable to them, sensibly organized, and arranged. With its help, we would also learn new things faster. In the survey questionnaire, 86% of VI confirmed the importance of text size and high contrast between text and background, 63% confirmed the importance of including graphic elements and 69% of their descriptions in e-learning material. The results indicate that the inclusion of graphic elements is not so important for the studied group. However, if they are present, it is vital that they contain an additional description.

Like the previous groups, in the group of ASD, we expected that the form of a template with a written form of providing information or visual communication with the help of multimedia media would affect the acceptance of the given content of e-learning materials and their understanding. Here, too, our expectations were justified, as the respondents with ASD confirmed that the form of the e-learning template influenced their acceptance of the given content of e-learning materials, as well as their understanding of this content. According to respondents with ASD, the adjusted handout was 1.5 degrees better than the unadjusted one in terms of transparency, interest, provision of information, number of interfering elements, meaningful layout, speed of memory, and comprehensibility and organization of information. Absolutely all respondents with ASD confirmed that the presence of definitions, vocabulary, and graphic elements in the e-learning material is essential. A total of 91% of respondents thought that they could ask for additional information at any time in the learning process, which indicates a tendency to use an avatar in e-learning material. However, just over half of them believe that navigation should be included in e-learning material.

4. Conclusion

When conducting the study, we found no standardized e-learning templates for SWD, except a few e-learning templates and quite a few recommendations [9, 30, 51]. However, it is very important to adhere to the provisions of the ETSI standard when creating e-learning materials and to consider that a multidisciplinary approach is then needed in designing, developing, and providing learning environments, learning materials and in the use of tools and devices if the aim is to consider all specific requirements in SWD e-learning [5].

The legislation also does not define how e-learning materials for SWD should be conceptualized and designed. We have found in the legislation only directives for the accessibility of PWD to the Internet. On 3 December 2012, on the International Day of Persons with Disabilities, the European Union adopted a Directive on the accessibility of websites of public sector bodies that provide essential information and services to citizens. The Directive stipulates that the Member States must take the necessary measures to ensure that public sector websites for PWD are accessible. In creating the accessibility of e-learning materials for SWD, we should also follow the recommendations and guidelines for the accessibility of websites, as both fall under ICT (recommendations such as text size, use of colors, etc., are the same for both online and e-learning materials).

The findings and recommendations presented in this study can help a variety of people who are actively involved in the implementation of the education process, particularly those who encounter PWD. In addition, the findings can also be a vital resource for e-learning content creators, as the technology has great potential for bringing information and knowledge closer to PWD. Because of this potential, it is essential that, in the future, the technology is even more adapted to SWD and facilitates or even overcomes barriers to access e-learning materials, e-learning and other electronic environments. A vivid example was given by Lynch [63] who foresees that in the future, professors may transform learning into an interactive experience using personal artificial intelligence tutors, helping SWD access lectures at their own pace with personalized artificial intelligence help.

In conducting the research, we found that the elements used in the case of electronic materials do not differ from the elements on the website, as the way of accessing information is the same, for example, computer. For this reason, the results of our analysis can also serve as recommendations for designers of websites aimed at SWD.

We suggest replicating the study for other SWD, for example, students with intellectual disabilities, speech and language disorders, mobility impairments, etc. Our study can be upgraded, and e-learning material, not only selected handouts, can be produced (with authentic video material of sign language interpreters, audio material of written text...). Based on these findings, an experiment could be performed, where, in addition to the acceptance of e-learning material, a difference in the effectiveness of e-learning material based on acquired new knowledge could be observed.

Acknowledgements

This research was funded by the European Commission under Erasmus+ programme project Trans2Work "School-to-Work Transition for Higher education students with disabilities in Serbia, Bosnia & Herzegovina and Montenegro" (Project Nr 561847-KA2-CBHE). It was co-financed by the Slovenian Research Agency, Ljubljana, Slovenia.

Author details

Peter Čakš[1]*, Monika Ferk[1], Matjaž Debevc[1], Julija Bele Lapuh[2] and Ines Kožuh[1]

1 University of Maribor, Maribor, Slovenia

2 B2 Ljubljana School of Business, Ljubljana, Slovenia

*Address all correspondence to: peter.caks@um.si

References

[1] Fichten CS, Ferraro V, Asuncion JV, Chwojka C, Barile M, Nguyen MN, et al. Disabilities and e-learning problems and solutions: An exploratory study. Educational Technology & Society. 2009;**12**(4):241-256

[2] Grammenos S. European comparative data on Europe 2020 & People with disabilities, Final Report, Academic Network of European Disability Experts; 2013. Available from: https://hdl.handle.net/1813/76816 [Accessed: December 1, 2021]

[3] World Health Organization (WHO). Disability and Health. 2021. Available from: https://www.who.int/news-room/fact-sheets/detail/disability-and-health [Accessed: December 1, 2021]

[4] Schelly CL, Davies PL, Spooner CL. Student perceptions of faculty implementation of Universal design for learning. Journal of Postsecondary Education and Disability. 2011;**24**(1):17-30

[5] Petretto DR, Carta SM, Cataudella S, Masala I, Mascia ML, Penna MP, et al. The use of distance learning and e-learning in students with learning disabilities: A review on the effects and some hint of analysis on the use during COVID-19 outbreak. Clinical Practice and Epidemiology in Mental Health: CP & EMH. 2021;**17**:92. DOI: 10.2174/1745017902117010092

[6] UNESCO. Guidelines for Accessible Information in Learning. 2015. Available from: https://www.european-agency.org/sites/default/files/Guidelines%20for%20Accessible%20Information_EN.pdf [Accessed: December 1, 2021]

[7] Khasnabis C, Mirza Z, MacLachlan M. Opening the GATE to inclusion for people with disabilities. The Lancet. 2015;**386**:2229-2230. DOI: 10.1016/s0140-6736(15)01093-4

[8] McNicholl A, Casey H, Desmond D, Gallagher P. The impact of assistive technology use for students with disabilities in higher education: A systematic review. Disability and Rehabilitation: Assistive Technology. 2021;**16**(2):130-143. DOI: 10.1080/17483107.2019.1642395

[9] Fichten C, Olenik-Shemesh D, Asuncion J, Jorgensen M, Colwell C. Higher Education, information and communication technologies, and students with disabilities: The good and the bad. In: Seale J, editor. Improving Accessible Digital Practices in Higher Education – Challenges and New Practices for Inclusion. Cham: Palgrave Pivot; 2020. pp. 21-44. DOI: 10.1007/978-3-030-37125-8

[10] Cidral WA, Oliveira T, Di Felice M, Aparicio M. E-learning success determinants: Brazilian empirical study. Computers & Education. 2018;**122**:273-290. DOI: 10.1016/j.compedu.2017.12.001

[11] Simsik D, Galajdova A, Onofrejova D. Some aspects in e-learning for persons with disabilities. In: Proceedings of the 15th International Conference on Emerging eLearning Technologies and Applications. New York: IEEE; 2017. pp. 1-7. DOI: 10.1109/ICETA.2017.8102527

[12] Cataudella S, Carta S, Mascia ML, Masala C, Petretto DR, Penna MP. Psychological Aspects of Students With Learning Disabilities in E-Environments: A Mini Review and Future Research Directions. Frontiers in Psychology. 2020;**11**:611818. DOI: 10.3389/fpsyg.2020.611818

[13] Kraleva R, Sabani M, Kralev V. An analysis of some learning management systems. International Journal on Advanced Science, Engineering and Information Technology. 2019;**9**(4):1190-1198. DOI: 10.18517/ijaseit.9.4.9437

[14] Moore JL, Dickson-Deane C, Galyen K. e-Learning, online learning, and distance learning environments: Are they the same? The Internet and higher education. 2011;**14**(2):129-135. DOI: 10.1016/j.iheduc.2010.10.001

[15] Alkahtani MA. E-learning for Students with Disabilities During COVID-19: Faculty Attitude and Perception. SAGE Open. 2021;**11**(4). DOI: 10.1177/21582440211054494

[16] Cinquin PA, Guitton P, Sauzéon H. Online e-learning and cognitive disabilities: A systematic review. Computers & Education. 2019;**130**:152-167. DOI: 10.1016/j.compedu.2018.12.004

[17] Calle-Jimenez T, Sanchez-Gordon S, Arias-Flores H. Profiling of e-learning users with accessibility needs. In: International Conference on Applied Human Factors and Ergonomics 2021. Cham: Springer; 2021. pp. 477-485. DOI: 10.1007/978-3-030-80091-8_56

[18] Seale J, Georgeson J, Mamas C, Swain J. Not the right kind of 'digital capital'? An examination of the complex relationship between disabled students, their technologies and higher education institutions. Computers & Education. 2015;**82**:118-128. DOI: 10.1016/j.compedu.2014.11.007

[19] Kajee L. Disability, social inclusion and technological positioning in a South African higher education institution: Carmen's story. Language Learning Journal. 2010;**38**(3):379-392. DOI: 10.1080/09571736.2010.511783

[20] Keeler CG, Horney M. Online course designs: Are special needs being met? The American Journal of Distance Education. 2007;**21**(2):61-75. DOI: 10.1080/08923640701298985

[21] Fresen JW, Hill RK, Geng F. A collection of suggested electronic course templates for use in higher education. Research in Learning Technology. 2014;**22**. DOI: 10.3402/rlt.v22.21669

[22] Hatipoglu N, Tosun N. The design of renewable and interactive e-book template for e-learning environments. Online Journal of Communication and Media Technologies. 2012;**2**(2):126. DOI: 10.29333/ojcmt/2382

[23] Savidis A, Grammenos D, Stephanidis C. Developing inclusive e-learning systems. Universal Access in the Information Society. 2006;**5**(1):51-72. DOI: 10.1007/s10209-006-0024-1

[24] Wen ZA, Silverstein E, Zhao Y, Amog AL, Garnett K, Azenkot S. Teacher views of math e-learning tools for students with specific learning disabilities. In: The 22nd International ACM SIGACCESS Conference on Computers and Accessibility. New York: ACM; 2020. pp. 1-13. DOI: 10.1145/3373625.3417029

[25] Smith C. Challenges and opportunities for teaching students with disabilities during the COVID-19 pandemic. International Journal of Multidisciplinary Perspectives in Higher Education. 2020;**5**(1):167-173

[26] Debevc M, Stjepanovič Z, Holzinger A. Development and evaluation of an e-learning course for deaf and hard of hearing based on the advanced Adapted Pedagogical Index method. Interactive learning environments. 2014;**22**(1):35-50. DOI: 10.1080/10494820.2011.641673

[27] European Telecommunications Standards Institute (ETS). Accessibility requirements suitable for public procurement of ICT products and services in Europe – EN 301 549 v.2.1.2. 2018. Available from: https://www.etsi.org/deliver/etsi_en/301500_301599/301549/02.01.02_60/en_301549v020102p.pdf [Accessed: December 1, 2021]

[28] Persson H, Åhman H, Yngling AA, Gulliksen J. Universal design, inclusive design, accessible design, design for all: different concepts—one goal? On the concept of accessibility—historical, methodological and philosophical aspects. Universal Access in the Information Society. 2015;**14**(4):505-526. DOI: 10.1007/s10209-014-0358-z

[29] Debevc M, Kožuh I, Raspopovic M, Kaplarski K, Ljubojevic D, Kartasidou L, et al. E-learning approaches for supporting higher education (HE) students with disabilities on transition planning. In: Ćirić T, Jovanović SM, editors. Proceedings of the Seventh International Conference on eLearnin. Belgrade, Serbia: Belgrade Metropolitan University; 2016. pp. 110-115

[30] Cooper M. Making online learning accessible to disabled students: an institutional case study. ALT-J. 2006;**14**(1):103-115. DOI: 10.1080/09687760500479779

[31] Khazanchi P, Khazanchi R. Pedagogical practices in teaching students with disabilities in inclusive education. In: Handbook of Research on Critical Issues in Special Education for School Rehabilitation Practices. Hershey, Pennsylvania: IGI Global; 2021. pp. 66-86. DOI: 10.4018/978-1-7998-7630-4.ch004

[32] Kelley P, Sanspree M, Davidson R. Vision impairment in children and youth. In: The Lighthouse Handbook of Vision Impairment and Vision Rehabilitation. Vol. 2. New York: Oxford University Press; 2000. pp. 1111-1128

[33] Permvattana R, Armstrong H, Murray I. Web-based learning environments for the vision impaired. In: Kommers P, Issa T, Isaias P, editors. Proceedings of the IADIS International Conference: Internet Technologies and Society. Perth: IADIS press; 2010. pp. 277-281

[34] Creed C. Assistive tools for disability arts: Collaborative experiences in working with disabled artists and stakeholders. Journal of Assistive Technologies. 2016;**10**(2):121-129. DOI: 10.1108/JAT-12-2015-0034

[35] Permvattana R, Armstrong H, Murray I. E-learning for the vision impaired: A holistic perspective. International Journal of Cyber Society and Education. 2013;**6**(1):15-30. DOI: 10.7903/ijcse.1029

[36] Kesič DM, Blažič M, Kavkler M. Vsi učenci so lahko uspešni: napotki za delo z učenci s posebnimi potrebami [All students can be successful: Guidelines for working with students with special needs.]. Ljubljana: Rokus Klett; 2010

[37] Stinson MS, Eisenberg S, Horn C, Larson J, Levitt H, Stuckless R. Real-time speech-to-text services. In: Stuckless R, editor. Reports of the National Task Force on Quality Services in Postsecondary Education of Deaf and Hard of Hearing Students. Rochester, New York: Northeast Technical Assistance Center, Rochester Institute of Technology; 1999. pp. 1-22

[38] Stinson MS, Elliot LB, Kelly RR, Liu Y. Deaf and hard-of-hearing students' memory of lectures with speech-to-text and interpreting/note taking services. The Journal of Special Education. 2009;**43**(1):52-64. DOI: 10.1177/0022466907313453

[39] Lartz MN, Stoner JB, Stout LJ. Perspectives of assistive technology from deaf students at a hearing university. Assistive Technology Outcomes and Benefits. 2008;**5**(1):72-91

[40] Kuzu A. The factors that motivate and hinder the students with hearing impairment to use mobile technology. The Turkish Online Journal of Educational Technology-TOJET. 2011;**10**(4):336-348

[41] Žagar D. Drugačni študenti [Different Students]. 1st ed. Ljubljana: Znanstvena založba Filozofske fakultete; 2012

[42] Ceranoglu TA. Autism spectrum disodrers and electronic media use: Empathy with avatars. Journal of the American Academy of Child & Adolescent Psychiatry. 2016;**10**(55):S70. DOI: 10.1016/j.jaac.2016.07.714

[43] Mantziou O, Vrellis I, Mikropoulos TA. Do children in the spectrum of autism interact with real-time emotionally expressive human controlled avatars? Procedia Computer Science. 2015;**67**:241-251. DOI: 10.1016/j.procs.2015.09.268

[44] Lombardi AR, Murray C, Gerdes H. College faculty and inclusive instruction: Self-reported attitudes and actions pertaining to Universal Design. Journal of Diversity in Higher Education. 2011;**4**(4):250. DOI: 10.1037/a0024961

[45] Clark RC, Mayer RE. E-Learning and the science of instruction: proven guidelines for consumers and designers of multimedia learning. San Francisco: John Wiley & Sons; 2016

[46] Lockwood F, editor. Open and Distance Learning Today. Routledge Studies in Distance Education. London: Routledge; 2013

[47] Dexter DD, Hughes CA. Graphic organizers and students with learning disabilities: A meta-analysis. Learning Disability Quarterly. 2011;**34**(1):51-72. DOI: 10.1177/073194871103400104

[48] Delisio LA, Bukaty CA, Taylor M. Effects of a graphic organizer intervention package on the mathematics word problem solving abilities of students with autism spectrum disorders. Journal of Special Education Apprenticeship. 2018;**7**(2):n2

[49] Wiebe EN, Annetta LA. Animation and narration: Using eye tracking to understand visual attention distribution. In: Annual meeting of the Americal Educational Research Association. Chicago: Department of Mathematics, Science and Technology Education; 2007

[50] Caldwell B, Cooper M, Reid LG, Vanderheiden G, Chisholm W, Slatin J, et al. Web content accessibility guidelines (WCAG) 2.0. WWW Consortium (W3C). 2008;**290**:1-34

[51] Center IRIS. Priporočila za oblikovanje besedila za tisk za populacijo slabovidnih oseb [Recommendations for drafting a print text for the visually impaired people]. 2017. Available from: http://center-iris.si/pomoc-inkluziji/pripomocki/priporocila-za-oblikovanje-besedila-za-tisk-za-populacijo-slabovidnih-oseb/ [Accessed: December 1, 2021]

[52] Fabri M, Andrews P. Evaluation of Course Scenario Prototypes with Representative Students and Autism Professionals. Leeds Beckett University. Report D3.2 autism&uni, 2015. Available from: https://www.autism-uni.org/wp-content/uploads/2015/10/D3.2-AutismUni-Evaluation-of-Prototype-Scenarios.pdf [Accessed: December 1, 2021]

[53] Riddell S, Weedon E. Disabled students in higher education: Discourses

of disability and the negotiation of identity. International Journal of Educational Research. 2014;**63**:38-46. DOI: 10.1016/j.ijer.2013.02.008

[54] Debevc M, Milošević D, Kožuh I. A comparison of comprehension processes in sign language interpreter videos with or without captions. PLoS One. 2015;**10**(5):e0127577. DOI: 10.1371/journal.pone.0127577

[55] Ministry of Public Administration of Republic of Slovenia – Administrative Academy. Navodila za izvajalce usposabljanj na upravni akademiji [Instructions for trainers at the Administrative Academy]. 2016. Available from: http://www.mju.gov.si/fileadmin/mju.gov.si/pageuploads/JAVNA_UPRAVA/Upravna_akademija/UA/Za_izvajalce/Navodila_za_izvajalce_usposabljanj_UA_okt2016__002_.pdf [Accessed: December 1, 2021]

[56] Gozd in gozdarstvo. Lipa [Linden]. 2017. Available from: https://www.gozd-les.com/slovenski-gozdovi/drevesa/lipa. [Accessed: December 1, 2021]

[57] World Medical Association. World Medical Association Declaration of Helsinki. Ethical principles for medical research involving human subjects. Bulletin of the World Health Organization. 2001;**79**(4):373

[58] American Psychological Association. Ethical Principles of Psychologists and Code of Conduct. 2017. Available from: https://www.apa.org/ethics/code/ [Accessed: December 1, 2021]

[59] Nemoto T, Beglar D. Likert-scale questionnaires. In: Sonda N, Krause A, editors. JALT 2013 Conference Proceedings. Tokyo: JALT; 2014. pp. 1-8

[60] Edutechwiki. Usability and User Experience Surveys. 2017. Available from: http://edutechwiki.unige.ch/en/Usability_and_user_experience_surveys [Accessed: December 1, 2021]

[61] Friedman HH, Herskovitz PJ, Pollack S. The biasing effects of scale-checking styles on response to a Likert scale. In: Proceedings of the American Statistical Association Annual Conference: Survey Research Methods. Vol. 792. 1994. pp. 792-795

[62] Brown S. Likert Scale Examples for Surveys. ANR Program Evaluation, Iowa State University, USA. 2010. Available from: https://www.extension.iastate.edu/Documents/ANR/LikertScaleExamplesforSurveys.pdf [Accessed: December 1, 2021]

[63] Lynch M. My Vision for the Future of the Assistive Technology in Education. Resource Document. The Edvocate. 2018. Available from: https://www.theedadvocate.org/vision-future-assistive-technology-education/ [Accessed: December 1, 2021]

Section 3

Future Education via Cloud Computing

Chapter 8

Workers' Education from the Cloud: Maximising Latest Technologies for Human Resource Development in Africa

Kehinde O. Kester and Solomon O. Ojedeji

Abstract

As the world is getting increasingly globalised as occasioned by rapid advancements in technology, so is the need for continuous skills enhancement on the part of the working population. What it takes to cope with the demands of the ever dynamic workplace in today's tech-driven world has kept changing. Therefore, a worker who refuses to up-skill in line with the changing demands of the workplace will soon become obsolete. This has an implication for workers' training and re-training towards skills enhancement which has some elements of digital skills acquisition. Meanwhile, cloud-based technology is increasingly being used in the education sector, and it is also considered to hold much promise for workers' education. Cloud computing systems provide a variety of opportunities for content delivery, as well as providing limitless access to information over the internet. This chapter, therefore, explores the workability of workers' education through the use of cloud computing systems, particularly in Africa in the face of her obvious challenges relating to a high level of poverty, epileptic power supply and poor internet connectivity, among others.

Keywords: workers' education, cloud computing, skills development, workplace, technology in Africa

1. Introduction

The world is becoming increasingly globalised as characterised by rapid information and communication technology. It has brought a change not only in the knowledge and skill requirements for most jobs across the world, but also brought about a huge change in the knowledge and skills required to meet up the demands of the twenty-first-century workplace. Therefore, it has become necessary for workers to continue to update their skills through on-the-job and off-the-job training programmes. More so, the knowledge and skills acquired through the regular schooling system are no longer sufficient to cope with the ever-growing demands of the world of work. For instance, even the patterns and trends of employment have changed over time, which is also connected to rapid advancements in technology [1]. It has increased the need to repackage workers' education in Africa to meet up with what is obtainable in the rest of the world. Newer skills needed to perform better and faster on the job, are emerging daily in the world of work as a result many skills becoming obsolete [2]. For this reason, it has become necessary for workers to continue to upgrade their knowledge and skills for optimum effectiveness on their jobs, and to continue to be relevant to their employers, as well as compete well with their counterparts across the world. Indeed today's world is a global village, occasioned by increasing globalisation and advancements in technology. Thus, the continent of Africa is faced with the huge task of enhancing the capacity of its workforce towards the development of the continent.

Since technology keeps advancing and also affecting the various job roles and working skills, so it is necessary to come up with specialised workers' education programmes that meet the regular up-skilling needs of the workforce. Similarly, this kind of education must have some elements of digital skills acquisition [3], which will make it possible for workers to continue to take advantage of technology for further training and re-training. However, this kind of education can effectively be provided when hinged on the principle of lifelong learning [4]. Therefore, an approach to workers education that maximises the affordances of the latest technologies, and that is based on the principle of lifelong learning is considered effective in this wise.

Interestingly, cloud computing is playing an important role in the development of Information and Communication Technology (ICT) today. Cloud computing simply refers to a combined system of networks, servers and computers tolls used to complete tasks over the internet [5]. Cloud computing systems have been used in various fields, including education, to deliver online instructions and they are considered capable of being used to deliver a high-quality learning experience, interaction, as well as knowledge and skills sharing within the shortest time possible [5, 6]. Cloud computing holds much promise for workers' online training because it is a new technology that can store data on cloud servers, which could be accessed anywhere and anytime on the internet using a digital device like a mobile phone. Similarly, cloud computing technology uses low-cost materials and equipment to construct an online platform within a short period of time, and it is very flexible in terms of deployment capacity [5]. All of these, and the fact that cloud computing provides rapid and reliable access to resources via the internet, make it a potential platform for floating online training programmes for different categories of workers in the African continent.

2. Need for workers' training and retraining in Africa

The heavy presence of technology in today's world and its consequent effects in the way things are done in various industries and organisations, have brought about a need for continuous training and retraining towards capacity enhancement of the human resource. For instance, see **Figure 1**, which shows the various things that people use their mobile phones for. It is worthy of note, however, that while globalisation and advancements in ICT have benefitted workers in most developed countries in terms of providing improved knowledge and skills and creating new job opportunities, the opposite has been the case in most developing countries. Several countries in Africa, for instance, have recorded a large number of workers' redundancy and retrenchment due to their inability to meet up the demands of the rapidly changing job description [2]. Many years back, researchers [7, 8] projected that a time would

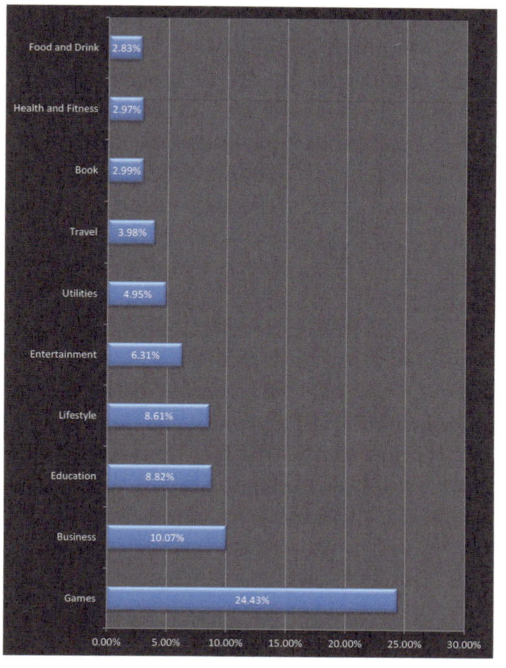

Figure 1.
What people use mobile phones for.

come when machines would be made to do the jobs primarily meant for humans; while this has not been totally true in most developed countries, it has indeed been the experience of workers in many developing countries. Yet, many more jobs may still be displaced due to a huge shift in the division of labour between humans and machines [2].

Today's workplace is a lot different from what it used to be. For instance, the world of work has gradually entered into what was predicted many years back regarding the adoption of technology, and how this can transform tasks, jobs, as well as skills [2]. However, it has also been noted that with the heavy presence of technology in today's place of work, as adopted by many companies, there also lies the possibility of the emergence of new roles requiring new skills. This has made some notable soft skills such as active listening, resilience, stress tolerance and flexibility to be in very high demand in the twenty-first-century workplace. This, therefore, suggests that there is generally higher demand for certain soft skills; just as some other skills are gradually going into extinction. This has serious implications on the knowledge and skills base of most workers, as workers who have access to training and retraining opportunities and maximise such soft skills will have an edge over others [9]. Therefore, any worker who will continue to retain his or her job or get new ones must continue to update his/her skills.

More so, we live in a globalised economy characterised by speedy, innovative and quality service delivery towards optimum customer satisfaction. This has also serious implications on the capacity of human resource. Aside from improvements in knowledge and skills of workers, therefore, there is also an expected transformation in their work attitudes, work habits, work choices and preferences, as well as work styles, among others. While many workers in the developed countries of the world have been able to go through this process of transformation by leveraging on the affordances of ICTs for continuous skills enhancement, many of their counterparts in most developing countries have not, particularly on the African continent. This gap is said to likely continue to increase except African countries, as well as other developing countries invest massively in continuous workers' education, training and skills enhancement towards higher rates of innovation and productivity [10].

The times have changed, and there are now a wide range of capabilities needed to cope with the emerging technological advancement, particularly as it affects the workplace. There is thus an urgent need for the labour force in Africa generally to be provided with knowledge, information and skills needed for coping with the ever-changing job roles and demands. It is obvious that Africa like the rest of the world is experiencing immense technological advancements, which is changing every facet of human existence. Therefore, the manner in which people go about their daily lives, as well as work has greatly been altered by the advancements in technology and cannot be overemphasised. This also has implications for increasing demand for new skills and competencies to continuously remain relevant in the ever-changing world.

On the account of the latest technologies, there are now newer ways of doing things and newer ways of solving human problems. We live in the information age where machines are used to do virtually everything, especially in the workplace. Thus, it is no longer sufficient for anyone to rely on working skills acquired many years ago to tackle the job demands of the twenty-first-century [4]. For this reason, providers of workers' education or training programmes must become more proactive in reviewing the content of workers education programmes, and particularly work towards the provision of specialised workers' training programmes that prepare workers for the changing work environment. Thus, the educational system in most African countries does not fully address the needs of workers [11]. For this reason, workers in Africa are considered to have special education requirements, especially in the area of work-related skills.

Meanwhile, the recent outbreak of the global pandemic of COVID-19 has given popularity to remote working, where workers are expected to work from home. Increasing advancements in technology, particularly in connectivity and communication technology, has laid the needed foundation for this new phase of work globally. Gone are the days when workers must converge at a specific location before they can perform their assigned tasks or work for an organisation. Nowadays, workers can work not only from home, but they can also work from anywhere [12]. The workplace, is, therefore, becoming increasingly dynamic, which is not likely to stop, with the current pace of advancements in technology. Thus, as technology continues to advance, so will the demands of the workplace, which has implications for the acquisition of new and marketable skills.

Over time, the school system has failed to transmit the skills, attitudes and abilities needed to function optimally in the workplace. This has shifted the attention of those responsible for training programmes to on-the-job training, particularly, effective and less costly approaches compared to institutional education. The kind of training that takes place at an ordinary workplace, making use of the job itself as part of the instruction given in the course of the training programme, as well as a means to acquiring practical work-related skills. This calls for repackaged and specialised training programmes which equip workers in Africa with skills necessary for the demands, as well as the peculiarities of the twenty-first-century workplace.

Interestingly, given the evolving nature of employment patterns, as well as continuous advancements in technology, a 'rejuvenated and repackaged workers' education' was suggested [1]. This suggestion was made with particularly emphasis on the need to remove the various barriers to continuous and lifelong learning, and skills enhancements for different categories of workers in Africa. It is believed that by so doing, workers will be able to effectively and efficiently carry on with whatever new responsibilities or challenges, as well as new job roles in the ever-changing and highly tech-driven twenty-first-century workplace.

3. Workers' education, the principle of lifelong learning and technology

Having established the fact that technology now drives a typical twenty-first-century workplace, and the implication of this on continuous knowledge and skills improvements on the part of workers, it has equally become imperative to consider what kind of educational programmes will be most needed for workers, particularly in the African context. One fact which cannot be overemphasised is that whatever kind of educational programmes provided for workers in the face of continuous advancement in technology must also be continuous in nature. The reason for this is not farfetched, since such workers' education is expected to equip workers with the necessary skills for meeting up with the demands of the ever-changing workplace as a result of rapid advancements in technology.

Thus, since workers' education has to be continuous in nature, it is also necessary that it be hinged on the principle of lifelong learning. By so doing, workers will be provided with opportunities to continue to learn throughout life; updating both knowledge and skills. This will allow individual workers to deal more confidently with socio-technology changes, as well as continue to seek knowledge throughout life independently and passionately [13]. The principle of lifelong learning is known to be important in providing opportunities for the enhancement of knowledge base, skills, as well as other competencies. Designing educational programmes that are based on the principle of lifelong learning, therefore, help to produce individuals who are continually relevant and active, since they are provided with opportunities to learn throughout their lifetime.

Lifelong learning is considered a viable framework for achieving sustainable national development [13]. This is considered so because it is believed that any nation that will truly develop must provide continuous learning opportunities for its citizenry which is crucial for producing self-reliant individuals. Lifelong learning is the learning that takes place throughout life. It is said to be a blend of formal, informal and non-formal education, which focuses on the provision of learning opportunities from birth till death [14]. This means that through lifelong learning, educational opportunities are provided to all categories of people beyond the four walls of a classroom or what is known as the conventional or regular school system. This is why lifelong learning is seen as truly crucial and important for human capital development and enhancement.

For a worker, learning does not terminate after school. As a matter of fact, for most professions, the end of school only marks the beginning of learning for a worker. This is so because most of the time the academic knowledge acquired in schools does not guarantee effectiveness on the job. For this reason, employers of labour always invest a lot to provide training or orientation programmes for new entrants in every organisation. Aside from orientation courses provided for new workers, most organisations also provide refresher training or on-the-job training programmes for their staff from time to time. This is always done in a bid to keep them updated and make them continuously relevant in their field. For this reason, workers' education itself is a lifelong learning process having elements of both intended and unintended learning. This kind of learning could also be on-the-job or off-the-job. For this reason, it is just perfect that efforts made in the direction of providing specialised training programmes for workers in Africa towards knowledge and skills enhancements must be rooted in the principles of lifelong learning [13].

Workers in Africa need to be provided with opportunities to learn independently to continue to acquire new knowledge and skills. The nature of most job roles today now places on workers a huge demand for the ability to seek relevant information from a variety of sources, the ability to access new ideas, as well as the ability to engage in self-directed learning. A key fact that cannot be overemphasised is that technology has come to stay, not only in the developed world but in the whole world, Africa inclusive. Interestingly, the major thrust of lifelong learning is in the fact that each individual ought to develop a mindset that is open to new ideas, skills, knowledge, attitude and behaviour [13]. More so, a major reason for continuous learning throughout life is not unconnected with the explosion of globalisation aided by rapid advancement in technology. Thus, lifelong learning may not be easily separated from technology.

Meanwhile, in clear terms, the principle of lifelong learning holds that an individual is capable of adjusting to socio-technological changes, as well as seeking knowledge independently throughout life [13]. Thus, if technology has altered the workplace in no little way, as well as placed a huge demand on workers in terms of job skills requirement, this could be an indication that technology could also be a viable means to the continuous improvement or upgrading of workers' skills. For instance, organisers of workers' education programmes could take advantage of the latest technologies towards the continuous enhancement of the knowledge and skills of workers. So that as workers are being exposed to limitless access to continuous training and retraining, their ICT skills are also being developed for continuous capacity enhancement. Thus, workers in Africa will be helped to compete well with their counterparts across the world, especially when they are provided with learning opportunities throughout their lifetime. This way, they will continue to update their knowledge and skills, enhance their career opportunities, as well as cope with new job demands.

Therefore, a viable and cost-effective approach to providing specialised workers' education that is rooted in the principles of lifelong learning could be through the use of the latest technologies. Information and Communication Technologies (ICTs) are considered capable of improving the quality and efficiency of educational and training programmes across the world [3]. ICTs are generally known to play a very useful role in the expansion of learning opportunities to all [15]. Therefore, whenever consideration is being given to equity, access and quality in the provision of learning and training programmes, the use of ICTs to drive or deliver such educational programmes is considered very useful. For this reason, ICTs have impacted the field of learning and training in no little way. As a matter of fact, there has been a growing trend in the integration of ICTs into teaching and training. There are now several new possibilities offered to providers of learning and training programmes that are powered by emerging technologies in our today's world. This could come in a range of new possibilities and tools, all geared towards providing hands-on and intensive learning-by-doing training courses for different categories of workers, particularly in Africa. For this reason, ICT is said to be changing the face of education generally in developing countries. ICT is capable of complimenting, enriching and transforming education for the better.

Thus, different ways through which technology can facilitate universal access to various forms of learning were highlighted, which include the fact that technology helps to bridge learning divides; supports the development of workers; enhances quality and relevance of learning and training content; strengthen inclusion; as well as improve the administration of learning and training programmes [15]. Interestingly, much evidence of successful integration of ICT in various forms of learning abound across the world – whether in schools located in high-resource or developed countries; schools located in low-resource or developing countries; or for workers' education and training [15]. Interestingly, the integration of some emerging technologies such as cloud computing has been noted for its ability to open up new learning and teaching opportunities and support lifelong learning [16, 17].

4. Harnessing the potentials of cloud computing for workers' training

The fact that workers need continuous up-skilling cannot be overemphasised. Yet, workers are those categories of people who are mostly busy either with their jobs, family commitments, religious or other engagements. Since workers' continuous education is a necessity, so providers of such programmes must arrange device training programmes for workers who do notgo outside their home or even their homecan not access to such training courses. More so, in today's world, we live a connected life, and in a highly connected society through the help of the Internet [15]. Therefore, through the use of an Internet-enabled computer, or even a mobile phone, we connect with people from far and near, and this has changed the way we communicate, consume and interact with varying degrees of information. So ICT and the Internet have 'invaded' and transformed virtually all aspects of our lives, such that we now live and work in an environment which is highly dominated by technology. Thus, technology and the Internet have really come to stay, and they have become very important parts of our everyday lives. Essentially, it is very expedient to take advantage of the latest technologies for driving the acquisition of life and work skills such that people are not disconnected and backward as the world is progressively advancing in the face of rapidly advancing technology. One of the well-known emerging technologies which could be maximised for workers' education is, therefore, cloud computing.

Cloud computing is an emerging technology amidst others such as new algorithms, Big Data, and the Internet of Things. It is a set of databases that provide information and services which could be accessed remotely over the Internet. Through the use of cloud computing, is it possible to create, store and retrieve information over the Internet using a digital device [17]. Cloud-based technologies have been extensively used by schools and universities across the world, especially in developed countries. Particularly during the emergence of COVID-19, cloud-based technology was extensively used to support e-learning and the transition from traditional lesson delivery to online or virtual lesson delivery [5].

Various cloud systems used by different educational institutions to communicate and interact with both learners and educators were reviewed and it was found that cloud-based computing systems are cost-effective, easy to use and very reliable [18]. They also found that through cloud-based computing, systems data is accessible over a large network along with enhanced security and privacy. For this reason, cloud computing is capable of being used to provide the delivery of quality and easily accessible online learning and training content. In addition, cloud computing allows multi-users to connect to a cloud platform, data or content at the same time.

This means that when training content are uploaded in the cloud, workers from different locations can access such content at the same time.

Meanwhile, the huge benefits of virtualisation technologies and cloud computing to educational and training programmes have been noted [5]. Such that virtualised, more sustainable and efficient training contents or resources are made available to workers through cloud-based applications which can be accessed anywhere and at any time through the internet. Over time and particularly with the emergence of COVID-19, many schools, universities, as well as other educational institutions have adopted cloud computing to offer e-Learning services to their learners. From its various uses for e-Learning, one major advantage of using cloud computing technology is the fact that it offers an interactive online platform whereby instructors can interact with their learners through technology-enhanced learning. Similarly, cloud computing technologies could be used for building the capacity of workers through an interactive online platform whereby the trainer interacts with trainees via a technology-enhanced training session.

Cloud computing is beneficial for online training because it is time-effective; less expensive compared to most conventional training programmes; accessible to various categories of workers; and also beneficial in terms of quality and performance [19, 20]. Some examples of cloud computing applications that have been used for online learning, which could also be maximised for online training include Google's Gmail, Google Meet, Microsoft Teams and Zoom platforms [21]. The greatest challenge to the use of cloud computing for learning has been reluctance on the part of users, as well as slow migration from traditional methods [22]. However, when used for online training, this challenge, as well as others could be surmounted through sufficient pre-training and orientation information for both intending trainers and trainees on how to use and interact with cloud systems. Similarly, as it is always the case with the use of technology for any form of learning activity, sufficient support will be provided, most especially to trainees all through the online training session. Also, given the peculiar African situation, users who neither have access to a digital device nor to internet connectivity would need to be provided with the needed support. For this reason, a discussion around ways to make the use of cloud computing technology for workers' training is very important.

Today, schools, universities, and other educational institutions are using cloud application systems like Zoom, Microsoft Teams and GoogleMeet to connect learners and instructors together for learning [23]. Similarly, cloud-based applications are being accessed in several forms such as the Email services like Gmail and Yahoo mail; Cloud Storage Platforms like Google Drive and Dropbox; and Functional Cloud Applications like Google Docs, Sky drive and [20]. All these provide different possibilities for innovative uses of cloud computing for the purpose of workers' education in Africa. The integration of cloud computing systems into e-Learning has brought several opportunities into the field of education, particular e-Learning [5]. This indicates that cloud computing systems, if properly harnessed, could also really transform the provision of workers' education, particularly in Africa. For instance, with cloud computing, data could be accessed anytime and from anywhere. This means that workers' education and training would no longer be limited to specific locations. Access will no longer be a problem, as different categories of workers will be able to gain access to training and training content at the comfort of their homes. This is really interesting because workers will become indeed reachable from any part of the world through the instrumentality of the internet, together with the use of other technological devices like the mobile phone. Thus, workers' education will be kept simple and very rich. It was submitted that knowledge, skills, awareness, data, as well as software applications, could be shared, monitored and accessed through cloud computing systems [5]. This has great potential for providing the needed quality in workers education in Africa. More so, as the case always is with using cloud computing systems for e-Learning, when used for workers' training, the quality of delivery will be greatly enhanced, and more room will be created for interaction between trainers and trainees.

Furthermore, cloud computing systems are known to provide great computing resources and storage capacity. With cloud computing, there is a high storage capacity, as well as efficient computing resources that could be accessed from a wide range of platforms. This is important for workers education and training, as it will be possible for workers to gain access to information or training content through different means such as the laptop, computer or the mobile phone. All that will be required of different categories of workers will simply be access to the internet from anywhere, and they will be able to take advantage of limitless workers' education from any part of the world.

The integration of e-Learning through cloud technology is also known to be highly cost-effective [5]. This will also be the case when used for workers' education. This is based on the fact that workers will not have to invest too much on highly technological devices or tools, as adopting cloud computing systems for workers' education does not require such [24]. Generally, cloud platforms can easily be accessed from simple digital devices such as mobile phones, tablets and PC which have a good internet connection. This means that the major cost in providing workers' education through the use of cloud computing systems will be in the area of good internet connection, as most workers are most likely to at least own a mobile phone. Interestingly also, since workers who are being trained using the cloud computing systems would not need to purchase any external storage devices such as memory cards or external hard drives, no additional cost will be incurred in this regard. The reason for this is simply because through the cloud computing system data can be created and stored on the cloud storage system itself. All that workers or trainees need to do is simply access the file or data which will be the training content in this wise at his or her convenience. This will also save a lot of money on the part of the employer or organiser of such a training programme that would have otherwise been used to do several other things. Things like payment for the venue; accommodation for both resource persons and trainees; food and refreshment; honorarium for resource persons; subsistence allowance for trainees; among others. As a matter of fact, all these are not directly linked with the training content, however, they take a huge part of the total amount budgeted for most training programmes. Adopting the cloud computing systems for workers' training, therefore, will help to save cost and maximise available resources for workers education.

5. Making workers' education through cloud computing systems workable in Africa

Despite its numerous potentials and advantages, it must be noted that the integration of cloud computing into learning and training has limitations. For example, some of the limitations in the use of cloud computing for workers' training could be related to lack of digital devices such as mobile phones or personal computers; and poor internet access. Given the peculiarities of most African countries characterised by a high level of poverty, illiteracy, epileptic power supply, and poor internet connectivity, among others, the situation can really be worsened. For this reason, ICT integration into workers' training can indeed be a 'muddy' environment if not carefully and properly planned and implemented, particularly in Africa [5]. This is why the use of cloud computing systems for workers' training, particularly in the African context must be approached with utmost carefulness so that the purpose for the use of this emerging technology is not defeated along the line. Because as gainful as the use of ICTs generally for learning and training, if we do not find a way to manage the various challenges associated with their uses, particularly within the African context, little or no positive results will be achieved. This is due to the fact that what works easily in many developed countries with respect to ICT use for workers' education or training may not work so easily in Africa. The reason for this is not farfetched, considering the main challenges faced by most African countries [25].

It is worthy of note that transitioning from the traditional method of workers' education delivery into an online system is a major shift. Hence, this needs to be well organised and planned for optimum results. This brings up the discussion of the workability of cloud-based workers' education, particularly within the African context. As the integration of ICTs into any learning or training programme in Africa is usually professionally and carefully done, bearing in mind the peculiarity of the environment. For instance, the major drive for the utilisation of cloud computing systems in the context of workers' education in Africa is simply to provide user-friendly media that allow knowledge and skills to be shared and accessed through technological devices such as mobile phones and laptops computers. To achieve success, therefore, in this way, the use of technology must be kept simple, and emphasis laid on the content and how they are delivered, rather than on the technicality of the medium of delivery. As technology itself is not capable of bringing about changes in learning outcomes [25, 26].

Therefore, virtually accessible training content could be delivered to workers within the African context through cloud-based computing systems using software applications, the internet and other web-based platforms. This way workers will be connected to an online-training platform from the comfort of their homes, rooms or even beds, at any time, and they will also be able to interact with other users from anywhere in the world.

6. Conclusion

The world is getting increasingly globalised occasioned by rapid advancements in technology. This has serious implications for continuous skills improvement for the working population, as what it takes to cope with the demands of the ever-changing world of work which is highly tech-driven, keeps changing. Therefore, a worker who refuses to keep up with the changing demands for newer working skills will soon become obsolete and unable to fit in, properly into the twenty-first-century workplace. There is, therefore, an increasing need for workers' training and re-training towards working skills enhancements that also have some elements of digital skills acquisition. This has particularly become important, as workers who possess digital skills will have the advantage to continuous skills improvements with further advancements in technology.

Meanwhile, cloud-based technology which is available and accessible to users across the globe, is increasingly being used in the education sector. Similarly, its use

DOI: http://dx.doi.org/10.5772/intechopen.102793

for workers' education holds much promise, particularly in Africa, if well planned and managed. This is so because cloud computing systems provide a variety of opportunities for content delivery, as well as provide limitless access to information over the internet through digital devices such as mobile phone and laptop computers. With the cloud computing systems, therefore, workers can gain access to training content anywhere and anytime, even from the comfort of their homes.

Given its great potential for workers education, the government in various African countries should make necessary policies towards the promotion of cloud computing systems for continuous working skills enhancements. Similarly, the government in various African countries should provide enabling environments for the adoption of cloud computing systems for workers' education. Particularly, steps must be taken to drastically reduce the various challenges facing the use of technology generally, and particularly the use of cloud computing systems for workers' education in Africa. For instance, issues related to the epileptic power supply and poor internet connectivity which seriously affects the result of the use of cloud computing systems for workers' education should be resolved as much as possible.

Author details

Kehinde O. Kester[1] and Solomon O. Ojedeji[2]*

1 Industrial Education and Training, Department of Adult Education, University of Ibadan, Ibadan, Nigeria

2 ICTs for Lifelong Learning and Training, Department of Adult Education, University of Ibadan, Ibadan, Nigeria

*Address all correspondence to: solomonojedeji@gmail.com

References

[1] Kester KO, Omoregie CO, Adeyeye JO. Rethinking worker' education in Africa. In: Okediran A, editor. Adult Education in Nigeria. Nigeria: NNCAE; 2006. pp. 241-248

[2] World Economic Forum. COVID-19 has Exposed the Education Divide in Nigeria. This is how we Can Close it. 2020

[3] Adelore OO, Ojedeji SO. Digital literacy: Key to equity and social justice in a tech-dependent world. In: Robinson PA, Williams KV, Stojanovic M, editors. Global Citizenship for Adult Education: Advancing Critical Literacies for Equity and Social Justice. USA: Routledge; 2022

[4] Kester KO, Bankole AR, Gbenro AI. Lifelong learning and the world of work in Africa: Realities, expectations and challenges. LASU Journal of Research in Educational Management. 2009;**2**(1):52-77

[5] Samyan N, St Flour PO. The impact of cloud computing on e-Learning during COVID-19 pandemic. International Journal of Studies in Education and Science (IJSES). 2021;**2**(2):146-172

[6] Bouyer A, Arasteh B. The necessity of using cloud computing in educational system. Procedia-Social and Behavioral Sciences. 2014;**143**:581-585

[7] Kope M. Understanding e-literacy. In: Martin A, Madigan D, editors. Digital Literacies for Learning. London: Facet Publishing; 2006. pp. 68-79

[8] Willams P, Minnian A. Exploring the challenges of developing digital literacy in the context of special educational needs communities. In: Andretta S, editor. Change and challenge: Information literacy for the 21st century. Adelaide: Auslb Press; 2007. pp. 115-144

[9] Akkermans J, Richardson J, Kraimer L. The covid-19 crisis as a career shock: Implications for careers and vocational behavior. Journal of Vacational Behavior. 2020;**119**:1-5

[10] Kester KO. Reframing training designs and functions in an emerging economy: Issues and perspectives. In: Onyeonoru IP, Olanrewaju J, Rafiq-Alaji F, Anisha T, editors. Perspectives in Nigeria Labour Market and The Global Economy. Ilorin: Michael Imodu National Institute for Labour Studies; 2011. pp. 109-120

[11] Kester KO. Transforming workers' education programmes through inclusive education system. Ibadan Journal of Educational Studies. 2002;**2**(2): 586-595

[12] Anseel F, and Ong M. Reflection: Behavioral strategies to structure and accelerate learning from experience. In: Harvery VS and De Meuse KP Eds. The Age of Agility: Building Learning Agile Leaders and Organizations. United Kingdom: SIOP Professional Practice Series – Oxford University Press; 2020

[13] Kester KO, Gbenro AI. Lifelong learning and national development in Nigeria. In: Omolewa M, editor. Comparative International Education: A Study of Selected National System. Ibadan: Laurel Educational Publishers Ltd.; 2021

[14] Iqbal MJ. Lifelong education: A conceptual debate. An International

Journal of Media Technology and Lifelong Learning. 2009;**5**(1):1-8

[15] UNESCO. Final Report: Planning Education in the AI Era: Lead the Leap. International Conference on Artificial Intelligence and Education. France: UNESCO Education Sector; 2019

[16] Alajmi QA, Kamaludin A, Abdullah R. The effectiveness of cloud-based e-learning towards quality of academic services: An Omanis' expert view. The International Journal of Advanced Computer Science and Applications (IJACSA). 2018;**9**(4):58

[17] Cheng X. Challenges of "School's out, But Class's on" to school education: Practical exploration of Chinese schools during the COVID-19 pandemic. Science Insights Education Frontiers, (SIEF). 2020;**5**(2):501-516. DOI: 10.15354/sief.20.ar043

[18] Madhumitha M, Rajbabu H, Purswani G. Impact of cloud computing in higher education: Amidst COVID-19. Utkal Historical Research Journal. 2021;**34**(7):146-172

[19] Nasri F. The Impact of Using Cloud Computing on Improving the Quality of Higher Education—Case Study: Electronic Ground for Dissemination of Lessons on Line Moodle. Algeria: The College of Economic, Business and Management Sciences; 2019

[20] Alhelou EM, Rashwan AR, Abu-Naser S. The role of cloud computing in improving the quality of accounting education in palestinian universities in light of the COVID-19 pandemic. The Journal of Economics, Finance and Accounting Studies (JEFAS). 2021;**3**(1); 11-32

[21] Bhardwaj AK, Garg L, Gard A, Gaip Y. E-learning during COVID-19 outbreak: Cloud computing adoption in Indian Public Universities. Computers, Materials and Continua (CMC). 2020;**66**(3):2471-2492

[22] Cheng YM. Can tasks and learning be balanced? A dual-pathway model of cloud-based e-learning continuance intention and performance outcomes. Kybernetes: The International Journal of Cybernetics, Systems and Management Sciences. 2021;**2**(2);146-172. DOI: 10.1108/K-07-2020-0440

[23] Azorín C. Beyond COVID-19 supernova. Is another education coming? Journal of Professional Capital and Community (JPCC). 2020;**5**(3):381-390

[24] Dahdouh K, Oughdir L, Dakak A. The integration of the cloud environment in e-learning systems. Transactions on Machine Learning and Artificial Intelligence (TMLAI). 2017;**5**(4):55-65

[25] Adelore OO, Ojedeji SO. Exploring the potentials of emerging technologies for literacy and skills development: Spotlight on artificial intelligence. International Journal of Literacy Education. 2019;**9**(2):246-260

[26] Adedoja GO, Adelore O, Egbokhare F, Oluleye A. Learners' acceptance of the use of mobile phones to deliver tutorials in a distance learning context: A case study at the University of Ibadan. African Journal of Information Systems. 2013;**5**(3):90-93

Chapter 9

Virtual Robotics in Hybrid Teaching and Learning

Sharon Mistretta

Abstract

Traditional robotics instruction in face-to-face classrooms, after-school clubs, and independent competition environments align with expensive, physical robot kits shared by students. Students or parent groups often elect themselves because of previous experience, expertise, or perceived technical ability to dominate the physical robotic platforms' planning, engineering, building, and subsequent programming. This self-elected grabbing of control leaves students who are not regarded as well-positioned to contribute sidelined to observe the self-appointed experts of the group. Virtual robotics platforms provide educators and coaches with the unique opportunity to give every student access to a robot. Each student learns programming, math, and scientific forces that impact robots through simulated physics algorithms. With their customizable virtual environments, virtual robotics platforms such as Vex VR and Robot Virtual Worlds level the playing field. All students can learn, practice, and subsequently contribute to robotics-centered group projects or competitive teams in meaningful ways. This book chapter delineates the strategies to implement virtual robotics in hybrid classroom environments supported by the Technological Pedagogical Content Knowledge (TPACK) framework. Additionally, this chapter reviews how computer-aided design and augmented reality platforms provide students with the opportunity to incorporate 3D objects into virtual worlds.

Keywords: virtual robotics, hybrid teaching environments, TPACK framework, computer-aided design, augmented reality

1. Introduction

Robotics courses, after-school programs, and teams are highly sought-after by school districts and parents who wish to provide their students with science, technology, engineering, and math (STEM) instruction to cultivate a foothold for children in future STEM majors and careers [1–3]. Acquiring physical robotic kits, tools, building and testing space, storage units, computer equipment, and software can be an expensive and time-consuming proposition. Funding for this scope of sustained classroom robotics ranges from well-organized parent-teacher committees [4], business sponsors in return for advertisements on t-shirts [5], and grants from non-profit robot competition entities such as Vex Robotics Education Competition Foundation [6].

The ratio of student-to-robot varies as children enroll in a class, program, or team. A small classroom bundle of robots, such as the Vex IQ, provides five kits, a 12-tile playfield, 18 generic game objects, storage bins, five "pin tools," and costs approximately $2250 [7]. In a classroom, club, or team of 20 students, this kit provides a 4:1 ratio of students to a robot. Classrooms and clubs can implement a generic "build" such as the Vex IQ Clawbot robot to practice fundamental robotics. Competitions, which change every year, require a custom build to enact the unique game established as a challenge by non-profit organizations such as Vex or FIRST Robotics. A team wishing to practice-to-win with their uniquely engineered robot could invest in a competition-size playfield and purchase the new game pieces each year.

With the physical requirements of robotics established, this still leaves teachers and parents with the imperative to provide all students with the opportunity to plan, engineer, build, program, and test a robot. Every physical robotic platform is a synthesis of hardware, software, and firmware. The definition of each of these terms is as follows:

- Hardware is the collection of the physical components of the robot. The robot's brain, sometimes called a brick, contains ports that connect to motors and sensors using cables of varying lengths and memory boards to house software instructions downloaded from the students' shared computer.

- Software is a general term that describes computer programs. The programs include the operating system that resides in the robot's brain to communicate with the programs we write in C, C++, or Python to instruct the robot to move and sense its surroundings.

- Firmware is the collection of instructions in the brain, motors, and sensors that allow the hardware to communicate and enact our programs.

Teachers, parents, and coaches are frequently at a loss of where to begin. This chapter delineates the implementation of virtual robotics as an on-ramp to familiarize educators and their stakeholders with the fundamentals of programming a robot to navigate a virtual world through a simulated physics algorithm. Virtual reality (VR) is a technology that immerses the user into a coded environment that employs visual output to depict different surroundings other than the real world. VR is typically associated with a headset such as Google Cardboard [8] or Merge VR headsets [9] that the user wears to block out the real world and experience new visual input. Vex VR and Robot Virtual Worlds are examples of virtual worlds that depict robots in a computer-generated environment without the use of goggles or headsets. The user observes the robot in an environment on their computer screen.

Virtual robotics provides educators, parents, and coaches with a 1:1 learner to robot ratio. Adults supporting robots in the classrooms, clubs, and competitions should understand the world of robots before making a substantial financial and time investment in physical kits, dedicated building & testing space, and the logistics to field a competition-ready team.

The following sections employ the technological pedagogical and content knowledge (TPACK) framework [10] that delineates the necessary knowledgebase to understand the *intersections* of teaching methods and content knowledge (**Figure 1**) to instruct with technology effectively. Robotics brings science and math instruction to the forefront as students must understand scientific *content* such as force and friction and mathematical concepts such as circle geometry. *Pedagogy* embodies the methods and teaching practices of the component disciplines of science, technology, and math. The ultimate intersection of technology, pedagogy, and content knowledge (TPACK) provides a solid on-ramp to robotics.

Figure 1.
Diagram of the intersections of the TPACK framework.

Using TPACK as a framework, the remaining sections of this chapter discuss the following virtual robotics platforms and supporting applications:

- Vex VR [11], a no-cost, browser-based virtual robotic platform.
- Robot Virtual Worlds [12], a licensed software package that includes a customizable virtual world called Level Builder.
- Tinkercad [13] – a computer-aided design (CAD) 3D modeling program offered by Autocad where students create objects to upload ".stl" files to Robot Virtual Worlds' [12] Level Builder.
- Merge Cube [14] – an augmented reality mobile application program that facilitates viewing student-designed 3D objects to "see" their creation before uploading to Level Builder or printing on a 3D printer.

This chapter concludes with a summary of virtual robotics and suggested transitions using a hybrid approach to virtual and physical robotics.

2. Vex VR

Vex VR is a browser-based virtual robot platform provided by the Vex Robotics Education & Competition (REC) Foundation. This platform is an ideal place to introduce students, teachers, parents, and coaches to the world of robotics. Educators can consider the VR Vex platform as a tool to use with students in face-to-face and synchronous or asynchronous online environments. The goal is to provide *all* students with the *same* learning opportunities. It is essential to consider how educators can use platforms such as Google Classroom [15] and Google Drive [16] to deliver supporting content, such as worksheets, to students. Online materials become accessible to all hybrid learners in the same room, joining via Google Meet [17], or who must enact the lessons when they have access to a shared home computer. Creating multiple entry points for students in a hybrid approach is the ultimate in student-centered learning.

With the hybrid "classroom" organization established, let us define programming. By this author's definition, programming is writing instructions to cause an object made of plastic, glass, rare metals, and electricity to solve logical and mathematical statements repetitively.

There are several ground rules for every programmer to consider as they journey into this fantastic field of coding and robotics. First and foremost, the program is doing what it is doing because that is what you told it to do. Programmers must think of how the computer interprets our instructions, not how we believe the code should work. Next, concise code is best. Programming is not a competition to write the most lines of code. Concise lines of instructions take up less of the computer's memory and will run faster. Persistent programmers write great programs. Finish a job. Be proud of your product. Finally, share what you know. Robotics communities have robust collaborative forums and videos on social media. Share techniques to help up-and-coming teams.

2.1 Vex VR technological knowledge (TK)

This section addresses the technical knowledge in the TPACK framework (**Figure 1**) necessary to implement the fundamentals of Vex VR. Since Vex VR is browser-based, there is no need to download software to each student's computer. A *browser* is software on your computer that communicates with a website's *server*, an extensive array of disk drives, that responds to your interactions when connected to the internet. Browsers such as Google Chrome [18] create a local, temporary file on each computer called *cache*. However, this temporary file resides on an individual computer and does not necessarily store a student's Vex VR ".vrblocks" file when the computer shuts down. The Vex VR software does allow students to export their developing program to the hard drive of their computer. At this juncture, educators should consider using Google Classroom [15] or the Google Drive [16] of their Gmail account to create folders for each student to upload their exported ".vrblocks" work-in-progress to their Google folder *each time* they finish a programming session. Using Google Drive to store files is particularly helpful if two students used the same device on different days or if a student is returning to school after working from home. Creating this workflow organization and reminding students to save, export, and upload their work to their Google folder saves time and frustration. Teach the students to rename each upload of their ".vrblocks" file with their name and date. For instance, Mistretta110921.vrblocks. Naming the file avoids confusion with prior iterations of the program and improves students' organizational skills. Google Drive [16] is capable of housing the ".vrblocks" file. One must download the file to your computer and import it to Vex VR to continue to program.

2.2 Vex VR content knowledge: science and math (CK)

This section addresses the science and math content knowledge in the TPACK framework (**Figure 1**) that underpin the natural forces and numeracy at work. Robotics is the glue that holds STEM together. The science topic of ultrasonic sound-waves correlates to the distance sensors on robots. The Vex VR software simulates the use of ultrasonic sound waves through a physics algorithm to measure the distance from an object in the robot's virtual environment. Educators can connect to the echo-location of bats and dolphins as an activity to explore the properties of ultrasound *before* teaching the blocks that detect the distance from an object to the robot's sensor. It is important to make these connections to students' *schema*, or prior knowledge, to other natural systems that use echolocation.

Kindly refer to **Video 1**, https://drive.google.com/file/d/1CuYGgckdw5xhYdXFu1jzvtdbHiyeJ8zg/view?usp=sharing and **Figure 2** as you read the following descriptions of the Vex VR platform. The Vex VR Playground [11], selected in the upper right-hand corner of the blue ribbon on the screen, provides challenges to practice moving the robot around obstacles. This author recommends the Wall Maze (not the Dynamic Wall maze that changes with each run of the program) as a good beginner activity to discover the capabilities of the virtual robot. The programmer has the option to reveal

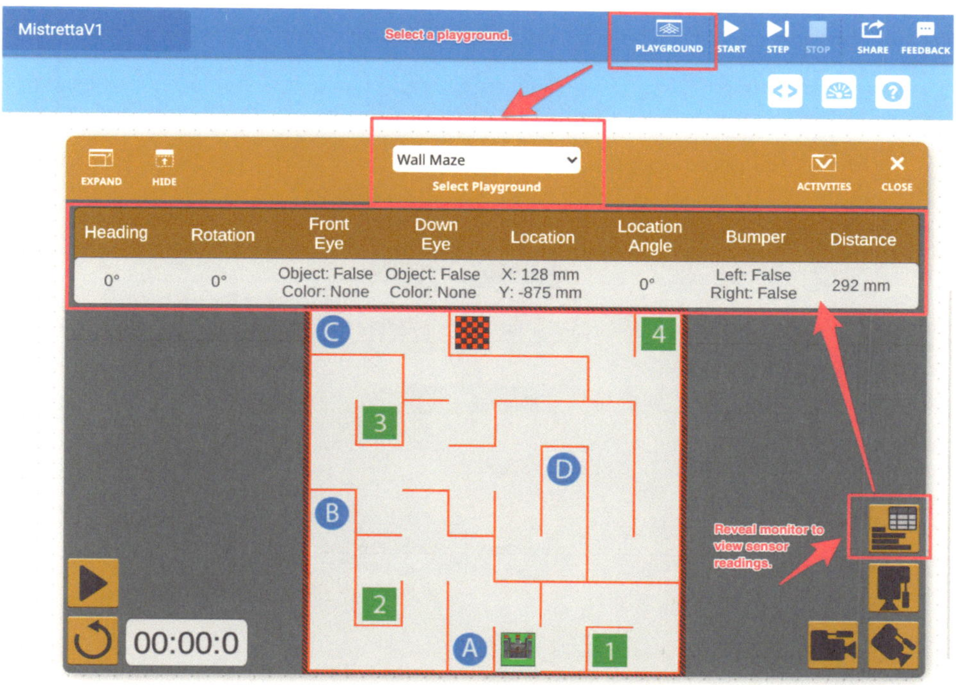

Figure 2.
VR vex platform. VR vex is a product of the Robotics Education & Competition (REC) foundation.

a monitor by clicking the button located just above the camera icons in the lower right-hand corner of the Playground pop up window to display the values of the following virtual sensors: front eye, down eye, XY axis location, location angle, bumper value, and distance in millimeters from an object. Based on the readout of the sensors, the programmer can code the robot to stop when the distance threshold is less than a number that they observe on the monitor. Writing code based on the sensor monitor is a tangible application of math to employ comparison operators to calculate when the robot must stop and turn.

2.3 Vex VR technological content knowledge (TCK)

This section elaborates on the intersections of technical and content knowledge (**Figure 1**) necessary to understand Vex VR. Students who have prior knowledge of programming on the Scratch platform [19], or other websites that use block coding, will recognize the structure of the Vex VR integrated development environment (IDE). Like Scratch programming [19], the code blocks are drag and drop puzzle pieces that join together in the large white work area that dominates the right two-thirds of the screen (**Figure 3**). Vex VR organizes the blocks into 10 categories: Drivetrain, Magnet, Looks, Events, Control, Sensing, Operators, Variables, My Blocks, and Comments. Vex VR provides you with the "when started" block. The programmer subsequently connects additional blocks based on planning strategies.

To learn more about each block, the programmer can click on the question mark in the upper right-hand corner of the screen (**Figure 2**) and then click on a block in the column that contains the puzzle pieces on the left of the screen. The "Help" column

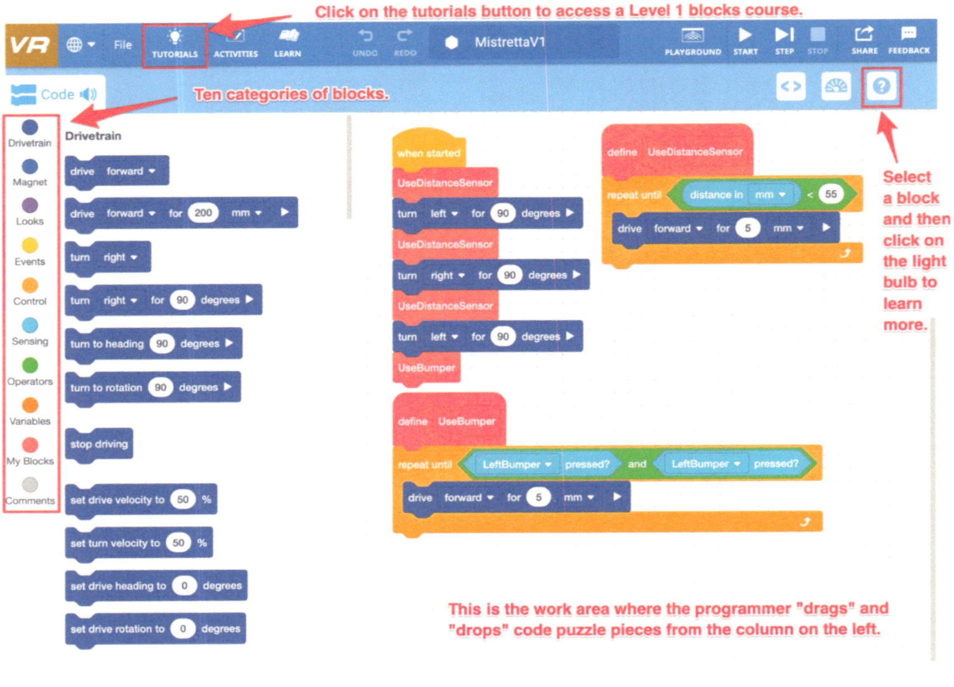

Figure 3.
VR vex work area, block categories, and resources. VR vex is a product of the Robotics Education & Competition (REC) foundation.

will populate with information about the selected block. To learn more about topics such as "Driving Forward and Backward" or "Turning," click on the "Tutorials" button under the lightbulb icon in the top blue "ribbon" of the screen. Vex VR provides a robust Level 1 Blocks Course collection to get the students started.

2.4 Vex VR pedagogical knowledge (PK): computational thinking

This section introduces the pedagogical, teaching methods, knowledge (**Figure 1**) necessary to instruct virtual robotics. Computational thinking is a mindset that is not limited to programming and computer science. It is a set of skills and attitudes that support students' creative solutions. Educators new to STEM might consider problem-solving as the only component of computational thinking. However, there are two additional skills: abstraction and algorithmic thinking [20]. Educators must emphasize that a computational thinking methodology is an *iterative* approach where mistakes and adjustments are an expected component of the process. **Table 1** summarizes the essential elements of the three computational thinking skills with examples based on the Vex VR Wall Maze challenge [11].

2.5 Vex VR pedagogical content knowledge (PCK)

This section addresses the intersection of pedagogy and content knowledge. Pedagogy is an art, especially when teaching technology. The methods of pedagogy seek multiple entry points to introduce content and provide all students with the opportunity to practice, make mistakes, revise, and reveal understanding. Giving guidance to each student is crucial to advance their knowledge of programming.

Skill	Sub-skill	Example
Problem solving	Decomposition	Student evaluates the Wall Maze to break down the entire maze (large problem) into smaller problems to navigate obstacles from start to finish.
	Redefine Problems	Student examines available code blocks and robot sensors.
	Strategic Decision Making	Student develops several possible solutions and decides which blocks and sensors to employ.
Abstraction	Modeling	Beginner programmer: Student programs a solution using multiple instances of the same blocks to navigate the maze. This can create a very long, concatenated grouping of code.
	Pattern Recognition	Intermediate programmer: Student recognizes that the same blocks are used repetitively.
	Modularity	Advanced programmer: Student identifies generalizable modules using the "My Blocks" feature that consolidates the movements of the robot into recognizing walls with the distance sensor, the bumper switch, left, and right turns.
Algorithmic Thinking	Algorithmic Design	Student develops a step-by-step strategy to call the "My Blocks" modules to create concise code (**Figure 3**).
	Incremental Design and Evaluation	Student designs, test, and revises code in an iterative approach to solve the maze.

Table 1.
Summary of three computational thinking skills.

Feed Up	**"Where am I going?" – Does the student's developing project exhibit an understanding of the goal of the assignment? Check the student's understanding before they potentially progress too far in the wrong direction.**
Feedback	"How am I going? – As students and educators, we are familiar with the prevailing direction of feedback that answers the questions, "What progress has the student made toward the goal?" With feedback, educators give students input to the overarching question, "How am I going?" that informs students about the trajectory of their work toward the goal. Students frequently ask, "Am I on the right track?"
Feed Forward	"Where to next?" – Offer substantive suggestions to inform students about specific activities that they need to undertake to make progress toward the goal.

Table 2.
Hattie and Temperly's tri-direction model [21].

Feedback, however, is only one of three components that comprise formative assessments. Hattie and Temperly [21] provide a tri-directional model of helpful feedback: feed up, feedback, and feed forward. **Table 2** elaborates on the three directions of formative assessments.

Hattie and Temperly's Tri-Direction Model [21].

2.6 Vex VR technological pedagogical knowledge (TPK)

This section discusses the intersections of pedagogy and technology to offer supporting applications to provide feed up, feedback, and feed forward guidance. There are several applications that assist teachers to provide impactful information

Application	Modality	Examples
Mote [22]	Audio Notes	Install the Chrome Mote extension on your computer. Share a worksheet in Google Docs with each student. Use the Mote audio feature in a new comment.
Loom [23]	Screen recording with voiceover and optional on-camera speaker.	Install the Chrome Loom extension on your computer. Download code from your student's Google folder and upload the ".vrblocks" file to the VR Vex in your browser. Review the program to formulate suggested revisions. Click on the Loom extension in your Chrome toolbar and screen record your feedback to your student. Click the Loom checkmark at the bottom of the screen to generate a URL to your feedback. Send the URL to the student via email.
	Small-skill videos	It is helpful to produce small skill videos (**Video 1**, https://drive.google.com/file/d/1CuYGgckdw5xhYdXFu1jzvtdbHiyeJ8zg/view?usp=sharing), using Loom, to share with students to cover programming techniques. Students can revisit a collection of educator-produced videos to review a skill or work ahead. This is helpful to bring new students up to speed or advanced students to progress ahead. Educators can archive the videos on Google Classroom [15], Google Site [24], or Wakelet [25].
Skitch [26]	Image Annotation	Skitch is part of the Evernote application. Download Skitch to your computer. Take a screenshot of your student's work with the Skitch application. Use the annotation and text tools to point out the areas of the program or assignment to revise. **Figures 2** and **3** are examples of Skitch annotations.

Table 3.
Feed up, feedback, and feed forward tools for educators.

to students. The categories are audio, screen recording with voiceover, and image annotation (**Table 3**). These tools work in face-to-face and online synchronous or asynchronous classwork.

2.7 Vex VR technological pedagogical content knowledge (TPACK)

The successful deployment of the Vex VR platform in a hybrid learning environment with face-to-face, synchronous, and asynchronous entry points compels teachers, coaches, and parents to understand the intersections of technology, pedagogy, and content knowledge. The on-ramp of the browser-based, virtual robotics, Vex VR platform transitions well to the next section that delineates Robomatter's Robot Virtual Worlds platform [12].

3. Robot virtual worlds

The Robot Virtual Worlds (RVW) product, offered by Robomatter, Inc., provides a powerful virtual robot platform [27] that gives programmers an option to run their code on a virtual *or* physical robot. The following information describes the setup of a Windows-based computer lab or laptop cart in *one* building. RVW is licensed software that has an option to obtain a 30-seat perpetual, one-time purchase for Vex or Lego Mindstorm robots [12]. Robomatter wrote RVW to work with the Windows operating system. One must download and install the licenses on *each* computer running the Windows operating system or to each Apple or Chrome computer running a Windows "partition" such as Parallels [28] software on a Mac OS or Chrome OS device. A *partition* is a region of your computer's memory dedicated to simulating the Windows operating system. The cost of a 30-seat, perpetual RVW license is approximately $600 with an available trial license to test-drive the software [12]. The Robot Virtual Worlds Level Builder, akin to the VR Vex playground, is free. Download a Level Builder package to each computer using Robot Virtual Worlds to "play" challenges or "build" a custom virtual world.

To facilitate students working from home, RVW offers homework pack licenses [12] to install on students' home computers running the Windows operating system. If a student owns a Mac or Chrome computer, the cost to the student for the partition software is approximately $80. Each student should download the free Level Builder software to facilitate "play" challenges or "build" custom activities. The following sections describe the RVW Vex IQ virtual robot.

3.1 RVW technological knowledge (TK)

This section addresses the technical knowledge in the TPACK framework (**Figure 1**) necessary to implement the fundamentals of the RVW RobotC programming software focusing on a Vex IQ virtual robot. The "C" programming language is an industry standard to program robots [29]. RVW provides a graphical user interface (GUI) with drag and drop blocks similar to VR Vex. Once installed on a computer, RVW provides a desktop icon named ROBOTC for Vex Robotics. Double click on this icon to invoke ROBOTC. Kindly refer to **Video 2**, https://drive.google.com/file/d/1Aj0sxMaZGRnMeIIa0Nijmis9fp7rQjj/view?usp=sharing and **Table 4** that contain suggested steps for educators to establish RVW on each licensed computer, to create a simple program, and to run this program in the *Turning Challenge* virtual world.

Task	Location in top gray row of the robotC Screen	Notes
1. Establish licenses	Help – Manage Licenses – Add License	One per computer.
2. RVW Package Manager to Install Level Builder	Help – Manage RVW Packages – Checkmark all Packages – Click Install/Update Selected	This is where you install Level Builder. One can also install the Vex IQ Competition Challenges [30] in virtual format here.
3. Review the Help Page	Help – (Choose language)	Review the extensive library of this user manual as needed.
4. Select the Virtual Robot	Robot – Compiler Target – Virtual Worlds	This will download your programs to the virtual robot. When one builds a Vex IQ, select Physical Robot and attach the Vex IQ with the USB cord.
5. Select the Platform Type	Robot – Platform Type – Vex IQ *and* Robot – Platform Type – Vex Robotics – Vex IQ	This example describes the Vex IQ virtual robot. The Vex Cortex virtual robot is also an option.
6. Select Virtual World to Use	Window – Select Virtual World to Use – RVW Level Builder	This menu option contains a “Download More Packages” option.
7. Select Menu Level	Window – Menu Level – Super User	The Super User options shows all available blocks.
8. Open a sample program	File – Open Sample Program	Select Moving Forward Rotations
9. Compile the Program	Click the Compile Program button at the top of the screen.	One must compile the program each time you make a change.
10. Download to the Virtual Robot	Click the Download to Robot button at the top of the screen	One must download the program each time you make a change. Click Play to reveal the Clawbot IQ page.
11. Select the Level	Select the Turning Challenge as a good beginner activity.	Click “Start Level” to reveal the virtual robot on the playfield. Notice the “play” button to the left of the robot. Click play to enact your program, click the rewind to return to the Start tile, click the “home” icon to return to the Select Level option.

Table 4.
Suggested sequence to establish RVW.

3.2 RVW content knowledge – sensors and geometry (CK)

This section addresses the engineering and geometry content knowledge in the TPACK framework (**Figure 1**) that underpin the robot’s build and associated properties of circle geometry at work. The RVW Vex IQ virtual robot has the same construction and sensors as the physical kit’s “Clawbot” build. A *sensor* is a device attached

Sensor	(P)urpose and (V)alues	Example
Bumper Switch	P: detect an obstacle V: pressed = 1 released = 0	&$$$; [29] This loop of code will move the robot forward one rotation at half power until the bumper switch is pressed indicating that it drove into an object.
Distance Sensor	P: Detects an obstacle with ultrasonic soundwaves V: Measures distance from 50 mm to 1 m	&$$$; [29] This loop of code will move the robot backward one rotation at half power until the distance sensor detects that an object is less than 300 millimeters away. Note: the virtual robot has its distance sensor on the back bumper. Hence, one must turn the robot to face the distance sensor toward the object that you wish to detect
Gyro Sensor	P: Measure the turn rate and calculates the direction of the robot. V: based on 360 degrees of a circle.	&$$$; [29] Always reset the gyro sensor (to 0) before turning the robot
		A gyro turning counterclockwise will increase its values. A gyro turning clockwise will decrease its values.
		This loop of code turns the robot to the left by setting the speed of the robot's left motor to −50 and the right motor to 50 until the gyro value is greater than 90 degrees.
Touch LED	P: In virtual robotics, set the LED to color to denote that a section of code is being enacted V: For example, colorRed, colorGreen.	&$$$; [29] For example, set the touch LED sensor to a different color for each section of code for a visual indication that a section of code is currently running.
Color Sensor	P: Detects the color of obstacles. V: Returns a color name or value of red, green, and blue in 256 levels.	&$$$; [29]
Smart Motors	P: Using an encoder within the motor, it measures speed, direction, time, revolutions, and degrees of turn. V: See example.	&$$$; [29] This block moves the robot forward for three rotations of the wheel at half power.

Table 5.
Robot sensors with examples.

to the robot's brain that detects the environment and sends numbers to the brain to report its findings. The programmer writes the code to respond to the robot's data to navigate the environment. **Table 5** lists the Vex IQ sensors, their purpose, and an example of how to use the sensor in a program.

It is necessary to understand circle geometry to employ the 360° properties of a circle to calculate the turns of the robot using the gyro. Additionally, students can arrive at the circumference of the robot's wheel to determine the distance in millimeters that the device travels in one rotation. Notice the length of the radius of the Clawbot IQ wheels on the start page of the Level Builder virtual robot (**Video 2**, https://drive.google.com/file/d/1Aj0sxMaZGRnMeIIa0Ni-jmis9fp7rQjj/view?usp=sharing). The radius of the wheel is 3.2 cm. Therefore, the diameter of this circle is 6.4 cm. Students can use the formula $\Pi * 6.4$ to calculate the circumference of the wheel to arrive at the distance that the robot wheel travels in one rotation. The circumference of the wheel in centimeters is approximately 20 cm or 200 mm. Using the measuring beam on the virtual robot, the student can calculate how many rotations it will take to travel the Turning Challenge depicted in **Video 2**, https://drive.google.com/file/d/1Aj0sxMaZGRnMeIIa0Ni-jmis9fp7rQjj/view?usp=sharing.

3.3 RVW technological content knowledge (TCK)

This section elaborates on the intersections of technical and content knowledge (**Figure 1**) necessary to understand Robot Virtual Worlds. Similar to the drag and drop code blocks described in Section 2.3, RVW is a robust platform that provides RobotC programming in 12 graphical functions categories (**Table 6**).

3.4 RVW pedagogical knowledge (PK) – perseverance rover

This section suggests a pedagogical method (**Figure 1**) to make real world connections to robotics as students program their virtual robot. The Mars Perseverance Rover is a robot launched by NASA in July of 2020 and deployed on Mars on February 18, 2021 [31]. The Perseverance mission team engineered the rover to utilize a

Graphical Function	Use
Program Flow	Contains blocks that the programmer to evaluate the data coming in from the sensors as the robot travels in an environment. The program flow blocks contain three components: the name of the sensor, a comparison symbol such as less than < or greater than >, and a threshold value such as a number, a color, or a Boolean value such as true or false.
	&$$$; [29] This program flow block evaluates the gyro sensor data and will turn the robot to the right until the value is less than −89.
Variables	The variable blocks allow the programmer to create a named location in the memory of the brain to store a value to use in a programming block.
	&$$$; [29] The programmer established the variable MyPower, set the value to 100, and then used the variable in the forward block. Using a variable in this manner standardizes the power. The programmer changes the value in one place and recompiles to change the speed of the robot throughout the program.
Simple Behaviors	Contains backward, forward, moveMotor, turnLeft, and turnRight commands. Use the Help – Command Library Vex IQ – Graphical – Simple Behaviors user manual to learn more.
Motor Commands	Contains blocks that address the encoder properties of the motor sensors. Use the Help – Command Library Vex IQ – Graphical – Motor Commands user manual to learn more.
Remote Control	Contains blocks to program the handheld controller that communicates via radio in *physical* robots.
Timing	Contains blocks to time or delay the program.
Line Tracking	Contains blocks to follow the edge of a line with the color sensor.
Datalog	Creates a graph of data from a selected sensor.
Display	Used to reveal controller, motor, or sensor values on the screen of the brain.
TouchLed	Changes the color on the TouchLED sensor
Distance and Gyro Sensor	Contains blocks to reset the distance and gyro sensors.

Table 6.
Robot virtual worlds 12 graphical function categories.

sophisticated collection of cameras and sensors to navigate the environment of Mars [32]. However, one simple calculation correlates directly to the students' virtual robot and circle geometry. The mission team calculated the distance that Perseverance travels in one rotation of the wheels, with no slippage on the rocky terrain of Mars, as 1.65 meters [33] using the same formula for the circumference of a circle demonstrated in Section 3.2 of this chapter. Educational philosopher John Dewey asserted that, "We do not learn from experience. We learn from reflecting on experience" [34]. Take the time to have the students pause and reflect on the rover on Mars to appreciate the skills that they are learning as actionable in future STEM careers.

3.5 RVW pedagogical content knowledge (PCK)

To achieve the intersections of pedagogy and content knowledge, teachers, coaches, and parents can reflect on the three types of problems delineated by Kirkley in the Principles for Teaching Problem Solving [35]. The students enacting virtual robotics will solve ill-structured problems without one solution. For every student in a class or on a team, they can develop a unique solution that solves the successful navigation of the virtual robot around the selected challenge. **Table 7** reveals three types of problems and the implications for instructing virtual robotics.

Type	Definition	Example	Pedagogy
Well-structured problem	The same step by step solution with one right answer.	Calculating the circumference of the wheel of a robot using Π * Diameter	Learner memorizes formula.
			Encourage reflection to real world contexts such as the Perseverance Rover.
Moderately structured problem	More than one acceptable solution with one right answer.	Turn the robot 90° to the right to navigate a maze. The learner can use the gyro sensor and setMotor blocks in a repeatUntil loop or a simple behavior of turnRight. Both solutions will turn the robot 90° to the right.	Learner selects a strategy to turn the robot to the right 90°. The solution using the gyro requires more analysis and abstract reasoning.
			Encourage students using the simple behavior to develop a solution to employ the gyro and motors.
Ill-structured problem	This is an open-ended problem with many correct solutions.	Challenge the students to move around a maze using all available sensors in their solution.	Students must plan the direction of the rover to move forward to use the bumper switch, backward to use the distance sensor, motor encoders to calculate distance traveled to navigate the robot to the finish block.

Table 7.
Three types of problems [35].

3.6 RVW technological pedagogical knowledge (TPK)

This section discusses the intersections of pedagogy and technology to offer supporting applications for students to develop their strategies to solve ill-structured problems. Students who complete the challenges provided within the RVW Level Builder software, such as the Turning Challenge, will be ready to create their own virtual environment. As previously demonstrated (**Video 2**, https://drive.google.com/file/d/1Aj0sxMaZGRnMeIIa0Ni-jmis9fp7rQjj/view?usp=sharing) there are two options to enact a program in RVW Level Builder. The first is "Play" and the second is "Build." When the programmer selects "Build", the system presents a blank playfield with one "Start" Block (**Figure 4**).

3.6.1 Level builder custom virtual environment

Students can customize their virtual Level Builder environment by dragging and dropping objects provided by RVW onto the playfield and saving their unique environment for continued development (**Figure 4**). Most exciting is that the student can create 3D objects using free online platforms such as Tinkercad [13] offered by Autodesk [Autodesk], export the resulting ".stl" file to the download folder of their computer, and import this file to Level Builder (**Video 3**, https://drive.google.com/file/d/1ddxnW7pp3KdELAbh53vAfdSC5spGUEp0/view?usp=sharing). Their custom 3D object becomes an obstacle to navigate around or an object to be "picked up" and carried by the arm and claw of the Clawbot Vex IQ virtual robot.

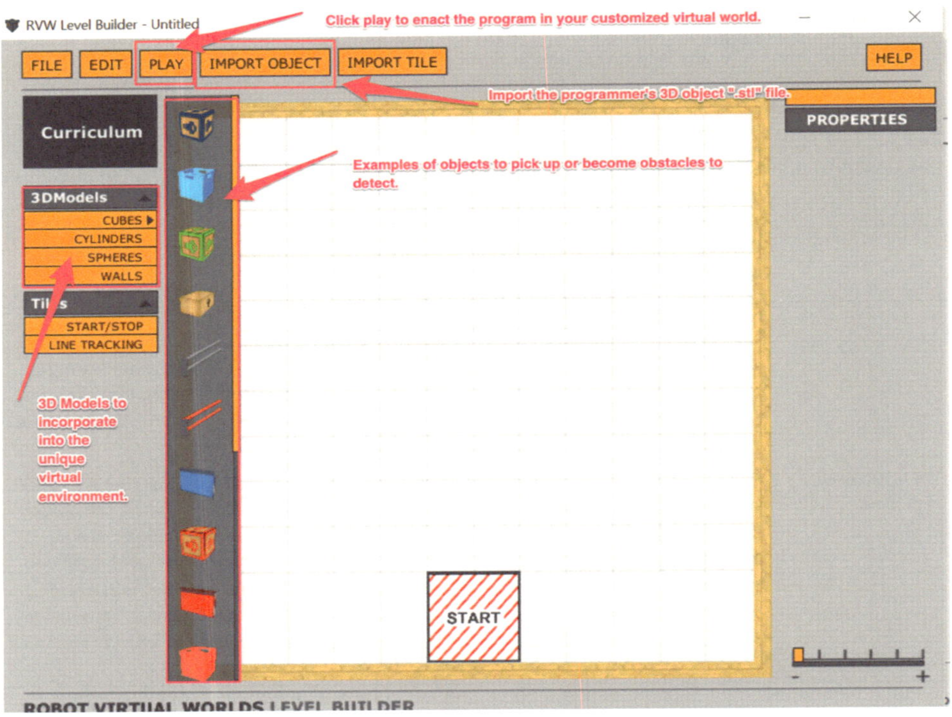

Figure 4.
Robot virtual worlds level builder – build option.

3.6.2 View custom 3D objects in augmented reality

Thus far, this chapter discussed the Vex VR and Robot Virtual Worlds virtual reality applications where the user observes a robot navigating a coded environment on a computer screen. Augmented Reality (AR) is a technology that overlays digital information into a user's real surroundings. Learners use a mobile phone or tablet running an application such as Merge Object Viewer [36] to facilitate the projection of objects onto a Merge Cube [14] into their current environment. This type of AR application is useful to students who designed a 3D object using Tinkercad and wish to view the object in their current environment before uploading it to Level Builder (**Video 4**, https://drive.google.com/file/d/1hTu_54BD9MkXa8bLj4brcMiG-8vw1p4K/view?usp=sharing). Additionally, the student can observe the object for size and expectations before upload to their custom Level Builder environment.

3.6.3 3D printing services

If the teacher, coach, or parent wants to print the student's custom 3D object, companies such as MakeXYZ [37] offer services to upload the.stl file, select inexpensive materials, and ship the resulting 3D object to you. The object can be used later with a Vex IQ robot on a physical playfield. Printing services provide several benefits to teachers, coaches, and parents who do not have access to a 3D printer and raw materials. Printing in 3D requires a large block of time, often overnight for one object. The extruder of the printer that melts the raw material filament can be approximately 280° C or 536° F [38], which requires adult supervision. If the roll of filament becomes jammed during printing, it can pull the extruder off the printer and ruin the printed object. Printing services provide access to 3D objects for students in face-to-face, synchronous, or asynchronous learning environments.

3.7 RVW technological pedagogical content knowledge (TPACK)

The RVW package provides *every* learner with an opportunity to code in RobotC, practice navigation in pre-packaged challenges, and create custom virtual worlds. The integration of student-created 3D objects into RVW with the option to observe and jury their creation using AR applications such as Merge prepares each student to become a producer of custom programs that transitions well to physical robotics.

4. Transition from virtual to physical robotics

Teachers, coaches, and parents who shepherd learners through the world of virtual robotics will be well-positioned to take the leap into physical robotics. The RVW package has a compiler target for a virtual or a physical robot. The students can compile and download the same program that they developed to navigate their custom Lebel Builder world to a physical Vex robot via a computer-to-robot USB cord. Obstacles crafted from recycled materials and placed on the floor of a classroom, community center, or home provides a workable test environment. It is helpful to create a "game" to have teams of students develop a scenario to have the robot gain "points" as the it navigates a custom, physical playfield. Example of games that this author's students developed included a home base for astronauts on the Moon and a distribution center for clean water in the aftermath of a natural disaster. Each time the robot accomplished a task using its sensors, the team gained points. It is important to note that teams can share the same physical robots by downloading their program to the robot brain. Sharing the same robots requires teams' agreement on the "build" of the robot to agree upon the location of the sensors.

5. Conclusion

Virtual robotics provides teachers, coaches, parents, and students with a unique opportunity to achieve a one-to-one ratio of robot to student. Vex VR and Robot Virtual Worlds provide students in face-to-face, asynchronous and synchronous settings with the opportunity to build upon their programming expertise while navigating a virtual robot in packaged and customized challenges.

Author details

Sharon Mistretta
Johns Hopkins University School of Education, Baltimore, Maryland, USA

*Address all correspondence to: cottagetechnology@gmail.com

References

[1] Burack C, Melchior A, Hoover M. Do after-school robotics programs expand the pipeline into STEM majors in college? (RTP). Proceedings of the ASEE Annual Conference & Exposition. 2018;**9**:1-25

[2] Costa C. Robotics K-12 and your district: The essence of STEM education and the E-ticket to unlimited possibilities. Leadership. 2017;**46**(4):32-35

[3] Nugent G, Barker B, Grandgenett N, Welch G. Robotics camps, clubs, and competitions: Results from a US robotics project. Robotics & Autonomous Systems. 2016;**75**:686-691

[4] We Robot. St. Vrain Valley Schools [Internet]. 2021 [cited 2021 Nov 7]. Available from: https://www.svvsd.org/2021/10/11/we-robot/

[5] Sysgen. SysGen [Internet]. 2014 [cited 2021 Nov 7]. Available from: https://sysgen.ca/sponsorship-robotics-club/

[6] REC Foundation. REC Foundation [Internet]. 2019 [cited 2021 Nov 7]. Available from: https://www.roboticseducation.org/team-resources/grants/

[7] VEX IQ Classroom Bundles (2nd generation) [Internet]. Vexrobotics.com; 2021 [cited 2021 Nov 7]. Available from: https://www.vexrobotics.com/iq-bundles.html?q=&locale.name=English

[8] Google Cardboard. Google VR [Internet]. Google.com; 2021 [cited 2021 Dec 1]. Available from: https://arvr.google.com/cardboard/

[9] Merge Headset. AR/VR Learning & Creation [Internet]. Merge. 2021 [cited 2021 Dec 1]. Available from: https://mergeedu.com/headset

[10] Koehler MJ, Mishra P, Cain W. What is technological pedagogical content knowledge (TPACK)? Journal of Education. 2013;**3**(3):13-19

[11] VEXcode VR. VEX Robotics [Internet]. Greenville, TX USA: Vexrobotics.com; 2021 [cited 2021 Nov 7]. Available from: https://www.vexrobotics.com/vexcode-vr?q=&locale.name=English

[12] Robot Virtual Worlds [Internet]. Robotvirtualworlds.com. 2021 [cited 2021 Nov 16]. Available from: https://www.robotvirtualworlds.com/

[13] Tinkercad. From mind to design in minutes [Internet]. San Rafael, CA, USA: Tinkercad. 2021 [cited 2021 Nov 7]. Available from: https://www.tinkercad.com/

[14] MergeEdu. AR/VR Learning & Creation [Internet]. San Antonio, TX, USA: Merge. 2021 [cited 2021 Nov 7]. Available from: https://mergeedu.com/

[15] Classroom. Google for Education. Classroom | Google for Education [Internet]. Mountain View, California USA: Google for Education. 2021 [cited 2021 Nov 29]. Available from: https://edu.google.com/intl/ALL_us/products/classroom/

[16] Google Drive [Internet]. Google.com. 2011 [cited 2021 Nov 29]. Available from: https://drive.google.com

[17] Google Meet [Internet]. Google.com. Google Meet; 2020 [cited 2021 Dec 2]. Available from: https://meet.google.com/

[18] Google Chrome. Download the Fast, Secure Browser from Google [Internet]. Google.com. Mountain View, California USA; 2017. [cited 2021 Dec 3]. Available from: https://www.google.com/chrome/

[19] Scratch. Educators [Internet]. Cambridge, MA, USA: Mit.edu. 2021 [cited 2021 Nov 8]. Available from: https://scratch.mit.edu/educators

[20] Computational Thinking Assessment Guide [Internet]. Available from: https://chrome.google.com/webstore/detail/mote-voice-notes-feedback/ajphlblkfpppdpkgokiejbjfohfohhmk?hl=en-US

[21] Hattie J, Timperley H. The Power of Feedback. Review of Educational Research. 2007;77(1):81-112

[22] Mote: Voice notes & feedback [Internet]. Mountain View, California, USA: chrome.google.com. Available from: https://chrome.google.com/webstore/detail/mote-voice-notes-feedback/ajphlblkfpppdpkgokiejbjfohfohhmk

[23] Loom. Send a video. Not a thousand words. [Internet]. San Francisco, CA USA: Loom. Loom; 2020 [cited 2021 Nov 8]. Available from: https://www.loom.com

[24] Google Sites [Internet]. Mountain View California, USA: Google.com. 2021 [cited 2021 Nov 29]. Available from: https://sites.google.com

[25] Wakelet. Save, organize and share content [Internet]. Manchester, United Kingdom: Wakelet.com. Wakelet; 2021 [cited 2021 Nov 29]. Available from: https://wakelet.com/

[26] Evernote [Internet]. Redwood City, California, USA: Evernote. 2018 [cited 2021 Nov 8]. Available from: https://evernote.com/products/skitch

[27] Robomatter [Internet]. Pittsburgh, PA USA: Robomatter.com. 2020 [cited 2021 Nov 16]. Available from: https://www.robomatter.com/

[28] Parallels: Mac & Windows Virtualization, Remote Application Server, Mac Management Solutions [Internet]. Seattle, Washington, USA: Parallels.com. 2021 [cited 2021 Nov 16]. Available from: https://www.parallels.com/

[29] ROBOTC for VEX Robotics 4.x (VEX Cortex & VEX IQ) [Internet]. Greenville, TX, USA: Vexrobotics.com. 2014 [cited 2021 Nov 17]. Available from: https://www.vexrobotics.com/robotc-vexedr-vexiq.html?q=&locale.name=English

[30] REC Foundation Competition History [Internet]. Greenville, TX USA: REC Foundation. 2019 [cited 2021 Nov 17]. Available from: https://www.roboticseducation.org/team-resources/competition-history/

[31] Watch in Person [Internet]. Pasadena California, United States: Nasa.gov. 2020 [cited 2021 Nov 30]. Available from: https://mars.nasa.gov/mars2020/timeline/launch/watch-in-person/

[32] Mission Overview [Internet]. Pasadena California, United States: Nasa.gov. 2020 [cited 2021 Nov 30]. Available from: https://mars.nasa.gov/mars2020/mission/overview/

[33] Rover Wheels [Internet]. Pasadena California, United States: Nasa.gov. 2020. [cited 2021 Nov 30]. Available from: https://mars.nasa.gov/mars2020/spacecraft/rover/wheels/

[34] The Collected Works of John Dewey, 1882-1953. Electronic Edition. The Later Works of John Dewey, 1925-1953. vol. 8: 1933, Essays, How We Think, revised

edition. How We Think [Internet]. Charlottesville, Virginia, USA: Jhu.edu. 2021. [cited 2021 Nov 30]. Available from: http://pm.nlx.com.proxy1.library.jhu.edu/xtf/view?docId=dewey/dewey.28.xml;chunk.id=div.lw.8.13;toc.depth=1;toc.id=div.lw.8.13;brand=default

[35] Kirkley J. Principles for Teaching Problem Solving. Bloomington, MN USA: University of Indiana; 2003. Technical Paper #4:1-16

[36] Merge Object Viewer [Internet]. San Antonio, TX USA: Merge Help Center. 2015. [cited 2021]. Available from: https://support.mergeedu.com/hc/en-us/articles/360052929752-Downloading-Merge-EDU-Apps

[37] Makexyz [Internet]. Tempe, AZ USA: Makexyz.com. 2018. [cited 2021 Dec 1]. Available from: https://www.makexyz.com

[38] Simplify 3D. [Internet]. Simplify3d.com. Cincinnati, OH USA; 2019. [cited 2021 Dec 2]. Available from: https://www.simplify3d.com/support/print-quality-troubleshooting/overheating/

Chapter 10

Emergency Remote Education Amid COVID-19 Pandemic

María de Jesús Araiza-Vazquez and Mariel García-Leal

Abstract

The COVID-19 health emergency has created an unprecedented crisis in many areas. In education, it caused the suspension of face-to-face classes at all educational levels to prevent the spread of the virus and mitigate its impact. In extraordinary circumstances, such as those faced since 2020, the governments and the corresponding educational authorities found it necessary to apply strategies that would allow continuity to the learning processes remotely, causing a series of changes. The teacher, for example, required a transformation in his/her role as part of the social isolation demanded by the pandemic, for which it should be noted, he/she was not prepared; compelling him/her to act mainly as a mediator in the teaching-learning processes, and rely on the use of technology as an educational resource. Therefore, given the particularities of the current context and the conditions required for students to adapt themselves to the challenges to come, the education needs to be structured according to the four pillars raised by Jaques Delors at the end of the last century; but from a different approach; which will be addressed through the next chapter.

Keywords: LMS platforms, canvas network, learning analytics, canvas learning analytics, academic development, academic performance

1. Introduction

The World Health Organization (WHO), on December 31, 2019, notified the outbreak of a new strain of coronavirus disease (COVID-19) in Wuhan, China [1]. The speed of spread of this infectious disease meant that a large part of the countries halted activities in both the public and private sectors and transferred them remotely.

Due to the very different strategies of facilitating learning remotely and without having teachers prepared to face this type of contingency, a new concept called Emergency Remote Education (ERE) was coined. According to Hodges et al. [2], ERE is a temporary and abrupt change in pedagogy due to crisis circumstances, involving the use of totally remote teaching solutions for instruction that would otherwise be taught in person or as combined or hybrid courses and that will return to that format once the emergency has subsided.

As a result of this extraordinary action, the work dynamics in the educational system have been modified to ensure that the curricular contents reach the entire school population. For which, home instruction has been taken as an emergent measure through the use of Information and Communication Technologies (ICT), diversifying their use.

2. Content

In this way, students have at their disposal a wide range of environments and tools from which they can draw during the educational process. So, today more than ever, learning must be flexible and adaptive. However, it must be remembered that the use of media does not guarantee the construction of knowledge, it is the activities designed to promote it that mark a differentiating point. Therefore, it becomes necessary to take into account the different learning styles that may be present in this type of educational environment, which are mainly based on sensory perceptions.

It must be remembered that sensory perceptions work as a function of the basic representational systems of neurolinguistic programming. It is important to point out that, although the student's profile must be considered for the planning of the educational process, a general rule cannot be established for the choice of representational systems. Their choice will largely depend on the discipline of study since these resources will serve different types of content depending on the learning objectives to be achieved. Representational systems are part of the VARK Model by Neil Fleming and Collen Mills, whose focus resides on the learner's sensory preference to process information in a simpler way, combining two elements—perception and memory, taking into account the following profiles:

- Visual: Better understand the content through visual illustrations, such as images, diagrams, videos, and brochures; since it allows you to relate them to previous ideas or concepts. Take into account shapes, sizes, distances, colors, and other physical characteristics; prefers to take notes.

- Auditory: Remember information more easily if it is addressed during an oral explanation. Consider the tone of voice, volume, timbre, pauses, tempo, and other nuances. You learn best through conversation, that is, speaking and listening. He likes to read aloud and use recordings, as a text may have little meaning to him until he hears it.

- Reader/Writer: Presents a greater ability to encode and understand messages through texts or readings.

- Kinesthetic: Optimally assimilates data through a manipulative approach, examining the physical world around them. It is difficult for him to sit for long periods and is often easily distracted by his need to explore. Be attentive to sensations and movements, which generates deeper learning that is difficult to forget [3].

That is movement, the senses, and even the emotions generated in the individual come into play since in one way or another these elements are involved in how the student internalizes the information. Although the data processing center is the brain, the whole body sends signals of the experiences lived.

To this should be added the student's own capacity for self-management, which translates into self-discipline, self-learning, critical thinking, and reflective analysis. Thus, students require direction to guide their development based on the use of media. Therefore, it will be necessary to promote the use of strategies capable of generating transformative experiences with diverse emphasis, inscribed in practices that allow active participation of the student in their own learning process so that it is authentic and meaningful.

The end is not only the communication or the distribution of the contents in a massive way through the use of different representational systems, but learning and skills development. These competencies will allow the integration of knowledge, skills, attitudes, and values that will train the student in knowing, doing, being and living together; being these basic pillars to achieve integral development in a complex, changing, diverse, and interconnected world like the one we live in today. The intention is that the student can function in various situations and contexts of personal, social, and work-life, where today the use of technology has taken on a highly important role.

This has required the teacher to make use of their digital skills, which were sometimes not well developed. Digital competence, as explained by Callejas et al. [4] "refers to a set of knowledge, capacities and attitudes, necessary to search, obtain and process information, as well as to use it critically and systematically."

The ideal is for teachers to use digital tools appropriately, which implies the development of strategies aimed at improving, expanding, and transforming learning through the combination of spaces, times, and technological resources. The DigComp Model proposes five categories for classifying digital skills:

1. *Navigation and data literacy*: Browse, search, select, analyze, classify, save, retrieve information and useful resources for your teaching procedure.

    - Data browsing, searching, and filtering.
    - Data evaluation.
    - Data management.

2. *Communication and collaboration*: Interact on social networks, establish communication with the group, share information and content of educational interest, participate in educational communities (pedagogical networks, for example), collaborate in a network, follow netiquette, respect the license of use, and manages the digital identity.

    - Interaction in social networks.
    - Share the content of educational interest.
    - Participation in educational communities.
    - Network collaboration.
    - Monitoring of netiquette.
    - Digital identity management.

3. *Creation of digital content*: Create educational content and share it. If required edit, adapt, or modify digital resources or content. Respect copyrights, as well as the corresponding licenses and configure programs or digital tools according to the agreed needs. Development of digital content.

    - Integration and adaptation of digital content.
    - Copyright and licensing.
    - Programming.

4. *Security*: Take care of electronic communication devices, protect data, know privacy policies, use digital tools responsibly, and promote their correct use and the reduction of energy consumption. Device protection.

    - Protection of personal data and privacy.
    - Protection of health and well-being.
    - Environmental protection.

5. *Problem solving*: Detects, identifies, and solves technical problems, and identifies and assigns tools for each declared objective, to meet particular learning needs (skills to be developed). He uses technology in a creative way, identifies both personal digital deficiencies and those present in the group, and seeks solutions to correct them.

    - Resolution of technical problems.
    - Identification of technological needs.
    - Creative use of digital technologies.
    - Identification of gaps related to digital skills [5].

Although we can identify a series of changes in education as a result of the health contingency, it must be remembered that the strategies corresponding to an ERE are not the same as those required by face-to-face education, which is why great efforts have been required, both of teachers, as well as students and parents to try to continue with training processes that ensure the acquisition of knowledge that, according to the study plans, should be acquired.

In the ERE, the learning process acquires a high presence and in turn a greater relevance. This is because the student must take a highly active role since he usually has to study alone. For this reason, the means of communication used by the teacher must fulfill a special function, facilitating the presentation of content, and learning resources, so that students do not require constant clarification or interpretation. Today, the environment demands that students be largely autonomous and actively participate in their educational process.

It should be clarified that the ERE is not synonymous with Distance Education (EaD). This last concept represents a planned experience that from the beginning has been conceived and designed through the use of communication media.

The educational process must be structured according to at least four fundamental learnings that in the course of each person's life will be their pillars of knowledge. Depending on its fulfillment, the challenges that the Mexican educational system will have to face in the face of the new global scenarios that this pandemic has brought with it and the current dynamism in science, technology, and knowledge must be recognized; requiring the development of transversal skills aimed at building the four pillars of knowledge that Jacques Delors spoke of.

- *Learning to know*: This is a means and an end of human life. As a means, it consists of learning to understand the world, at least enough to live with dignity, develop professional skills, and communicate with others. As an end, its justification lies in the pleasure of discovering and understanding. This supposes in the first instance the exercise of attention, thought, and memory. This is because the dizzying succession of information from the media threatens the discovery process, which requires a deepening of the information captured for its subsequent permanence.

- *Learning to do*: This notion demands the development of skills that enable the individual's ability to cope with a wide range of situations to be able to influence their own environment. The main purpose is that the student can develop in terms of autonomy, judgment, and personal responsibility.

- *Learning to live together*: It implies achieving values of pluralism, mutual understanding, and peace, to promote the participation and cooperation of individuals in all human activities for the subsequent development of common projects.

- *Learning to be*: This abstraction requires the development and promotion of imagination and creativity in children and young people, as well as their freedom of thought, judgment, and feelings. The intention is to ensure that these develop a comprehensive way so that they can reach fullness [6].

Given that the ERE requires a series of conditions and capacities to enable independent study, it is essential that the teacher provides the student with sufficient materials, information search strategies, examples of the use of technological resources, and the necessary motivation for the student to commit to your own learning. In this sense, the guidance provided by the teacher is very important. This is why the teaching-learning strategies, the preparation of materials, and the evaluation process are elements that should be oriented considering the context and the particularities that this new reality implies. The student can develop her autonomy and the well-designed learning environment enables self-instruction, so study methods play a crucial role. Each student can explore different learning styles through a process of introspection and based on this, look for better alternatives that allow them to enhance the acquisition of knowledge.

Taking into account the changes that the ERE demands in the current educational system, the exchange of experiences among the teaching staff becomes a core element to enrich, correct, and strengthen the dynamics corresponding to the teaching-learning process; particularly in terms of access and use of media, evident in the current digital divides.

Although, many of the schools and educational institutions worldwide have opted for online resources as support instruments; according to the UNESCO Institute for Statistics (UIS) and Teacher Task Force, approximately 50% (826 million) of students who have been out of class as a result of the pandemic do not have a computer at home, and 43% (706 million) do not have internet access. Some of them (56 million) do not even live in regions served by mobile networks [7].

While, in Mexico, according to the National Survey on the Availability and Use of Information Technologies in Households (ENDUTIH) carried out by the National Institute of Statistics and Geography (INEGI), before the pandemic only 56% of households had fixed or mobile internet connection, 44% had a computer, and only 45% used it as a support tool for school purposes [8].

Considering the existing technological gap in the country, to give continuity with remote learning in basic education, the use of television and radio programs has been used as the main means, being that television was already a medium present in 93% of households [8]. The interest of these broadcasts goes beyond the needs of the students, seeking to provide intergenerational learning where health and emotional well-being issues must be considered [9], mainly with the intention of providing support for the entire population affected by COVID-19. However, the use of these two media as tools for remote teaching delivery has represented a series of challenges for the federal government that go beyond accessibility; highlighting among them:

- The generation of significant content in quantity and quality in such a short period of time.

- The level of competencies required by teachers and students to move from a face-to-face teaching-learning process to a remote one.

- The importance of carrying out an adaptation of the evaluation process.

- The need to provide greater attention to students in situations of vulnerability, since there is a risk of increasing inequalities within the system, generating lag and dropout.

- The very reduction and bureaucratization of the educational messages that the student receives. This is because in face-to-face teaching the teacher not only transmits knowledge but also values and forms of behavior; basic elements to guide the integral development and structuring of the "learning to be" pillar.

Although the use of radio and television has proven to be highly suitable means of addressing the digital divide in the education sector, important questions remain to be reviewed. Therefore, it is necessary to plan on the current reality and the experiences lived, recognizing the need to take into account the lessons learned, reinvent ourselves, and strengthen our educational system in the long term; for which dialog and horizontal participation play a crucial role.

According to Castro et al. [10], "horizontal participation promotes free, responsible, and respectful dialog between the different people who participate, everyone has the possibility to share, raise their ideas, be heard and valued" (p. 39). The emphasis on learning is placed on the quality of the arguments and not on the hierarchical position of the speaker. In this sense, dialog is conceived not only as a communicative act of interaction but intentional actions of all members of the group are crystallized, which are oriented toward the common good.

To adapt the current work methodology to the needs of the present educational context, it is necessary on the part of the teachers and the corresponding managers, a restructuring in terms of leadership. This restoration in terms of leadership derives from the need to achieve the design of best and new practices with an emphasis on dialog and horizontal participation that enables permanent analysis and discussion of the local, national, and international reality.

Teachers have faced great challenges having to transition from a face-to-face education to a remote one in such a short period of time. While, within a classroom, the teacher has the immediacy of communication that allows the creation of close links; in a remote education event, this interaction depends on other elements, such as media availability, connectivity, data transmission speed, and connection quality. This flow of communication, which implies a space–time disparity, generates psychological exhaustion, both in the teacher and the group; particularly because a greater effort is needed to establish communication, to be able to express oneself correctly to transmit the desired message and to be able to understand the other. Therefore, even communication loses spontaneity, requiring prior planning. This, in turn, becomes more complex depending on the level of digital competencies maintained by the group and the parents or guardians in charge of providing support, particularly in the early stages of training, since it represents a core factor in the determination of the learning tools to use and, to a large extent, the success they achieve. Time also plays a crucial role during the interaction, mainly in the resolution of doubts; since there may be a time lag as a consequence of the teacher's schedule and the availability of the technological medium in the home, especially if it is shared among several members of the family.

Children and young people face taking their classes in an environment full of distractions, such as television, food preparation, cleaning the house, and the noise from the interaction between other members of the home; which generates anxiety and emotional disorder. Therefore, teachers have faced the challenge of maintaining student interest through the implementation of mostly interactive dynamics and exercises.

In the understanding that virtuality is now the new reality, at least temporarily; the change of environment where the place has become the classroom is also a factor to consider. The home has become the space where all the activities of the day are carried out, including study, work, leisure, and rest. This change, from the emotional aspect, also denotes being somewhat complex; so, it is an element that must be assumed, understood, and worked on.

The ERE has aroused tensions between students, parents, and teachers. The change generated breaks in routines that demand adaptation to a new reality, from which learning is expected to help improve education through the use of technology. Additionally, to this are added other challenges of comparable importance, in which the classroom can influence to improve education; including:

- Narrow the current digital divide: This health contingency has exposed the notable inequalities that the country faces in terms of access and use of media.

- Promote a relevant motivation: The isolation or the feeling of loneliness, feelings generated as a result of the pandemic, has caused some children and young people to present symptoms of demotivation.

- Take advantage of digital resources: Teachers have had to adapt their work methodology, transferring content to remote-learning environments through the use of media; to guarantee comprehensive training capable of coping with the social and technological changes present in today's environment.

- Increase socialization: Since confinement has largely isolated us from our family circle, this has had a considerable impact on children in the early stages of formation. So, it becomes necessary to re-educate in collaborative work to find that social cohesion, necessary even in remote-learning environments.

- Reduce early school-leaving rates: Students with the highest risk of dropping out of school are those with whom direct contact has not been established to continue the educational process. In this regard, the United Nations Organization for Education, Science, and Culture (UNESCO) declares that projections worldwide manage to indicate that almost 24 million children and young people from primary to university could drop out of classes [7].

It must be remembered that the incorporation of virtual learning environments should not arise from a transfer of what occurs in a face-to-face environment. It requires the work of experts in the field of education that enable the design of an adequate structure to achieve timely monitoring of each of the work stages, ensuring a study sequence through the use of quality resources that allows the achievement of an optimal learning experience.

- Provide a punctual accompaniment to the students who need it most: It must be remembered that remote education represents a challenge not only for students but also for their families. Not all of them can provide children and young people with a punctual accompaniment or a space free from distractions. There are even students who, given the current economic situation, have had to leave their school activities to enter the world of work, mainly to support their homes; which could lead to an educational lag if the corresponding proactive measures are not taken. • Manage time based on fundamental learning: When students have fewer hours for study, it is a priority to dedicate them to addressing fundamental learning for life.

- Support the final grade students of each educational level: Likewise, it is advisable to prioritize this accompaniment in children and young people who are in their last grades of each educational level; for example, the third year of preschool, sixth of primary, third of secondary and last grade of upper secondary, since these students will hardly be able to recover the learning lost in the next school year, due to changing educational level.

- Make the most of the resources available at home: The intention is to achieve an experiential education, even remotely. Therefore, it is necessary for each family to take advantage of the available resources to reinforce the educational process. These resources are not only technological means but also the knowledge of parents or guardians can be beneficial for the learning of children and young people, since their experience can be taken as part of a process of development and growth. Other resources are books and games available at home, which if used appropriately may have the potential to serve an educational purpose. Daily activities can even be useful to develop observation, analysis, and reflection.

- Strengthen the culture of care and prevention: Although all the points that we have just mentioned are fundamental from an academic and emotional point of view, it is also very important to promote health care in our children and young people. Try to reinforce prevention and care habits in your group, such as keeping a healthy distance and washing your hands frequently; during the time recommended by the health authorities, avoid touching your face and do not leave the house.

- Use technology: One of the most valuable resources available today is the internet. This is why, as a consequence of the pandemic, many countries have launched valuable educational platforms and open resources, such as those presented in the previous section. One of the tools that have gained a greater presence in Mexico is Google Classroom, offered by Google for education in collaboration with the SEP, which has allowed the preparation of classes, the development of activities, and their evaluation. There are also some other tools that you could use.

    - For example, to teach online classes you can use Teams, Google Meets, Facebook Live, Zoom, or Skype; all with free versions that allow you to develop videoconferences.

    - To send or receive tasks you can use Google Drive, Dropbox, or Mega.

    - In case you or your students do not have an Office 365 license to use Word, Excel, or PowerPoint, you can use or suggest the Open Office option, which is free.

    - And to maintain an immediate communication flow for the resolution of doubts or to follow up with your group, you can resort to the use of instant messaging applications such as WhatsApp, Telegram, or Facebook Messenger.

- Provide and receive emotional support: Currently, we are in times of stress and uncertainty not only because of the fear that contagion represents, but also as a result of the abrupt changes that this health contingency has brought with it, such as confinement and social isolation, increased responsibilities, job instability, the current financial crisis, or caring for sick family members. These are elements that can affect the learning capacity. That is why, as teachers, we must take into account the emotional and mental state in which our students are, to be able to support them and provide them with the necessary tools that allow them to restore their well-being. For which, in the first instance, we must practice self-care since a teacher in a state of stress will hardly be able to provide effective support.

As mentioned at the beginning of this chapter, the ERE maintains a series of peculiarities; for example, didactic processes. These processes include the way in which classes are approached, the use of TAC, the dynamics of group participation, and the methods for evaluating performance. These changes and transformations arise mainly from the communication media used in this type of study.

- *Printed*: Considering paper materials used for educational purposes, such as books, manuals, or workbooks.

- *Radiophonic*: They use only sound elements, so the production of this type of material is easier. An example is educational programs broadcast on the radio.
- *Audiovisual*: They are based on the use of images and sound for the transmission of content, such as educational television.
- *Digital*: Include resources encoded in a machine-readable format, such as videos, audio or digital images, computer programs (software), video games, pages and websites, social networks, and blogs [11].

At no time in our recent history have TACs been more in demand than they are today. By tradition and prior to the pandemic faced worldwide, technology has served as a facilitator of education. However, today, the educational process is intrinsically dependent on it. As social isolation prevails, technology can no longer be viewed as a peripheral instrument, but as a basic element to make education viable.

In recent decades, the use of technology in education has gained a high profile. Particularly in the international context, this transformation reached its peak in the 1990s. However, in Mexico, the integration of these resources over the years has been slower. It is that these efforts have been oriented to cover access to technological resources, however, students and teachers also require the coverage of other types of more basic needs, such as access to electricity; particularly in remote rural communities.

It must be remembered that remote education is not exempt from being affected by the social and economic context. For what will have to be recognized in the first instance, the characteristics of each region, and on the other the attributes of the family and community environment; since the intention is to reduce the gap in access or appropriation to resources, not to increase it. The implementation of technological programs, without a pertinent diagnosis and adequate planning that enables an improvement in educational conditions, can generate situations of inequality and lag. Technology represents an element of high value today to create an environment in which the needs of the context can be efficiently addressed, highlighting TACs in this category.

Although education outside of face-to-face education in Mexico has already been on a path that consists of more than 50 years, it is still a modality in deployment that requires a process of evaluation, analysis, and continuous improvement in more than one aspect; particularly in basic education. This is because formal education involves more than overcoming the physical barrier that exists between the teacher and her group. It requires the application of relevant strategies that go beyond generating a temporary solution for an extraordinary situation. It needs planning and development that does not appear overnight.

This modality implies generating a space that enables the achievement of authentic and meaningful learning through the meaningful use of the means and available resources, placing them in the corresponding context.

In this time of school isolation, it has become urgent that our basic, upper secondary, and higher education teachers get ahead in the use of means and resources; specifically in digital matters. It is the characteristics of remote education that differentiate it from face-to-face education that have an impact on the teaching-learning process, as well as on the actions of the teacher and the didactic strategies of it.

Today's teacher has put his creativity to the test in preparing his classes and for the first time, they are experiencing all the potential afforded by one of the greatest distractions present in the classroom environment—cell phones; since mobile telephony is today one of the main instruments for accessing digital content.

The presence of technology has driven society to move towards a 180-degree change in its daily life. These transformations have not only had an impact on technical issues, since the use of these devices goes beyond the instrumental nature; it represents a decisive element in the system of relationships, customs, and knowledge of each individual.

Therefore, in this time of change and transformation, digital skills together with advanced cognitive skills, such as communication, teamwork, creativity, critical thinking for problem solving, and the ability to aspire to learn throughout life; and emotional skills, such as empathy, adaptation, perseverance, and resilience; they are the best buffer to deal with uncertainty [12].

Each medium has a symbolic system, a technological potential, and a processing power that affect the interpretation and construction of mental models. Therefore, different types of content merit the use of different resources and involve different ways of learning them to achieve a meaningful experience.

TACs cannot be perceived as mere vehicles to transport information and make access to content feasible; Hand in hand with a good method, a relevant instructional design, and an adequate learning environment, they can contribute to greater cognitive efficiency [13]. As explained by Aguirre, et al. [13], this cognitive efficiency represents "a lower use of brain resources obtaining a better execution." (p.16).

While TACs have become a common fixture in education today, many other key pieces have remained largely unchanged, including the curriculum and teacher pedagogy. In this sense, its selection should require a detailed review, since this type of technology is capable of modifying the way in which students construct their own learning by connecting them with their context and with previously acquired knowledge. It does not mean that this technology is the key to knowledge, represents only a support to enable an optimal work methodology, especially if we consider that education does not focus solely on the content, on the teacher, or on the students; rather, it contemplates a comprehensive vision.

Therefore, at this time, it is necessary to have a coherent proposal to this vision and the present needs, both of the students, the teacher, and the community. It will be necessary to take into account individual trajectories, depending on which one must opt, among other things, for personalization. Prior to the pandemic, these valuable resources have enabled educators to scale-up education intervention and reach normally excluded areas. However, in contemporaneity, few countries have managed to take optimal advantage of it to better respond to the current situation facing the educational system. No country was prepared to respond to the abrupt change that this event has brought with it, however, some have managed to experience more favorable results.

As we previously reviewed at the beginning of the chapter, remote education strategies differ from face-to-face education. Although they may maintain common aspects, the logic behind planning, the use of resources, as well as the role that each of the agents involved maintain are elements of each modality. However, in remote education, these must be analyzed with dedication and diligence; since face-to-face communication is eliminated. In function of all the present changes, one of the indisputable properties that current education must maintain is adaptability; a concept defined as "the ability to respond adequately to the demands of the environment, regulating behavior to achieve homeostasis" ([14], p.68).

But not only teachers must be willing to change traditional teaching strategies and urge more participatory roles. It is also important that students seek new transformations that allow them to translate the current situation, generated by the pandemic, into a change at the educational level that lasts over time; aiming at improving educational quality. And it is that this health emergency has brought to the fore a series of elements that are worth adapting to consolidate an educational culture focused on the skills demanded by the 21st century:

- *Learning and innovation skills*: prepare for the increasing complexity of life and work environments. Consider creativity and innovation, critical thinking and problem solving, communication and collaboration.

- *Skills related to information, media, and technology*: typical of the environments in which we live today, marked by technologies and access to a large amount of information. They include information literacy, media literacy, and digital literacy.

- *Life and career skills*: they have a social and emotional character, allowing us to navigate the complexity of the environments in which we develop. They include flexibility and adaptability, initiative and independence, social and cross-cultural skills, productivity, leadership, and responsibility [15].

Even in remote mode, these skills can be worked to a lesser or greater degree by involving the student not only with their cognition but also with their senses and emotions. As you reviewed in the previous topics: we learn with the whole body! T.

Therefore, in these times of change, the purpose is to promote comprehensive training and encourage adaptability and resilience in our students, this being the "ability to adapt effectively to adverse, traumatic or highly stressful situations, even learning from they are already improving" [16].

As Maggio [15] explained, a resilient individual has the ability to face adversity, has self-control and autonomy, optimistically faces the future, openly manifests his feelings, develops empathy, maintains a good mood, is persistent in failure, and has the ability to constructively handle pain, anger, frustration, and other upsetting aspects. So, it is conceivable that a resilient individual is a person with good emotional health. Due to COVID-19, the social environment and consequently, the school environment have been changed abruptly. Normality as we knew it before is likely not to return for some time, so the way in which this social distancing is faced represents a challenge for children, youth, and adults. However, this scenario can result in individual, family, and even community strength if we know how to properly manage change and learn from it. In other words, resilience is a function of adaptive capacity.

3. Study

The effect of teaching online education on the study skills of postgraduate students was investigated. A sample composed of two groups of students who were enrolled in a Project Management course offered at a business school was considered. This course was randomly assigned as an experimental group (N = 20); while the other was considered as a control group (N = 27). The control group was traditionally taught using a textbook-focused lecture and the LCD screen/projector was used from time to time, quizzes and paper assignments were used frequently. The same content in the textbook was used for the experimental group, but in electronic format using the e-learning platform. Moodle was the LMS used, in the second semester of 2021 and was the space used for the delivery of the course requirements. A validated scale consisting of 60 items covering nine dimensions of study skills was administered to the two groups before and after treatment. Statistically, significant differences were found between the groups on the pretest. As a result, multivariate analysis of covariance was used for the post-test data analysis controlling for differences in the pre-test. The differences between the experimental and control groups in their performance on the post-test appeared to be statistically significant on all dimensions. All these differences were in favor of the experimental group.

The study shows that the use of an LMS in instruction seems to be able to improve skills as the experimental group outperformed the control group with statistically significant differences in all dimensions of study skills if we control for the difference in their performance on the pretest from one dimension to another. All these differences were in favor of the experimental group.

It is worth noting that although the experimental group outperformed the control group in all dimensions of study skills, a decline was reflected in their performance with a statistically significant difference in two dimensions, which were—essay writing and effective listening. The decline in essay writing may be due to the nature of the course selected to be taught on Moodle. The Project Management course where less effort is given to report writing and more effort is given to hands-on activities using the software. In terms of the experimental group's decrease in effective listening, it could be explained based on the fact that teaching in an LMS gives little emphasis on listening, which is a crucial factor in the traditional lecture method. Therefore, it is logical to obtain such a result.

The study showed that the LMS was influential in improving most of the dimensions (6 out of 9) of study skills, the overall improvement of the experimental group was not statistically significant. The implication of this finding is that researchers should always verify the effect of any new instructional method on the subfactors and dimensions of the target variable or aspect. The overall effect could be masked by one dimension over the others.

Finally, although the results of this study support the use of an LMS in graduate-level instruction, more research is needed in several courses before a conservative generalization can be made.

4. Recommendations

Thus, it becomes crucial to generate a community residence, this is the "capacity of the social system to respond to the adversities that are affecting the community at the same time and in a similar way, while the resources that already exist are developed and strengthened, to reorganize" [9]. It is worth noting that this concept is not only aimed at an individual, but also at a community facing social adversity. As the Government of Mexico explains, it is possible to reach a state of community resilience. This community resilience can be built on a day-to-day basis when we engage to improve. We can overcome the negative feelings that this contingency has brought with it through a series of compensation mechanisms, such as the following:

- Performing self-confirmation behaviors.

- Exalting own values.

- Increasing our participation.
- Acknowledging our emotions and expressing them.
- Seeking to be more assertive.
- Avoiding physical and emotional overload.
- Consulting official sources of information and sharing them with our students and fellow teachers.
- Speaking with reliable data and clear language to our group, remembering that the mental health of our children and young people also depends on our actions.

Author details

María de Jesús Araiza-Vazquez* and Mariel García-Leal
UANL, Monterrey, México

*Address all correspondence to: araizav@gmail.com

References

[1] WHO. Coronavirus Disease (CoViD-19) Outbreak. QUIEN: World Health Organization; 2020

[2] Hodges C, Moore S, Lockee B, Trust T, Bond A. The Difference between Emergency Remote Teaching and Online Learning. United States: Educause Review; 2020

[3] Fleming N, Baume D. Learning styles Agin: VARKing up the right tree. Educational Developments. 2006;7(4):4-7

[4] Callejas, A.I., Salido, J.V. and Jerez, O. Digital competence and information processing: Learning in the 21st century. Edition of the University of Castilla-La Mancha; 2016

[5] Carter S, Vuorikari R, Punie Y. DigComp 2.1 the Digital Competence Framework for Citizens. Spain: Joint Research Centre; 2017

[6] Delors J. The four pillars of education. In: Education Contains a Treasure. France: The UNESCO Courier; 1994

[7] UNESCO. Alarming Digital Divides Emerge in Distance Learning. Scientific and Cultural Organization: United Nations Educational; 2020

[8] INEGI. ICTs in Homes. Mexico: National Institute of Statistic and Geography; 2019

[9] Government of Mexico. Community Resilience in Times of CoViD-19. Mexico: National Institute for Older Adults; 2020

[10] Castro Medina C, Quintero Reyes CY, Ramírez Monroy CG, Gollás Núñez IY, Carrillo Sánchez MG. Learning communities in and for life. SEEJ. 2020;7(3):1-18

[11] Sanchis L, Megias D. Organization and Management of Actions to Stimulate Information for Young People. Spain: Publisher CEP; 2016

[12] Inter-American Development Bank. What you Can and can't Do for Education: A Comparison of Five Success Stories. United States: IDB; 2020

[13] Aguirre N, Cruz ÁJ, Miró A, Bueichekú E, Solozano N, Broseta R, et al. Working memory training improves cognitive efficiency in multiple sclerosis patients. Dis Cli Neuro Journal. 2018;**5**(2):16-25

[14] Mamani TH. Characterization of adaptability through multivariate analysis and its value as a predictor of academic performance. Cepies Scientific Magazine. 2017;**3**(1):68-75

[15] Maggio M. 21st Century Skills: When the Future Is Today. Mexico: Santillana Foundation; 2018

[16] SEP. Programa del curso optativo: Enfoque de resiliencia. Mexico: DGESPE; 2020